Poland and Spain
in Contemporary World

·COLECCIÓN UNIVERSIDAD·2·

Edited by
Małgorzata Mizerska-Wrotkowska
José Luis Orella Martínez

Poland and Spain
in Contemporary World

·SCHEDAS·

·COLECCIÓN UNIVERSIDAD·2·

Poland and Spain in Contemporary World

Edited by
Małgorzata Mizerska-Wrotkowska
José Luis Orella Martínez

© 2014, The authors

© 2014, SCHEDAS, S.L.

    Paseo Imperial 43C, 6ºD. 28005-Madrid.

    www.schedas.com Tel. 911264770 ofi@schedas.com

This book was published as a result of an international research project conducted by the Institute of European Studies in the Department of Journalism and Political Science at the University of Warsaw, and the CEU History Studies Institute.

This publication was co-financed by the Department of Journalism and Political Science at the University of Warsaw and the CEU History Studies Institute.

Reviewers:

Radosław Zenderowski – full professor (Cardinal Stefan Wyszyński University in Warsaw)
Álvaro Ferray – full professor (University of Navarra)

This book consists of 14 publishing sheets.

Traslation courtesy of arbil.org FORO ARBIL

ISBN (paper): 978-84-942256-4-2
ISBN (EPUB): 978-84-942256-5-9
ISBN (MOBI Kindle): 978-84-942256-6-6
Printed: CreateSpace

GENERAL INDEX

Preface
ÁLVARO FERRARY 13
Introduction
MAŁGORZATA MIZERSKA-WROTKOWSKA
JOSÉ LUIS ORELLA MARTÍNEZ 19
Poland's Foreign Policy in the Years 1945-1980
JÓZEF TYMANOWSKI 23
    1. Poland in the international political arena after World War II ... 23
    2. Poland's foreign policy under the government of Władysław Gomułka ... 27
    3. Poland's foreign policy under Edward Gierek's leadership ... 37
    4. Conclusions ... 41
    5. Bibliography ... 43
Spain's Foreign Policy in the Years 1945-1975
MAŁGORZATA MIZERSKA-WROTKOWSKA 45
    1. Spain on the international stage in the aftermath of World War II ... 45
    2. Spain's foreign policy 1953-69 ... 49
    3. Spanish foreign policy 1969-75 ... 57
    4. Conclusions ... 64
    5. Bibliography ... 64
Poland's Security Policy after the Second World War
JACEK CZAPUTOWICZ 69
    1. Security policy during the Cold War ... 70
    2. Security policy after achievement of independence in 1989 ... 72
    3. Poland and the European Security and Defence Policy ... 77
    4. Poland's security policy in strategic documents ... 81
    5. Conclusions ... 84
    6. Bibliography ... 86
Defence Policy and Safety Perceptions in Franco's Spain
JUAN CARLOS JIMÉNEZ REDONDO 93
    1. The basis of the safety and defence policy in Spain 1945-1975 ... 93
    2. Potential sources of thread ... 109

3. Methods and instruments of the safety policy 116
  4. Conclusions 121
  5. Bibliography 124

Danubian and Polish Exile in Contemporary Spain
José Luis Orella 127
  1. Spain and Central European delegations 128
  2. Colegio Mayor Santiago Apóstol 131
  3. The new emigration to democratic Spain 143
  4. Bibliography 145

The Spanish Exile in Poland (1939-1955)
Cristina Barreiro 147
  1. Spain 1939: starting point to the exodus 147
  2. The Spanish government in exile and the Central and Eastern Europe: the Polish legacy 150
  3. Spanish exile in Poland: post operation Bolero-Paprika refugees 153
  4. Bibliography 157

Questions of Polish Identity in the Context of European Integration
Konstanty Adam Wojtaszczyk 159
  1. National identity - conceptualization of the concept 159
  2. The origins and development of Polish national identity 160
  3. The European identity 167
  4. Polish national identity and European identity 170
  5. Poland vis-a-vis the European Union's development dilemmas 171
  6. Conclusions 172
  7. Bibliography 173

Spain – Europe: a Strange Relationship
José Díaz Nieva 177
  1. Introduction 177
  2. Today's Spain 178
  3. Spain and Europe yesterday 184
  4. The complex of Spain 188
  5. Spain and Europe today 190
  6. Spain – Latin America 193
  7. Conclusion 195
  8. Bibliography 195

The Euro Area Crisis: Selected Problems of Institutional Solutions. Implications for Poland
Jan Misiuna & Kamil Zajączkowski 197
  1. EU's position towards the crisis of the euro area 198

2. The European Stability Mechanism	201
3. Single Supervisory Mechanism	204
4. Single Resolution Mechanism	206
5. Implications of the Euro Area Crisis for Poland	210
6. Conclusions	219
7. Bibliography	219

Spanish and Polish Economies: Two Faces of Great Recession in Europe

José Manuel Cansino & Manuel Ordóñez — 225

1. Introduction	225
2. A comparative macroeconomic overview	226
3. Database	230
4. Methodology	232
5. Results	235
6. Conclusions	243
7. Acknowledgements	245
8. Bibliography	245

Information about the Authors

Małgorzata Mizerska-Wrotkowska	249
José Luis Orella	249
Józef Tymanowski	249
Jacek Czaputowicz	249
Juan Carlos Jiménez Redondo	249
Konstanty Adam Wojtaszczyk	250
José Díaz Nieva	250
Cristina Barreiro	250
Jan Misiuna	250
Kamil Zajączkowski	250
José Manuel Cansino	250
Manuel Ordóñez	250

Preface

Preface

ÁLVARO FERRARY

If the aim of comparative history is to achieve a better understanding of historical institutions or ideas by seeing how they differ between different countries and societies across time, we should conclude that with "Poland and Spain in Contemporary World" the main objectives and the justification involved in this kind of historical approach are fully reached.

Through ten contributions from twelve Polish and Spanish specialists in contemporary history the study encompasses a large number of key questions concerning the recent history of both countries.

In "Poland's Foreign Policy in the Years 1945-1980", a chapter centred on the so-called 'lost' period of a Poland dominated by the USSR, **Józef Tymanowski** stresses the relevant steps taken by Władysław Gomułka during his time of government in order to endow Poland with an active stance within the communist system in external issues, which unquestionably meant a progress in comparison to the previous Stalinist era. The 1956 Hungarian Uprising nevertheless, Tymanowski points out, cleared up where the limits were laid by Moscow, demonstrating that for Poland during those years a real independent foreign policy was not possible. The 60's and 70's, despite Edward's and Gomulka's illusions about a distinctive Polish foreign policy coming into being, functioned virtually as a confirmation of the aforementioned fact.

Passing from Poland to Spain, it could be said that a notably fine balance between calculation and pragmatism defined Francisco Franco's political behaviour in external, as well as in internal, matters. The chapter dedicated to Spain's Foreign Policy by **Małgorzata Mizerska-Wrotkowska** is a good, and certainly brilliant, example of the aforementioned Franco's personal political features. Because of its close ties with the Axis Powers, isolation and an international embargo was imposed to the Spanish regimen in 1945. Franco's response was twofold:

to exploit Spain's anticommunism stance and to proceed to a political reshuffle, in a successful effort of readapting Spanish regime's image to an international context soon split by the outbreak of Cold War. As Mizerska-Wrotkowska rightly concludes, although Spain was always obliged to pay a fee because of its non democratic nature, Madrid's increasing cooperation with the Western governments certainly paved the way for Spain's total integration in the Western Security System, quickly accomplished few years after Franco's death.

Once regained its strategic independence after the events of 1989, it came the time for the Polish Republic to redefine its security policy from a new basis. As **Jacek Czaputowicz** points out, NATO and European Union membership was the Polish response to the need of basing strategic culture on national interest. As a result of its new international status, and in the face of the political and social volatility installed beyond its Eastern borders following the Soviet collapse, Poland, concludes de author, became a firm advocator of the creation of a Collective Security System through the reinforcement of NATO's military structures or strengthening the ESDP.

Returning to Spanish affairs, **Juan Carlos Jiménez Redondo** explores how the balance of power which the Fracoist regime was based on started to change in the fifties as a result of Spain's integration in the Western Defence System. A final outcome of that process consisted in an increasing contrast between the regime and the State, concludes the author.

Meanwhile, in "Danubian and Polish Exile in Contemporary Spain", **José Luis Orella** lights up a unexplored terrain: the action implemented since 1946 by the Obra Católica de Asistencia Universitaria in order to help academics and university students prosecuted because of its religious faith with economic assistance and accommodation facilities in Spain for the implementation of their respective careers. Along his grounded text, Orella stresses the point of the not in the least irrelevant contribution due to these conspicuous exiles from East and Balkan Europe to the Spanish cultural and social panorama.

From a reversed angle, **Cristina Barreiro** penetrates into the subject of Spanish exile to Poland following the end of Spanish Civil War. As Barreiro illustrates, the tiny Spanish community in Poland was to be increased at the beginning of the fifties because of the political measures taken against the communists in France and in other Western countries, starting up henceforth a second exile, more political, and affecting mainly to communist militants.

Based on a consistent empirical analysis and a set of well defined theoretical assumptions, **Konstanty Adam Wojtaszczyk** poses the question -or questions, the author remarks- of Polish identity in the context of European integration. According to Wojtaszczyk, the patterns and models of Western democracy represent a challenge to Polish national identity, formed historically around language and religion as key factors.

In his stimulating contribution, **José Díaz Nieva** deals with the sometimes too thorny subjects of the meaning of Spain and the endless debate around its political and historical identity. Under the cover of the disproportionate Europeanism felt by a large number of Spaniards, Díaz Nieva states, lies a disturbing loss of identity, even to the point of one be tempted to reformulate Europeanism as a useful and convenient artefact for filling the void left by a slow and permanent identity loss.

Even though the crisis in the EU has been generally felt in considerably much broader terms, and more intense and deeper that predicted, its direct influence in the Polish economy has been lesser in comparative terms. This is the main argument developed by **Jan Misiuna** and **Kamil Zajączkowski** in their important contribution. As the authors show throughout their remarkably consistent research, during the last two decades the Polish economic development has been faster when comparing to the rest of the Euro Area and the EU as whole, meanwhile for the next two years a GPD growth and a low inflation are expected, albeit the unemployment rate seems to remain stagnant at around 10%.

Despite the common bonds shared between Poland and Spain in terms of cultural backgrounds, demographic as well as other geo-economics aspects, their respective economies exhibited a remarkable different behaviour facing the international monetary crisis or in order to overcome its effects. This formula could be the main conclusion drawn by **Juan Manuel Cansino** and **Manuel Ordóñez** in the last chapter. According to Cansino and Ordóñez, in the role played for the foreign sectors, both in the Spanish and Polish economy, could be found the key elements for providing a convincing explanation of the different, and even contrasting, ways in which these two economies reacted to the great recession.

Introduction

Introduction

MAŁGORZATA MIZERSKA-WROTKOWSKA
UNIVERSITY OF WARSAW

JOSÉ LUIS ORELLA MARTÍNEZ
CEU SAN PABLO UNIVERSITY

Relationships between Spain and Poland have always been scarce and distant. However, when the sun never set in Spain, there was an initial relationship between both countries, whose Golden Age years clashed. Later, both the periods of the War of Independence and the cruel Spanish Civil War would become the most frequent fields of study about Spain in Poland as well as serving as basis for further comparison.

The first precedent would be in the 19th century with Joachim Lelewel, heir to a romantic 11th century, who prepared a comparative standpoint as the method of historical knowledge with his work *Historyczna paralela Hiszpanii z Polską w XVI, XVII i XVIII w.*[1] Some decades later, the presence of Spanish communists in communist Poland and Polish exiles in Franco´s Spain would spread new horizons both in the historic and literary fields despite their very different points of view. It will not be long until the arrival in Spain of Jan Kieniewicz, Head Professor of History and first ambassador of Democratic Poland, who used the Study Centre on Ancient Traditions in Poland, Central and Eastern Europe of Warsaw University (OBTA[2]), also named *"Corpus Diplomaticum hispano-polaco"*, to encourage the academic relationships between both countries, write numerous works and establish a school of Spanish history lovers[3].

---

1 W. Stefański, Poznań 1845 or Wydawnictwo DiG, OBTA UW, Warszawa 2006.
2 OBTA – Ośrodek Badań nad Tradycją Antyczną w Polsce i Europie Środkowo-Wschodniej.
3 For example: *La obra de Joachim Lelewel, 'Paralelo histórico entre España y Polonia en los siglos XVI, XVII y XVIII' (1831)*, "Hispania. Revista Española de Historia", LI/1991: 695-734; *Dantisco: diálogo y futuro de las relaciones hispano-polacas*, "Estudios Hispánicos" 6/1997: 29-40; *Polonia y España desde la perspectiva histórica*, "Estudios Hispánicos. Hispano-Polonica: Homenaje a Piotr Sawicki", 15/2007: 193-199.

As a result, Jerzy Axer and Antonio Fontán´s (eds.) *Españoles y polacos en la corte de Carlos V*[4] would be released to study the abundant correspondence by Juan Dantisco in the Imperial Spain. Another institution which has joined this approach is the History Institute of the Science Polish Academy (IH PAN) of Warsaw, which has also collaborated with the History Institute of CSIC[5] on research on the phenomenon of migratory movements. One of these results can be found in Elda González Martínez and Malgorzata Nalewajko´s *España y Polonia: los encuentros*[6]. Another fruitful collaboration will be that of the Catholic University of Lublin (KUL) with La Rioja University, after the initial approach by Cezary Taracha´s (coord.), *We wspólnej Europie. Polska-Hiszpania XVI-XX wiek*[7]. Professor Taracha had already published the names of those Poles who had consulted the Spanish funds in the 19th century in *Źródła do dziejów Polski i polonika w archiwach hiszpańskich*[8].

In Wroclaw, with Piotr Sawicki and the "Estudios Hispánicos" journal, and at Jagellónica Universiy of Krakow, with Teresa Eminowicz and the "Studia Iberystyczne" journal interesting works have been fostered. An example is *Olivares, Wazowie i Bałtyk: Polska w polityce zagranicznej Hiszpanii w latach 1620-1632*[9] by Ryszard Skowron, focusing on a modern history which still hides interesting chapters between both countries. Other relationships are increasing like that of Poznań University with the Basque Country University or that of Copernicus University in Toruń with Navarra University.

However, contemporary history, particularly in the 20th century, has nourished a bigger mutual interest as it has been shown by Lidia Mularska-Andziak´s works, *Franco*[10] and *Dyktatura generała Prima de Rivery a hiszpańskie tradycje imperialne 1923-1930*[11]. Also, Pawel Skibinski´s *Państwo generała Franco. Ustrój Hiszpanii w latach 1936-1967*[12] whose author has contributed to "Arbil" journal with several articles on some Poles´ lives such as Cardinal Wyszynski and St. Maximilian Kolbe. Besides, Franciszek Ryszka´s *W kręgu zbiorowych złudzeń. Z dziejów hiszpańskiego anarchizmu*

---

4 Alianza Editorial, Madrid 1994.
5 CSIC – Consejo Superior de Investigaciones Científicas.
6 CSIC, Madrid 2005.
7 Redakcja Wydawnictw KUL, Lublin 2001.
8 „Kwartalnik Historyczny" 103/1996, z. 2: 45-46.
9 „Historia Iagellonica", Kraków 2002 (Spanish version: Wydawnictwo DiG, Warszawa 2008).
10 Wydawnictwo Puls, London 1994.
11 Wyższa Szkoła Humanistyczna w Pułtusku – Instytut Historyczny UW, Pułtusk-Warszawa 1999.
12 Arcana, Kraków 2004.

1868-1939[13] deals with purely Spanish phenomena such as the study of Hispanic anarchism.

As for the relationship between both countries during the Second World War, Jan Ciechanowski has recovered a period of intrigue and secrecy reminding us of detective stories with a historical background[14]. Transition to democratic regimes in both countries from formerly different experiences required an enriching comparison whose first results came from Bogusława Dobek-Ostrowska´s *Hiszpania i Polska: elity polityczne w okresie przejscia do demokracji. Analiza porównawcza*[15] and Eugeniusz Górski´s *España y Polonia: sus identidades democráticas*[16].

But, as it can be seen at this stage of the introduction, this comparative study is assymetrical in favour of Poles, who are usually bilingual, unlike Spaniards´ lack of fluency in such a difficult language like Polish. However, Felipe Ruíz Martín, Antonio Domínguez Ortiz, Rafael Ródenas Vilar and José Alcalá Zamora discussed the existing connections between both countries in their works. At present, we cannot help quoting Fernando Presa and Tania Dimitrova Láleva´s (eds.) *España y el mundo eslavo. Relaciones culturales, literarias y lingüísticas*[17]; Matilde Eiroa y Dolores Ferrero´s *Las relaciones de España con Europa centro oriental (1939-1975)*[18] and Gregorio Bak, a Pole living in Spain, who discovers Josef Lobodovski´s poetic work and the Hispanic literary world around him.

On leading this new way by philologists, sociologists and historians. We expect to broaden the comparative enrichment of our nations in the 20th and 21st century.

* * * * *

This monograph is a product of an international research project conducted by the Institute of European Studies at the Faculty of Journalism and Political Science, Warsaw University, and the History Studies Institute of the University of San Pablo CEU (Madrid).

---

13 Ośrodek Badań Społecznych, Warszawa 1991.
14 For example: *Azyl dyplomatyczny w poselstwie Rzeczypospolitej Polskiej w czasie hiszpańskiej wojny domowej (1936-1939)*, „Przegląd Historyczny", t. XCI, 4/2000: 551-584; *Działalność wywiadu polskiego w Portugalii i Hiszpanii w czasie II wojny światowej* [in:] *Wkład polskiego wywiadu w zwycięstwo aliantów w II wojnie światowej*, ed. by Z.J. Kapera, Wydawnictwo PAU, Kraków 2004: 83-114.
15 Wydawnictwo Uniwersytetu Wrocławskiego, Wrocław 1996.
16 [in:] *Identidades: etnias, culturas, naciones*, ed. by M. Nalewajko, Uniwersytet Warszawski, Instytut Studiów Iberyjskich i Iberoamerykańskich, Warszawa 2004: 51-65.
17 Gram, Madrid 2002.
18 *"Ayer"* 67 (3)/2007.

The aim of the authors is to place Poland and Spain in a modern historical perspective. The authors focus on five main themes. The first two chapters deal with Polish and Spanish foreign policy from World War II until its democratic transition. The following two chapters are devoted to the security policy of both countries in the same period. Throughout this book, the authors analyse the causes of migration and activities of Poles in Spain and Spaniards in Poland and the problems of identity the two countries have faced in the context of European integration. The final two chapters address the contemporary economic crisis and methods of combating it.

The book's structure is that of a mirror image, each of the main themes being addressed in the context of both Poland and Spain. The authors sought to answer the following questions: (1) What were the circumstances surrounding Polish foreign policy and manifestations of that policy during communism? (2) How was Spain's foreign characterized in the "Franco era"? (3) How did Polish security policy evolve after World War II and what new challenges does it face? (4) How did an authoritarian system of government influence the security policy of Spain? (5) How has Polish national identity evolved, starting from the beginning of Poland's statehood? (6) How has Europeanization influenced Spanish national identity? (7) What has been the scale of Polish emigration to Spain and what have those immigrants done? (8) How did Poland adopt its Spanish refugees after the loss of the civil war? (9) What means has Poland used in its fight against the economic crisis? (10) What has Spain achieved in this respect?

In addition to articles by academics from Warsaw University and the University of San Pablo CEU, to this book contains contributions from eminent experts from the University of Seville, Warsaw School of Economics and Santo Tomás University in Santiago de Chile.

Poland's Foreign Policy in the Years 1945-1980

JÓZEF TYMANOWSKI
UNIVERSITY OF WARSAW

1. Poland in the international political arena after World War II

The end of the Second World War, symbolised by Germany's signing of the German Instrument of Surrender on 8th May 1945, was an extremely difficult period, both for forming the political structures of the Polish Republic and for elaborating effective means and instruments for realizing the country's foreign policy. Despite the joy following the end of this barbaric war, freedom and sovereignty did not come to Poland; its territory and internal political system was now determined by the USSR. Following World War II, Moscow dominated almost all of the countries of Central Eastern Europe, forcing upon many of them its own political and economic system, as well as political and military alliances.

The determinants of external policy of this period significantly influenced not only the choice of Polish policy's basic directions, but also the degree to which it was independent in the time of 1945-1980 (Skrzypek 2010: 98-123).

The "lost" years of Poland fall into three distinct periods. The first relates to the immediate post-war period (1945-1948) when Stalin had not yet ascertained whether plans to form a communist system in Central Europe would succeed, while the major part of the political elites and Polish society persisted in the delusion that Poland could be protected from communism. Nevertheless, in this period a pretence of democracy held, expressed through the existence of opposition parties. Other than the Polish Workers' Party there were also other parties controlled by communists: the Polish Socialist Party, the People's Party and the Democratic Party, as well as an independent peasant movement represented by the Polish People's Party.

The second period begins with the years 1948-1956 when the communists united to form the Polish United Workers' Party (PUWP). Following Leninist-Stalinist assumptions and using the 'proletarian dictatorship', PUWP initiated a cult of Bierut and a Stalinist system which was not negated until 1956. The second half of this period was 1956 to 1970, when Polish politics were significantly influenced by Władysław Gomułka. It could be posited that this chapter of Polish politics was an unsuccessful attempt to create a Polish route to socialism.

Finally, the third period was set between 1970 and 1980, dominated by Edward Gierek. Gierek searched for a means to get closer to the West. Generally, it is agreed that the 'lost' period of Poland dates from the victory on 9th May 1945 to the final dissolution of the United Soviet Socialist Republic in December 1991.

The fact that the final composition of the Provisional Government of National Unity (PGNU) announced to the public on 28th June 1945 was agreed in Moscow illustrates that Poland at that time was not making sovereign decisions. The position of Prime Minister was given to Edward Osóbka-Morawski, the positions of Deputy Prime Ministers to Władysław Gomułka and Stanisław Mikołajczyk. Being the former Prime Minister of the Polish Republic in Exile, Mikołajczyk openly accepted the decision of the Yalta conference and entered the new government in the hope that a democratic system would be created in Poland. Other members of the Polish Government in Exile condemned Mikołajczyk for accepting the position of Deputy Prime Minister, seeing his step as constituting moral consent to the functioning of the communist system. The composition of PGNU was dominated by the communists (17 members out of 21). In June 1945 the Provisional Government of National Unity was recognised by France and Sweden, in July by the Great Britain and the USA, and thereafter by other countries. This international recognition was tantamount to the outlawing of the Government in Exile (Śniegocki 2006: 222-232).

In 1945 it was not clear whether Stalin's aim was the progressive incorporation of the Central European countries into the USSR or to allow them some form of autonomy. After winning victory over Germany, the USSR no longer had to reckon with the Western alliances. Even so, in the territory ruled by the Red Army existed some social, economic, political and cultural structures and their transformation would take time. To this end Stalin used a temporary form of state called 'people's democracy'.

People's democracy as 'a transitory system to socialism' functioned as a screen behind which to hide preparations for complete sovietization. Communist ideology, which rested upon lies and coercion, created an artificial world in which 'democracy' meant strict dictatorship, 'progress' the abolition of values and absolute power, and 'knowledge' primitive faith in ideologists' charms. Many dilemmas in the communist world were rooted in the discord between utopian but nice-sounding theory and cruel practices of the government.

Polish foreign policy was during this time completely dominated by the USSR which, after the Second World War, created the political system in Central and Eastern Europe. This system lasted until the end of 1980s and was united by bilateral and multilateral bonds in the political-military dimension (the Warsaw Pact), the economic dimension (the Council for Mutual Economic Assistance) and the ideological dimension (in the years 1954-1977 Kominform, and later other cooperation forms of communist parties). In the political sphere Polish foreign policy's most important pact was the bilateral alliance with the USSR. Polish side of the treaty was signed in April of 1945 by Bolesław Bierut, a man who had no legal authority to do so and who was appointed for the Head of the State National Council (SNC) by Moscow (before the Polish Government was created under the Yalta agreements). At the time Charles de Gaulle would say it was how "Stalin made alliances with himself" (Kuźniar 2001: 53-58).

This pact was to make the West aware that the USSR saw the Provisional Government of the Polish Republic as the only alternative for the basis of realising the Yalta formula.

The pact had the character of an valid regulation, its significance extending beyond the sphere of bilateral relations. The USSR's signing of such an agreement with the Provisional Government of the Polish Republic was an undoubted gesture of defiance of the allies. The agreement flew in the face of the Yalta formula, which stated that Poland could become a party to such an agreement only after achieving a separation of powers and after their 'reorganization'. However, the reorganization happened much later, at the end of June 1945. It is therefore not surprising that following the announcement of the Polish-Soviet pact, both Anglo-Saxon powers accelerated their diplomatic interventions, pointing out the fact that Moscow's actions could complicate the formation of a cabinet of national unity, and breached the principle of a common policy of the powers towards the region (Materski, Michnowicz: 89-94).

Poland, as a Russian vassal state, was deprived of the benefits of sovereignty and unable to conduct its own foreign policy. The position of a country in international relations is based on a number of determinants: objective and subjective, internal and external. In the case of Poland the following determinants have been significant: geopolitical determinants, material-social (economic, scientific-technical and military potential); subjective determinants which are important in the group of internal determinants, structural determinants (existence of different kinds of inner system bonds, political and military organizations), as well as functional determinants (different types of states of international relations) which indicate the level of a country's foreign policy (i.e. cooperation, relaxation, tensions, wars). These determinants, as pointed out by Teresa Łoś-Nowak, influenced the essence, character and directions of the Polish foreign policy during the whole post-war 40-year period (Łoś-Nowak 1992: 215-219).

The foreign policy of the Polish People's Republic was one of a dependent country whose interests were determined by the rules of socialist internationalism laid down by Moscow, not by the Polish *raison d'état*. The scope and character of Polish foreign policy was a consequence of both the division of Moscow's sphere of influence, which contained Poland, and of political, economic, military and ideological connections imposed on Poland by its Eastern neighbour.

The situation largely limited, and often precluded Poland's chances to conduct a fully sovereign (independent) external policy, placing Poland as it did in the position of a satellite state, with all the consequences of this role and its position on the continent. However, the essence and character of foreign policy is usually a result of a number of factors: international relations, capability, readiness and opportunity to choose a fundamental behavioural paradigm in the surrounding international environment, and thus, a certain type of foreign policy.

Only a completely sovereign country can decide what the essence of its foreign policy will be and by what means to conduct this policy. The main factor in this process is, on the one hand, a state's readiness (or lack thereof) and its adaptability in the international environment, and on the other, signals sent or specifically received by this environment. Poland's "historical bad luck" in the years 1944-1945 was that before managing to free itself from German occupation and restore complete freedom and independence, Poland found itself in the zone of "historically justified Soviet security interests".

The new-created political order, known as the Yalta-Potsdam territorial and political order, the formula for which Poland had no influence over, was a consequence of compromise between the great superpowers, leading countries and anti-Hitler coalitions and interests. While both sides of the coalition were interested in maintaining order, its consequence for Poland was absolutely disadvantageous political and geopolitical decisions. In general conclusion we can say that if Poland had been restored to independence, it would have been equivalent to breaking the balance between the already-shaped East and West (Łoś-Nowak 1992: 215-219).

This fact influenced Poland's behaviour in the international arena, the essence, character and directions of its external policy since the choice of a certain strategy and tactics is usually made under the influence of factors of internal and external character. So often these factors overlap, or one dominates the other, thereby determining the essential conditions for formulating foreign policy (Łoś-Nowak 1992: 215-219).

This is what happened in Poland throughout the 40-year post-war period. A particularly significant time, important because of the efforts taken by Polish diplomacy to free Poland from the strengthening USSR political domination, was the years 1945-1948. Hopeful and confident in the promises of the West, Poland sought during this time to achieve the position of an independent country with sovereign rights to decide on own interests and foreign policy. These attempts came to nothing.

The basis of Polish foreign policy was constituted by its alliance with the USSR and other socialist states. The Treaty of Friendship, Cooperation and Mutual Assistance was signed in 1945 and prolonged in 1965 for the next 20 years. The USSR had also become Poland's most important partner in all economic aspects. Treaties of Friendship and Cooperation were also concluded with other socialist states (Topolski 1986: 253-259).

Therefore, to judge the Polish foreign policy after 1945 we have to take into consideration that its scope and character were rather influenced by external rather than internal factors. As a "hostage" of the Yalta-Potsdam system, Poland was forced to create its policies in accordance with Moscow's interests, but also indirectly to sanction the international order of Yalta and Potsdam.

2. Poland's foreign policy under the government of Władysław Gomułka

During the time Władysław Gomułka had decisive power to govern, Polish foreign policy was characterized by two ideological trends that were both exclusive and complementary. The first of these was inspired by the Communist Information Bureau (Kominform - established in 1947), which was supposed to coordinate actions across the communist states. Its general aim was to transfer Soviet experiences related to the political and economic system and to root them in the actions of other communist states.

In order to support this aim, in 1948, with the participation of the USSR, Poland, Czechoslovakia, Hungary, Bulgaria, Romania and Albania, the Council for Mutual Economic Assistance (CMEA) was created. The USSR took effective steps to make sure that in the organization's structures the models of "socialist industrialization" applied, models which had a dominant influence on the scope of Poland's cooperation in the international arena.

The CMEA was the first organization of multilateral cooperation of the people's democracy countries and the USSR, and it constituted an important step in the direction of the so-called socialist community. The first article of the CMEA charter provided for support for the development of member states' national economies (Łaptos, Mania 2010: 298-307). The CMEA was an effective tool of maintaining USSR domination over the Central Eastern Europe countries and so shaped the directions of Polish foreign policy.

The second tool supporting the Soviet vision of worldwide socialism was establishment of Warsaw Pact Organization in 1955. As with the CMEA, its creation was motivated by propaganda more than real defence needs (Czubiński 2003: 533-535). Firstly, the existing network of bilateral agreements between the USSR and satellite countries guaranteed their siding with the Russian side in any war. Secondly, the USSR knew that the fact that West Germany joined NATO and the West European Union (WEU) - an indirect cause of the conclusion of the Warsaw Pact - did not affect the defensive character of the North Atlantic Treaty. Thirdly, the establishment of the Warsaw Pact Organization did not significantly raise the Eastern block's fighting value, which NATO already to be powerful enough on the basis of its nuclear capability (Parzymies 2004: 78-82).

The actions of all organisations - the Communist Information Bureau, the CMEA and the Warsaw Pact - limited the sovereign decisions of communist countries. Poland in its foreign policy had to take into consideration political, economic and military structures which primarily realised Russian goals.

The second ideological trend which had a strong influence, albeit not as strong as the first, was "the Polish road to socialism". According to his idea, Gomułka (fruitlessly) tried to build communism on the basis of spiritual and national heritage. Soon in consequence, the General Secretary of the Polish People's Party (PPP) Gomułka, Marian Spychalski, Zenon Kliszko and other communists of similar views were accused of right-wing nationalist deviation. In November 1949 during the third plenary session of the Central Committee of Polish United Workers' Party, established in December 1948 as a result of a merger of the Polish People's Party and Polish Socialist Party (PSP), Gomułka, Spychalski and Kliszko were dismissed from the Central Committee of the party (Paczkowski 1996: 216-223).

On the back of these changes, both in the USSR after the 20th convention of the Communist Party of the Soviet Union (CPSU) and in Poland, where there was a wave of score-settling after the death of Stalin and Bierut, surprisingly Gomułka, identified as the spokesman for Polish road to socialism, regained power as the First Secretary of the PUWP. Along came hope for democratic changes in the internal system (Friszke 2003: 105-135). Foreign policy became a field for independent proceedings (for instance, the 1957 Rapacki Plan to create a nuclear-free zone; the 1964 Gomułka Plan regarding freezing nuclear armaments) (Materski, Michnowicz 2010: 496-508).

While W. Gomułka was in legally in power, Polish foreign policy concentrated on a small number of the most important directions, including:
• strengthening the formation of socialism in Poland through institutionalization of bilateral and multilateral relations with the USSR and other socialist countries,
• opening to the West and the attempt to develop political partnership-style relations,
• taking initiatives with the West in order to acknowledge Poland's western borders.

2.1. Poland-USSR relations

Since 30th October 1956, relationships between Poland and the USSR had theoretically been determined by the declaration of the CPSU government of progress and further strengthening of friendship and cooperation between the USSR and other socialist countries. Although, in the declaration Kremlin mentioned about the principle of national sovereignty and equality in economic relations, in practical terms Moscow did not plan to take its own words seriously (Materski, Michnowicz 2010: 496-508).

Regardless of meaning and inter-party connections, especially at the leadership level, after October of 1956, diplomacy gained ever more power in the relationships between the Polish People's Republic and Central Party of the Soviet Union. For ideological, strategic, political and economic reasons, Moscow did not intend to give up its influence over the biggest satellite state in Europe. When Marshal Rokossowski and his Soviet army advisors left the territory of Poland, the Kremlin's influence over decision making was reduced. The first half of 1957 was a time when modified forms of Poland's dependency on the USSR were shaped. In spite of a strong resistance against Chruszczow, Władysław Gomułka did not intend to openly oppose USSR policies in the international arena. As Moscow never trusted Gomułka, he tried to deal with problems in the bilateral contacts and he never disclosed any difficulties to the public as doing so would have strengthened the anti-Soviet tendencies in Polish society (Materski, Michnowicz 2010: 496-508).

In the case of diplomatic relationships with Warsaw, Moscow had to get used to using persuasion, instead of Stalinist dictator-style methods, which were still visible in the actions of the USSR Embassy before October 1956. Nevertheless, the significant growth of Polish diplomacy in relations with Kremlin did not mean that it took part in all decision-making. Intergovernmental negotiations played a significant role in economic relations. Being deprived of a charter until 1959, the Council of Mutual Economic Assistance was not a body that was able to decide upon the character of economic relations between socialist countries. A more effective strategy was to build the military and political structures of Warsaw Pact. Poland tried to make these structures more equal for all the member states; however, the USSR did not plan to maintain its influence by creating another NATO. Nevertheless, in the field of defence, bilateral contacts between the USSR and certain members of Warsaw Treaty were more important, a fact borne out by the agreement regarding stationing of Soviet army in Poland, which complemented cooperation in this agency (Jarząbek 2008: 21-26).

Despite arguments between Gomułka and USSR leaders, Polish-Soviet relations improved. Though Poland was far from attaining complete independence, it did gain freedom to act within the realm of the communist system, which meant progress in comparison to the previous Stalin era. The future of Polish diplomacy rested upon Gomułka's actions and his ability to seize upon the existing chances. With his firm stature in October 1956 Gomułka gained a position beyond the reach of any other communist leader in Europe. This fact limited the USSR's influence on PPR diplomatic the activities as respect for the USSR standpoint – and avoiding disputes with the Soviet leaders – was Poland's overarching aim. Although Polish diplomacy did not refer to the Kremlin as a vassal of the Kremlin, as it did in Stalin's day, in most cases regarding international issues, particularly regarding contacts with the West, Poland used the agency of the PPR Embassy in Moscow to inquire of the "Soviets" whether they had any "suggestions" with regard to the question at hand (Winiewicz 2010: 496-508).

Polish-Soviet relationships at this time were on the up because, according to Western diplomats, Gomułka's foreign policy in mid-1958 achieved convergence with that of Moscow. The Kremlin had also noticed that fact, which explains the invitation sent to the First Secretary of CK PUWP to pay a "visit of friendship" to the USSR. This visit took place on 24th October 1958 (Skrzypek 2005: 171-173).

Gomułka's attempt to build a more independent Polish foreign policy was not possible due to the bonds and ties of socialist internationalism, which precluded self-reliance in this respect. The Hungarian Uprising and its bloody repression by the Soviet Army in 1956 (Polish leaders remaining passive) made it clear that any potential attempts to change the system in this part of Europe were doomed to failure. Another inglorious symbol of Poland's participation in maintenance of the *status quo* was Poland's active participation in the putting down of the Prague Spring in Czechoslovakia in 1968. The situation took place in connection with internal factors which generated events in March 1968. It is characteristic that the more and more conservative behaviour of Gomułka, which in fact led to his losing power in 1970, coincided with his greatest foreign policy success – the conclusion of a very important Polish-German treaty regarding the basis for normalising bilateral relations (Szczepanik 2012: 195-202).

It is a paradox that after October 1956, Polish relations with many non-communist countries, including NATO members largely improved, while at the same relations with Poland's so-called sister countries of the Warsaw Pact deteriorated, those allies observing the Gomułka government with suspicion. PPR diplomacy encountered various difficulties in the socialist capitals, sometimes even while addressing problems that had previously been viewed as routine. Diplomats coming from Czechoslovakia, Hungary, Bulgaria, Romania and (in those rare cases when they were recognised) from GDR exercised caution in their dealings with representatives of the People's Poland (Materski, Michnowicz 2010: 508-526).

The aim of PPR diplomacy was normalisation of relations with socialist countries. Alliances with them constituted a basic element of PPR foreign policy. Gomułka understood that the significance of Poland in Europe and worldwide was a function of PPR's relations with the USSR and other socialist countries. The confirmation that "the Polish route to socialism" had its limitations became visible when PUWP with Gomułka supported a Moscow declaration in November 1957. The phrase Gomułka disliked, "a socialist group with the USSR in the lead," appeared in the text only once; repeatedly used were his expressions showing the USSR as the first and the most powerful socialist country. PPR diplomacy was tasked with downplaying with Western partners the significance of the declaration by pointing to the party character of the document while not giving the impression that Gomułka had been forced to sign the declaration (*Naszkowski to Spasowski...* 1956).

The aim and character of Polish foreign policy after 1956 was shaped under the dominating influence of Moscow. Even if disagreements between Gomułka and the USSR leaders arose regarding Poland's foreign policy, such disagreements related rather to the choice of tools and instruments for realising that foreign policy rather than the question of finding alternative policy in comparison to the assumptions of Marxism-Leninism principles which Gomułka in principle attempted to obey. It is also undeniable that the Polish October of 1956 created the conditions to depart from the uncompromising rules of Stalin-era politics, although this did not mean a move towards pluralism of a Western kind, but rather a slightly different approach to forming socialism in Poland.

2.2. The opening in relations with the West

Poland's foreign policy after 1957 focused both on improving the role of the socialist country in the international context and on minimizing East-West tension. However, Poland's reliance on the USSR political, economic and military structures significantly limited the extent to which these tasks could be realised.

Gomułka's Poland was perceived as the country where "national communism" was born, one which would constitute a model for other Warsaw Pact members to follow. In relation to PPR, countries of the West intended to conduct policy that would develop as far-reaching contacts as possible in almost every sphere, and to encourage the communist authorities to maintain their independence of Kremlin. After discussion with the USA, the main role within NATO for formulating politics of "discreet" support for Gomułka was taken up by Great Britain. During a meeting in Bonn on 2nd May 1957, NATO Prime Ministers adopted a document on policy regarding satellite countries, which repeated the British theses saying that it is necessary to support Gomułka and to support creation of national communist regimes in the Eastern Europe. Potentially, Poland was the most disintegrating force within the Soviet bloc. Eventually, NATO abandoned the policy of liberty as it realised that stirring up military conflicts in this part of Europe was not in the West's interests (cf. Materski, Michnowicz 2010: 526-543).

For reasons of prestige and propaganda, after October 1956 PPR diplomacy was interested in far-reaching contacts with Western European countries, including NATO members, who, despite treating PPR as a unique Soviet bloc's country, were initially cautious towards Warsaw's political initiatives, especially where they concerned ministerial visits, or constituted a risk of conflict with FRG. Polish diplomacy tried to conduct "an active policy of coexistence with capitalist countries". Peaceful coexistence with the West was supposed to end with socialism's victory over capitalism. However, the more PPR citizens experienced the West, the more they were fascinated with it. During a press conference in autumn of 1957, Gomułka expressed concern about the lack of control over the visits of artists and scientists to capitalist countries. He criticised them for unreasonable admiration for the West and a lack of national pride (Nurek 2003: 212).

After October 1956 Great Britain became one of the most important fields of activity for PPR diplomacy. This was prompted by London's favourable response to changes in Poland, its position in the Western alliance, and Warsaw's hope that the Labour Party would soon take power. Some obstacles that might have hindered the development of closer ties were successfully removed before 1956. In 1954 Polish diplomacy negotiated a favourable agreement on compensation for the nationalised property of British citizens. This agreement and another, which regulated repayment of Polish World War II loans from Britain, signed on 24th June 1946, removed barriers in economic relations (Materski, Michnowicz 2010: 526-554).

Polish-French relationships were strongly burdened by the Stalin period. Within exception of the USA, the PPR's political relations in the early 1950s were not as bad with any other Western country. From 1954 a gradual improvement took place within a certain thawing in the Western superpowers' relations with Moscow; but above all, Moscow assigned new tasks to PPR diplomacy regarding France. These tasks, the aim of which was to undermine attempts to build Western European Unity, meant supporting the French Communist Party, an important role for PUWP, and developing contacts with other political powers unwilling to ratify the treaty of the European Defence Community (Pasztor, Jarosz 2001: 20-31).

Another difficulty for PPR diplomacy in relations with France was the Suez Crisis. In its support of Egypt, Poland, was among those nations that criticised actions of Paris. Despite these international burdens, in the period before Gomułka became leader, Polish diplomats believed that relations with France had improved remarkably. Although Warsaw was aware of Paris's pro-Atlantic policy, which limited Polish political initiatives, economic relations developed well. It was also believed that Poland and France could develop academic and cultural cooperation. At that point, the Polish Ministry of Foreign Affairs was ready to accept the re-opening of the French Institute in Poland, in exchange for regaining control over the Polish Library in Paris (*Note of 13th October 1956*).

Neither were Polish-Italian relationships easy. The Stalinist period damaged bilateral relations. What Gomułka above all aimed at was obtaining loans and modern technology for the Polish economy. Not insignificant for Polish diplomacy was the question of its Western borders, acknowledgment of which Gomułka was fighting for in the West.

PPR diplomacy did have some instruments for applying political pressure on Italy. The problem of South Tyrol, inhabited mainly by German speakers and claimed by Austria, resulted in attempts by Rome to gain Polish support since the end of 1950s. Vienna attempted to generate international debate on this matter and bring the case of the ethnic Germans to the United Nations. As Rome preferred not to make the affair international, the language of Italian diplomats regarding Austrian policy resembled the attitude of Polish diplomacy towards the threat of West German revisionism. The USSR believed that the problem of South Tyrol was between Italy and Austria alone and was for them to settle without international intervention. The Kremlin's position obliged PPR to support bilateral talks and to resist any idea to internationalise the issue. Both Moscow and Warsaw were against changes in Europe's borders, a fact that determined their attitude towards this dispute between the NATO state and the neutral country. Paradoxically, this led to Polish-Russian supported for the latter (Materski, Michnowicz 2010: 541-543).

After October 1956 Polish-USA relationships improved significantly, driven by the USA's belief that Gomułka had been able to distance himself from Moscow politics. This warming of relations aroused suspicion among other communist countries.

Even though Gomułka held himself officially aloof towards any Western help, the government in Warsaw wanted to build its contacts with highly-developed capitalist countries and to obtain loans on favourable terms – provided such loans were not termed "aid". PPR diplomats did not know exactly what lay beneath U.S. policy towards Poland but drew their conclusions from talks with Western representatives, press conferences and the overtone of propaganda directed at the Polish nation. In a memorandum agreed with the UK's Foreign Office, the State Department described Poland as an unusual communist country which had achieved a degree of independence from the USSR. The USA intended to support Gomułka through financial aid and trade development to lessen Poland's economic dependence on Soviet Russia. The USA did not make any difficulties regarding the exchange of academics and engineers. Similarly, when it came to cultural connections, the USA enabled Poles to experience the West and maintain ties there (Materski, Michnowicz 2010: 556-568).

Lacking the attributes of a sovereign state, Poland was limited in its opportunities to interact in the West for the purposes of realizing its socialist interests. Gomułka wanted the West to acknowledge Poland's identity as a sovereign country and to create partnership relations with Western states but this proved impossible due to the dominating political, economic and USSR security position. According to Marxist-Leninism assumptions, the aim of Polish-Western co-existence was a victory over capitalism. As such, partnership was out of the question and Moscow was the only alternative for Poland's development.

2.3. Initiative for Poland's western borders acknowledgment

In the overall politics of Gomułka from 1956 until the end of his career in 1970 the matter of Poland's Western borders was a top priority.

Political changes in Polish People's Republic made it possible to establish diplomatic relations with the Federal Republic of Germany. Even before October 1956, Warsaw was ready for normalisation with Bonn but, as it turned out, the first unconfirmed signals from Western Germany diplomacy came in late 1956. Poland made it clear the Western border was inviolable but did not make the establishment of diplomatic relations dependent on "any preliminary terms". Nevertheless, PPR diplomats wanted to establish full diplomatic relations, not only a substitute for them in the form of economic representatives or political missions lacking a full diplomatic status (*Jeleń to Spasowski...* 1956).

The record of Polish-Western German contacts in the end of 1956 and in the first months of 1957 is dense, ranging from press conferences to diplomatic meetings. Bonn declared its good will but also the necessity to correct the border in favour of FRG. Using its good diplomatic relations with West Germany, Yugoslavia tried to mediate in Warsaw's favour, though Warsaw was reserved to being with. Finally, in January 1957 Poland agreed to open unofficial talks in Washington between an advisor of PPR Embassy, Henryk Jaroszek, and Plenipotentiary Minister of the FRG Embassy Albrecht von Kessel. This dialogue did not bear substantial fruit (Jarząbek 2001: 116-118).

Polish diplomacy met with considerable difficulties when it tried to persuade the USA, Great Britain and France to take a more favourable stance regarding Poland's Western border. Due to the great importance of relations with FRG and its growing significance in NATO, Western superpowers did not want to jeopardise their relations with Bonn. On the other hand, Warsaw could see that Great Britain was its greatest supporter. However, October events in 1956 in Poland did not change London's position, as it turned out on 10th July 1957 when a Labourite, Konni Zilliacus, asked whether the British Government planned to accept the border on Oder-Neisse line and whether it supported German unification only within the borders of FRG and GDR. The chief of British diplomacy, Selwyn Lloyd, answered that, in accordance with Potsdam Treaty, the final determination of borders should be conducted through a peace treaty. He also mentioned Bonn's opinion that only the government of a united Germany could make a decision regarding its borders. The same formal standpoint was shared by other Western superpowers and NATO countries (Materski, Michnowicz 2010: 481-496).

On the question of Poland's Western borders, Gomułka mistrusted Moscow, believing that Moscow would be ready to correct Polish borders as a price of German unification. Since the end of the war, the PPR communist regime had referred to anti-German attitudes in Polish society. When in 1963 Kremlin manifested a tendency to lessen tensions in Europe mainly by changing its policy towards FRG, Gomułka reacted negatively, afraid of German unification. Gomułka estimated that the Polish People's Republic, whose territory was in large part guaranteed only by the USSR, should support FRG as a buffer state in Germany. In January 1963 Gomułka violently attacked Bonn and simultaneously presented a program of maintaining the *status quo* in Central Europe (Radziwił, Roszkowski 1994: 188-189).

Under Gomułka's leadership, Polish foreign policy underwent several chapters of progress. After 1957 it was a time when Poland tried to emphasize a certain independence from Moscow and maintain unity with the USSR. This led the West, especially the USA, to believe that Poland was searching for its own path to development. The second chapter opened in the 1960s, when Polish and Moscow foreign policy were visibly aligned and any appearance of independence vanished; Gomułka became a fundamental interpreter of Marxism-Leninism as a consequence of his dogmatic attitude towards shaping socialism in Poland. The third chapter began with the Warsaw Pact countries' use of armed intervention in Czechoslovakia in 1968 and during events in Poland in March that year, in which Gomułka can be seen as a man dependent on Moscow's decisions and deprived of free will to lead his country's policy - as was the case following October 1956.

3. Poland's foreign policy under Edward Gierek's leadership

The years of 1970-1980 are conventionally called the era of Edward Gierek (Friszke 2003: 309-366). In the international arena it was a time of the normalization of East-West relations as they took on a less confrontational character (Helsinki Final Act of OSCE, 1975) (Zając, Zięba 2005: 114-117). These circumstances were take advantage of by Gierek, Poland's new leader, who promoted not only the political opening of Poland to the West but a economic opening too (Borodziej 2005: 15-33). Gierek believed that borrowing in order to invest would help modernize the Polish economy and make a great 'civilizational leap'. His first few triumphs increased public support for the government. Participation in the international arena was a new challenge because it required more activity to create economic and trade ties. Simultaneously, there was growing pressure from the People's Party to take more control over the organizational aspect of Polish-Western relations (*On coordination principles...* 1973: 13-53).

Polish foreign policy in the 1970s was to a large degree derived from the world's division into blocs. Though it can be assumed that international organizations and conferences constituted a good place for dialogue (including bilateral talks, which for political reasons were difficult to organize), casting votes depended on the bloc thinking. A further example of Polish diplomatic multilateral functioning is its participation in the United Nations Organization. In 1970 and 1971, Poland sat on the UN Security Council as a rotating, non-permanent member. This created certain additional opportunities regarding participation in discussions and consultations on numerous international issues. However, in this field of PPR diplomatic activity too, there were certain limitations. They were noted by the permanent PPR ambassador to UN Eugeniusz Kułaga who wrote: *we should not forget about very serious limitations in activities of a particular Council's members resulting from the role of this organ, but also from the political position of a given country, its membership of certain treaties or groups, and finally – from topics discussed in the Security Council in a given period* (Jarząbek 2010: 663).

In this period, the priority tasks for Poland's international policy was to acknowledge the Oder-Neisse border, constitute diplomatic relations with FRG and repay debts that emburdened bilateral relations, i.e. rent arrears, compensations for the victims of the Third Reich, or campaign to reunite families. Even though Moscow tried to discourage Warsaw from signing an independent pact with Bonn, after signing a treaty on the basis for normalising relations with PPR and FRG it did not interfere into bilateral politics, even when there were consultations regarding Polish-West German relations. PPR leaders and the diplomatic service of the period was able to influence how relations were normalised, which is did by seeking support in other countries (cf. Jarzabek 2010: 663).

The enthusiasm and support for Gierek from the first half of the 1970s fell systematically in the latter half of the decade as the first results of "debt spiral" hit. Ever since that time, two questions have gone unanswered: To what degree was Poland's foreign policy used to muffle unresolved domestic problems? And, was Poland a bridge or dam in relations between the USSR and the West in this period? (cf. Szczepanik 2012: 199).

A very important point for Polish diplomacy was the signing of the Final Act of OSCE, which Edward Gierek hoped to use to deepen Poland's relations with both East and West. Poland was aware that a policy of detente could greatly boost its development. Moreover, by signing the OSCE Final Act Poland had gained some acceptance for its identity as Polish state and guaranteed the stability of Oder-Neisse border.

Because of Poland's dependence, Soviet diplomacy was the most important partner for Polish diplomacy. Forced to hold a course set by Moscow, Poles carefully observed the direction taken by the Russians on matters ranging from the strategic to the local. The former was commonly-known; the latter was reflected in the language repeatedly used in instructions sent to the most remote diplomatic posts: "consult with the a local Soviet Representative on the matter" or "behave as a Soviet Representative should". PPR diplomacy was also obliged to promote the current ideas of Soviet policy. In strategic issues, Poland tried to see the Moscow course in the widest possible way, making use of fair winds in the USSR's relations with a superpower to conduct business on issues in its own interest. The field of operations was at the highest level, included meetings of summits party-state members, deliberations of Soviet bloc ministers, bilateral meetings of party leaders, and bilateral consultations of ministers and conferences of experts. Relations with Soviet bloc countries were maintained according to the norms described by this community, relations with other communist parties as China or Yugoslavia, according to principles similar to relations of countries from the opposing bloc (cf. Skrzypek 2010: 732).

The most significant place in relations between Poland and the West still belonged to France, creating a particular insurance policy. On actions with respect to GDR, Paris was to be consulted, although, of course, Moscow came first. PPR leaders planned to fight German reunification, supporting FRG, and connecting it with the socialist community by signing a new treaty of friendship. The OSCE Final Act, and Gierek's declaration of 8th and 9th of October 1974 while in America, constituted the background of relations with the USA. Poland was still to strive for economic progress with the West, including being granted access to scientific achievements which would allow modernization. A detailed instruction to Polish diplomacy was to fight back attempts to conjoin economic cooperation and human rights. For this purpose Moscow recommended further work on the provisions of the OSCE Final Act (*The Act of 20 March 1976...*).

In the mid-1970s Poland began to experience economic difficulties, resulting from bad policy. An ill-conceived decision of Prime Minister

Piotr Jaroszewicz in December 1976 to increase in the price of meat by and average of 69 per cent and to double the price of sugar provoked an avalanche of protest from much of Polish society. In many Polish towns a general strike was declared against government's decisions. As communist leaders could not overpower society, they decided to use repression, making mutual relations even worse.

In the face of the beating of detainees, unjust trials and workers being dismissed from work, there appeared public appeals in the name of the repressed. Jacek Kuroń wrote an open letter to the General Secretary of the Italian Communist Party Enrico Berlinguer and asked him to influence PPR leaders. Berlinger made an appeal (Roszkowski 2007: 335-338). Communist leaders of the time could not stop the process of relaxation and so the leadership of the PUWP started to lose influence over its own members. The deepening economic crisis released many negative reactions from society, slowly but surely weakening the political system.

In spite of difficulties in Poland, Gierek demonstrated his openness to the world. Over 15th to 17th September 1976 he welcomed Giscard d'Estaing on a private visit. In their conversations the guest promoted European integration in the shape of a European union based on the European Economic Community. Polish diplomacy related to these plans with growing understanding. Neither did Polish diplomacy object to leadership of this structure belonging to France, Great Britain or GDR, politicians seeing here an alternative to a Germany-dominated EU. There was less enthusiasm for France deepening ties with the USA and NATO, but it was hoped that the increasing significance of the French political left would ameliorate this trend (cf. Skrzypek 2010: 750).

The active years of Polish diplomacy after the crisis of 1976 were even more connected with Gierek's loss of influence in Moscow, who viewed Polish reforms as too domestic and not international enough. On the other hand, following the USSR's armed intervention in Afghanistan, the West hardened its attitude to Moscow and those countries cooperating and dependent on the USSR.

The sequence of events which started in Poland in the beginning of July 1980 and which was to lead to systemic transformation put PPR diplomacy in a difficult situation within previously unknown challenges. In the second half of 1976 Polish diplomacy was "dominated by attempts to counteract" negative foreign reactions connected with the way Poland had repressed workers' protests in June. In the following years similar activities were necessary in the face of the West's reaction to the appearance of a democratic opposition and repression of its participants. However, the spirit of ongoing *detente* and the fact that the initiatives were of a social rather than official character (such as letters of protest, press articles), there was no need to take particularly complicated diplomatic action (cf. Paczkowski 2010: 821).

Foreign policy of the People's Poland in the time of Gierek's leadership was concentrated on opening up to the West, since the West could help to modernize the country much faster than either bilateral relations with the USSR or multilateral relations within CMEA. Taking into consideration context in which Gierek was active, a period when CPSU leaders in Moscow had to be consulted (and negotiated with) on key political decisions, we should assume that his decisions were both bold and reckless. Even today scholars discuss the moment in which the limit of the People's Poland's indebtedness was crossed - the consequences were felt by society for decades. The effect was an onerous national debt, economic destabilization at the end of the 1980s and the emigration of hundreds of thousands of Poles. As the consequence of economic and political crises during Gierek's leadership, the communists gave up power.

It is also a certain historical paradox that economic and political crises in Poland (1956, 1968, 1970, 1976, 1980/81) significantly contributed to the creation of the strong "Solidarity" social movement, resulting an the handover of power in Poland, peaceful revolution in Central and Eastern European countries and the end of bi-polar system. The USSR's dissolution opened a new chapter in the history of international relations. Finally, the Republic of Poland as a completely sovereign entity could realize its own political, economic and security aims which were parallel with its national interest.

4. Conclusions

In the 1980s, following another change of the leader, Poland faced ever worse consequences of social unrest, in the form of demonstrations in August 1980 and development of Solidarity. The atmosphere in the relations between the East and West cooled, which fact the USSR exploited once again for the purposes of internal integration. Pressure in this respect, allied with the Polish authorities' fear of losing its grip on power resulted in the declaration of martial law in Poland in

December 1981 (Bahr 1985: 196-202). The consequence was Poland's international isolation in relations both with the West and socialist states (Zając, Zięba 2005: 131-136, 180-185), forcing the Polish Foreign Service to operate in difficult conditions. The idea to develop relations with non-European countries (e.g. the visit of General Jaruzelski in India, Algeria, Libya) was an attempt to solve the problem of isolation (Noworyta 2008: 118-132).

Declaration of martial law in Poland not only froze relations with the West but above all resulted in economic and political destabilization. Foreign policy lost its efficient instruments of interests realization in the USSR while "sister" socialist states distanced themselves from Warsaw in fear of Solidarity's ideas. As a result of Michaił Gorbaczov's reform in the USSR, the change in PRP policy and readiness to compromise in the governmental system, made the "round table" possible in 1989. Peaceful dialogue with Solidarity marked the beginning of the transfer of power to Poland's political opposition.

Even today we still question whether the most significant changes and social tensions of this era (1956-1989) were caused by transformations and social conflicts in Poland or whether they were a consequence of a change in the international arena, especially Gorbaczov's policy of *perestroika* in the USSR.

The very real domination of the USSR in the socialist countries' system of cooperation limited Poland's own foreign policy sovereignty. This situation was caused by the change in Poland's geopolitical position after 1945 (its borders subject to the decisions of the great superpowers and the ruling bi-polar system in Europe and worldwide in the period of 1945-1989) and so East-West relations were dominated by international European relations. Therefore, they had an attribute of a strong bloc character which precluded the building of bilateral relations based on real national interests (Szczepanik 2012: 195-202).

In assessing two personalities – Władysław Gomułka and Edward Gierek – who dominated PPR politics and the formulation of its foreign policy, it must be conceded that both politicians operated in the realm of a lack of sovereignty. On the one hand, Gomułka sought to build Polish socialism and sometimes disagree with Soviet leaders but only in the Marxism-Leninism matters. His ultimate intention was to modernize the country. On the other hand was Edward Gierek who tried to modernize Poland using East-West cooperation to strengthen socialism.

5. Bibliography

Bahr J. 1985, *Wspomnienie z teraźniejszości*, „Zeszyty Historyczne" 72: 196-202.

Borodziej W. 2005, *Polityka zagraniczna Polskiej Rzeczypospolitej Ludowej w roku 1972-szkice do dyskusji*, „Polski Przegląd Dyplomatyczny" 1(23): 15-33.

Czubiński A. 2003, *Historia powszechna XX wieku*, Poznań: Wydawnictwo Poznańskie.

Friszke A. 2003, *Polska. Losy Państwa i Narodu 1939-1989*, Warszawa: ISKRY.

Jarząbek W. 2010, *Dyplomacja polska w warunkach odprężenia*, [in:] *Historia dyplomacji polskiej*. Tom VI 1944-1945-1989, ed. by W. Materski, W. Michowicz, Warszawa: PISM: 662-732.

Jarząbek W. 2008, *PRL w politycznych strukturach Układu Warszawskiego w latach 1955-1980*, Warszawa: Wydawnictwo Instytut Studiów Politycznych PAN.

Jarząbek W. 2001, *Problem niemiecki w polskiej polityce zagranicznej w latach 1956-1958*, „Dzieje Najnowsze" 1: 16-28.

Jeleń do Spasowskiego z 29 VIII 1956, Archiwum MSZ, w. 52, t. 678.

Kuźniar R. 2001, *Polska polityka bezpieczeństwa 1989-2000*, Warszawa: Wydawnictwo Naukowe Scholar.

Łaptos J., Mania A., 2010. *Dyplomacja polska wobec zimnowojennego podziału świata (marzec 1947-grudzień 1955)*, [in:] *Historia dyplomacji polskiej*, Tom VI 1944-1945-1989, ed. by W. Materski, W. Michowicz, Warszawa: Wydawnictwo PISM: 279-444.

Łoś-Nowak T. 1992, *Współczesne stosunki międzynarodowe*, Wrocław: Wydawnictwo Uniwersytetu Wrocławskiego: 51-62.

Materski W., Michowicz W. 2010 (eds.), *Historia dyplomacji polskiej*, Tom VI 1944/1945-1989, Warszawa: Wydawnictwo PISM.

Naszkowski do Spasowskiego z 17 XII 1956 r. „Zbiór Dokumentów" w. 56, t. 763: Archiwum MSZ, 1956.

Notatka z 13 X 1956, Archiwum MSZ, w. 9, t. 78, z. 23.

Noworyta E. 2008. *Polityka i dyplomacja – wspomnienia ambasadora*, Łódź: Wydawnictwo Społecznej Wyższej Szkoły Przedsiębiorczości i Zarządzania.

Nurek M. 2003, *Raporty roczne ambasady brytyjskiej w Warszawie 1945-1970*, Warszawa: Wydawnictwo Naczelnej Dyrekcji Archiwów Państwowych.

O zasadach koordynacji i organizacji stosunków z zagranicą, Uchwała Biura Politycznego KC PZPR z 30 stycznia 1973 roku, Archiwum Akt Nowych, KC PZPR, sygn. 1766, Protokół nr 59 Biura Politycznego.

Paczkowski A. 2010, *Dyplomacja polska czasów kryzysu (1980-1989)*, [in:] *Historia dyplomacji polskiej*, Tom VI 1944-1945-1989, ed. by W. Materski, W. Michowicz, Warszawa: Wydawnictwo PISM: 821-855.

Paczkowski A. 1996, *Pół wieku dziejów Polski 1939-1989*, Warszawa: Wydawnictwo Naukowe PWN.

Parzymies S. 2004, *Stosunki międzynarodowe w Europie 1945-2004*, Warszawa: Wydawnictwo Akademickie Dialog.

Pasztor M., Jarosz D.,2001. *Robineau, Bassaler i inni. Z dziejów stosunków polsko-francuskich w latach 1948-1953*. Toruń: Wydawnictwo Adam Marszałek.

Radziwiłł A., Roszkowski W. 1994, *Historia 1945-1990*, Warszawa: Wydawnictwo Szkolne PWN.

Roszkowski W. 2007, *Historia Polski 1914-2005*, Warszawa: Wydawnictwo Naukowe PWN.

Topolski J.1986, *Zarys dziejów Polski*, Warszawa: Wydawnictwo Interpres.

Skrzypek A. 2010, *Dyplomatyczne dzieje PRL w latach 1956-1989*, Pułtusk-Warszawa: Wydawnictwo Akademii Humanistycznej w Pułtusku.

Skrzypek A. 2010, *Dyplomacja polska między Wschodem a Zachodem (1976-1981)*, [in:] *Historia dyplomacji polskiej*, Tom VI 1944-1945-1989, ed. by W. Materski, W. Michowicz, Warszawa: Wydawnictwo PISM: 731 – 816.

Skrzypek A. 2005, *Mechanizmy autonomii. Stosunki polsko-radzieckie 1956-1965*, Pułtusk-Warszawa: Wydawnictwo Wyższa Szkoła Humanistyczna w Pułtusku.

Szczepanik K. 2012, *Organizacja polskiej służby zagranicznej 1918-2010*, Warszawa: Wydawnictwo Naukowe ASKON.

Śniegocki R. 2006, *Historia-burzliwy wiek XX*, Warszawa: Wydawnictwo Nowa era.

Uchwała z 20 III 1976 w sprawach głównych kierunków działania w związku z realizacją AK KBWE, Archiwum MSZ, Dep. IV, z. 31/81, w. 2.

Winiewicz J. 2010, *Notatka z 1 VIII 1957*, [in:] *Historia dyplomacji polskiej*, Tom VI 1944-1945-1989, ed. by W. Materski, W. Michowicz, Warszawa: Wydawnictwo PISM: 161 – 197.

Zając J., Zięba R. 2005, *Polska w stosunkach międzynarodowych 1945-1989*, Toruń: Wydawnictwo Adam Marszałek.

Spain's Foreign Policy in the Years 1945-1975

MAŁGORZATA MIZERSKA-WROTKOWSKA
UNIVERSITY OF WARSAW

The aim of this chapter is to present Spain's foreign policy after World War II, up to the death of General Francisco Franco and the beginning of democratization. It covers research into the following questions: (1) What were the causes and manifestations of Spain's international isolation immediately following World War II? (2) How did Spain succeed in normalizing foreign relations? (3) What were the main foreign policy directions of "Franco era"? (4) Which measures were successful - and which not? This chapter utilizes the method of analysing and criticising sources and a making a comparative analysis of available information, primarily Spanish-speaking.

1. Spain on the international stage in the aftermath of World War II

In 1945 the former Foreign Minister of Spain, JF de Lequerica, was sent to Washington, where he took up the rather unusual position of Inspector of Embassies (*Inspector de Embajadas*). Alberto Martín Álvarez-Artajo was appointed new minister, before whom stood the unenviable task of softening the image of Franco's regime internationally. The minister enjoyed a large degree of autonomy thanks to the aversion of leaders of many countries to the dictator, which forced General Franco to limit his personal involvement in foreign policy (Olivié 2004: 33; Huguet 2003: 500; Calduch 1994: 115-117; Pereira 1983: 185).

The so-called Big Three did not speak with one voice when it came to Spain; in Potsdam Winston Churchill, the British Premier, opposed Stalin's idea of introducing sanctions against Spain. Churchill believed that sanctions would, rather than weaken the regime, strengthen the relationship of Spain's citizens with its dictator. Harry Truman, President of USA, on the other hand, initially advocated Stalin's concept, but with the escalating conflict with the Soviet Union, he finally sided with the United Kingdom (Calduch 1994: 117-118). USA and the United Kingdom feared that intervention in Spain could lead to another civil war, handing power to a Communist government (Huguet 2003: 500)[1].

1.1. Sanctions against Spain

On 9 February 1946 the UN General Assembly at the request of Panama (supported by Mexico, Venezuela, Bolivia and Guatemala) issued Resolution 32 (I), which included a recommendation that in relations with Spain UN Member States act in the spirit of the Declarations of San Francisco and Potsdam and not support its admission to the UN.

At the time Spanish relations with France were not going well. This was due to the actions of partisans (*maquis*) consisting of Spanish emigrants intent on the armed overthrow of Franco's government. France closed its border with Spain on 1 March 1946 (Calduch 1994: 118-120). After some days, France, USA and the United Kingdom issued the so-called London Declaration, condemning the Franco regime and stating the terms under which Spain could end its international isolation (Powell 1995: 36-37; Pereira 1983: 185). On the other hand, the signatories of the Declaration assured that they did not support any form of intervention in Spain's internal affairs (though they were not initially unanimous on this - de Gaulle had been calling for) (Huguet 2003: 501; Olivié 2004: 32-33).

Meanwhile, in the UN Security Council, on the initiative of the Soviet Union and Poland a committee was formed to determine whether the existence of the Francoist regime constituted a threat to international peace and security. On the committee sat representatives of Australia, Brazil, China, France and Poland. Its report rejected the possibility of intervention in Spain, suggesting only a severance of diplomatic relations. Upon a motion of Poland this proposition was considered by the General Assembly, which subsequently, in Resolution 39 (I) of 12 December 1946, suggested that accredited ambassadors be withdrawn from the Spanish capital, Madrid, and that Spain be excluded from all initiatives and organizations

---

[1] On this period, see also: Martínez Lillo 2000; Espadas Burgos 1998; del Río Cisneros 1965.

affiliated with the UN system (Spain was, for instance, a member of the Universal Postal Union, the International Telecommunication Union and the International Labour Organisation). A number of countries – Argentina, Portugal, Dominican Republic, Switzerland, Ireland and the Vatican – elected not to comply with these recommendations. At the same time representatives of republican exiles in Mexico were gaining attention and support. These activists not only proclaimed a plan to restore the Spanish republic, but even formed a government headed by José Giral, which until 1946, was supported by 11 countries.

Spain's international isolation after World War II was not complete. Argentina, ruled by General Juan Peron, gave Spain commercial and financial support. On 30 October 1946, Spain signed an agreement with Argentina providing for 350 million pesos' credit for the import of Argentinian food. Thanks to loans Spain received 700 thousand tons of wheat (Pereira 1983: 186). Additionally, the Western powers – in particular the United States - never actually reduced to zero the supply of crude oil and other raw materials and food to Spain. Spanish diplomacy with exceptional skill manoeuvred between the Cold War blocs until the country get itself out of international isolation and normalized relations with key countries (Calduch 1994: 118-120).

1.2. Signs of normalization of Spain's international situation

On 31 March 1947 the Spanish Succession Act was issued (*Ley de Sucesión a la Jefatura del Estado*) and in June that year approved by citizens in a referendum. According to this document, Spain became a kingdom, and Franco Regent, authorized to designate the future king. The succession procedure at the end of the dictatorship was the subject of conversation between Franco and John Bourbon at the end of August 1948 (Wacławczyk 2004: 109-110). At the same time the first symptoms were appearing of Spain's emergence from international isolation. This had been made possible by changes in the international arena, where anti-fascism was being replaced by anti-communism (Pereira 1983: 186).

At that time, Franco decided to deepen relations with the countries of Latin America, whose representatives were sympathetic to "the Spanish question" at the UN. He had also been forced to seek new allies; quite unexpectedly, Franco turned his attention to the Arab states. It turned out that most of them, as conservative monarchies, shared Franco's anticommunist views. Also not without significance was the fact that Israel had refused to establish diplomatic relations with Spain because of its association with the Axis during the war. As a result, Franco supported the Arab states in the Middle East conflict, and in 1946 recognised the League of Arab States. Interestingly, the Arab states have never voiced dissatisfaction with the Spanish presence in North Africa. What's more, Abdullah, the King of Jordan, was the first head of state to visit Spain since 1939 (his visit took place in 1949), and thanks to the Sultan of Morocco, Spain was allowed in 1952 to resume its place in the international administration of Tangier (Powell 1995: 38-39).

The US president, Harry Truman, announced in 1947 his famous "the doctrine of containment" (otherwise known as the "Truman doctrine")[2]. The United States were now supposed to help countries at risk of communist invasion. Fortunately for Spain, finding itself under Franco's rule, anti-communism had become they key determinant of American foreign policy, and brought the two countries closer together. In January 1948, Truman approved the suggestion of the National Security Council to normalize political and economic relations with Spain. Soon after France re-opened its border with Spain.

Spain - in marked contrast to Portugal - was not invited in 1949 to join the North Atlantic Alliance. This is even more surprising given that the regime of Antonio Salazar did not differ significantly from that of Franco. Researchers suggest, however, that Portugal's foreign policy during World War II was characterized by greater discretion and balance in its relations with the parties to the conflict than was the case with Spain (Olivié 2004: 31; Powell 1995: 37). Still, the new circumstances, did not compromise the Iberian Pact: Spain and Portugal renewed their 1939 mutual assistance agreement.

At the same time U.S. banks (the Export-Import Bank, Chale National Bank, National City Bank) decided to grant Spain its first lines of credit after international criticism forced the U.S. House of Representatives to retreat from the idea of excluding Spain from among the beneficiaries of the Marshall Plan. A further economic assistance agreement with Portugal was concluded and trade relations with Britain and France were opened, the latter deciding to expel from its territory the leaders of the Spanish Communist Party, which supported the "maquis" (Powell 1995: 38).

---

[2] The thinking underlying this policy was presented in 1946 by the American diplomat George Kennan, first in the so-called "long telegram" and then in the pages of *Foreign Affairs*.

1.3. Cancellation of the sanctioning resolutions

On 4 November 1950, the UN General Assembly, at the request of a group of Latin American countries (Brazil, Bolivia, Colombia and Peru), the Arab states, and with strong support from the United States, approved Resolution 386 (V) cancelling the sanction resolutions of 1946. This decision led to the dissolution of the Spanish government in exile (Huguet 2003: 515). Ambassadors of different countries could now return to Spain, and Spain in turn could join the UN's specialized agencies. In 1950 Spain joined the ICAO and the FAO, in 1951 - to the WHO, UPU and ITU, and in 1952, UNESCO[3]. Nevertheless, the obstacles remained to Spanish accession to the UN itself and to the Council of Europe. The biggest objections in this respect from among the Western bloc countries came from Norway and the Benelux countries (Powell 1995: 38). Nineteen fifty one was the year of "the return of the ambassadors". To Madrid came representatives of the U.S. (Santon Griffis) and the UK (John Balfour). Ambassador of France was Bernard Harion, who had previously been the *chargé d'affaires* (Calduch 1994: 122).

In summary, it can be said that paradoxically the isolation of Spain in the international arena did not contribute to the weakening of the Franco dictatorship. Isolation awoke xenophobic sentiment in Spaniards, many of whom blamed foreigners for the situation. For many Franco personified the national interest. Moreover, while defeat of the Axis in World War II led to the international isolation of Spain, the outbreak of the Cold War proved the salvation of Franco and his system (Powell 1995: 37). Western powers turned a blind eye to the actions of the Franco regime during the war, acknowledging instead his anti-communism. Spain's re-admission to international bodies and the assumption of cooperation was the price for keeping the country to beyond the influence of the Soviet Union.

2. Spain's foreign policy 1953-69

2.1. The first international agreements and membership in the United Nations

The year 1953 was a turning point for Spain's foreign policy in the period in question. On 27 August 1953, Spain signed a concordat with

---

[3] ICAO - *International Civil Aviation Organization*; FAO - *Food and Agriculture Organization*; WHO - *World Health Organization*; UPU - *Universal Postal Union*; ITU - *International Telecommunication Union*; UNESCO - *United Nations Educational Scientific and Cultural Organization* (Granell 2011).

the Vatican. Previously Church-state relations had been governed by several separate agreements and declarations. By signing the Concordat, Pius XII proved his support for the government of General Franco. The latter immediately reciprocated, granting the Church new privileges or maintaining many new ones, such as economic support for future dioceses; legal immunity for priests, creation of church assets and state financing for the Church from compensation for earlier expropriation of property, tax relief, civil validity of effect of church weddings, compulsory teaching of religion, the right to establish different levels of state schools and to request the withdrawal from circulation of the publications conflicting with to the principles of faith. As can be seen, the Concordat resulted in major concessions being made to the Church. This comes as no surprise, however, since the Church was one of the main pillars on which the Franco government rested (Pereira 1983: 187-188; Powell 1995: 39). With the Concordat the government attained is own kind of legitimacy in the eyes of Spanish Catholics, while Franco himself gained control over the church hierarchy through his right to put forward candidates for bishops[4].

In 1953 another important document was signed – agreements with the U.S. paving the way, for the location of U.S. military bases on Spanish soil. These agreements were concluded for ten years and consisted of three parts: the Technical Support Agreement (*Asistencia Técnica*), the Assistance for the Common Defence (*Ayuda para la Defensa Mutua*) and the Agreement on economic aid (*ayuda sobre Convenio económica*) for the supply of military equipment (Huguet 2003: 503-504; del Rocío Álvarez Piñeiro 2006: 178-180). It was agreed that "the time and form of the use of military force will be determined by mutual agreement"(Article 3 of the disclosed part of these agreements). Such wording could not raise objections among the public. Nevertheless, the agreement was accompanied by a secret additional protocol, giving the U.S. the right to unilaterally decide to use bases in the case of communist aggression (*agresión Comunista*) that would jeopardize Western security. Many scholars equate this with a loss of Spanish independence through the limitation of its territorial sovereignty. Moreover, Madrid, Zaragoza and Cadiz found themselves in real danger due to storage in close vicinity of a nuclear weapons (Pereira 1983: 189-190; Powell 1995: 40; Huguet 2003: 504). These concessions were the price Spain paid to obtain the status of

---

[4] On the subject of relations between Spain and the Vatican under the Franco government, see Laboa 2000; Espada Burgos 1998: 140-152; Rodríguez Nieto 2007: 171-180.

U.S. ally, the economic benefits from U.S. aid and the development of strategically important infrastructure (Caluduch 1994: 122-125; Sagredo Santos 2004: 125-129; also se de Areilza 1984: 79-140; Viñas 1981, Vázquez Montalbán 1974 Cortada 1978: 205-273).

The Spanish-American agreements of 1953 were decisive in Spain's return to the international political stage. All that remained for Spain to be truly satisfied, however, was the country's admission as a member of the United Nations. In the early 50s this was impossible, as both the United States and the Soviet Union exercised their Security Council veto to block the candidacy of countries from the opposing bloc. It was only in 1955, following the death of Stalin, that a US-Soviet agreement enabled 14 countries to join the U.N. Spain was among these countries, officially applying on 27 September that year. But still Spain remained outside the Council of Europe, NATO and the European Communities (Calduch 1994: 125-126).

Spain showed a willingness to withdraw from Morocco[5], but left the initiative in this respect to the French, who controlled most of that territory. Franco also advocated that negotiations be conducted separately with each of the two countries governing the protectorate. Finally, Spain recognized Moroccan independence in early April 1956 during the visit of the Moroccan sultan to Madrid. An additional protocol to that agreement contains a provision stating that Spain will support Morocco in the organization of an army. Cooperation in this respect became a key pillar of the relations between the two states. Nevertheless, a shadow was cast over Spanish-Moroccan relations during that period by the crisis in Sidi Ifni – a Spanish-controlled town in the southwest Morocco. Under an earlier agreement Spain had decided to give away all of its possessions in Morocco except for Ceuta, Melilla, Sidi Ifni and the Tarfaja region[6]. It also retained sovereignty over Western Sahara. Offensive operations against the Spanish forces and pressure from the Rabat government calling for the immediate handover of Sidi Ifni caused the outbreak of war, lasting from November 1957 to February 1958. During the conflict Spain received significant French support.

In 1958, at the initiative of Admiral Luis Carrero Blanco, Sidi Ifni and Western Sahara were transformed into Spanish provinces. The Admiral had wanted to maintain sovereignty over the territories to help guarantee

---

5 On Spanish policy towards Morocco in the years prior to the granting of Moroccan independence, see Elkin 2004.
6 Spain finally withdrew from the region in 1958.

the security of the Canary Islands. However, the complete withdrawal of Spanish forces from the former Protectorate in 1961 resulted in increased pressure from Morocco to hand back Spain's remaining possessions in North Africa. Additionally, the Moroccan state unilaterally extended its territorial waters to 12 nautical miles, thus harming Spanish fishing interests. Finally the Sidi Ifni question went before the UN, where in December 1967 the General Assembly issued Resolution 2354 (XXII) confirming the right of Sidi Ifni to self-determination and calling for Spain to accelerate its decolonization efforts. On the basis of the Treaty of Fez (1969) Spain declared its transfer of its disputed region of Morocco. However, it failed to ratify the document within the prescribed term, forcing Morocco to file a formal complaint with the UN. Finally, the Spanish Cortes ratified the agreement and Sidi Infi became part of Morocco (Calduch 1994: 126-128; Pereira 1983: 193; Powell 1995: 46; Huguet 2003: 508-509). Even so, Spain managed to keep the Western Sahara for a further seventeen years.

By contrast, Equatorial Guinea's tendencies towards independence emerged in the early 1960s, and organizations seeking to independence from Spain in the country could count on the support of the Organisation for African Unity and neighbouring countries: Cameroon and Gabon. Interestingly, during this period, two key figures in Franco's government had differing views on the future of the province. These men were Franco's right-hand man since 1967 and vice-Prime Minister, Luis Carrero Blanco and Spanish Prime Minister and Minister of Foreign Affairs in the years 1957-1969, Fernando María Castiella[7]. While the former was for the introduction of broad political autonomy for Cameroon and maintaining Spanish economic influence, the latter advocated a peaceful movement towards independence. The situation was further complicated by traditional inter-ethnic rivalries in the Cameroon independence camp. In 1963, following a plebiscite, Spain granted Cameroon political autonomy. However, these concessions did not calm the situation and, on 12 October 1968, after the adoption of a new constitution in a state referendum, Spain agreed to grant the colony independence. This did not, however, lead to improved mutual relations. President Francisco Macías Nguema introduced a dictatorship, fighting the opposition and questioning the rights of Spanish landowners. This ultimately led to a

---

[7] On Spanish foreign policy while Castielli was in power, see Olivié 2004: 36-52; Espadas Burgos 1998: 222-244; Pardo Sanz 2000.

rupturing of diplomatic relations with Cameroon and the return to Spain of the Spanish colonists (Calduch 1994: 131-132; Powell 1995: 46-47)[8].

2.2. Relations with the Latin America and Arab countries

While Castiella was in power Spain sought to develop good relations with Latin America as compensation for its reduced activity on the European continent. Until the end of the 1950s, relations with Latin America mainly concerned culture and were realised through the Spanish Cultural Institute (*Instituto de Cultura Hispánica*) and the high-level visits of Latin American politicians to Spain (Pereira 1983: 193). However, in 1960s economic relations began to develop. In 1966, Latin American countries were already buying 17 per cent of Spanish exports (in 1975 the rate was 10 per cent). Spain aspired to become a bridge between the European Communities and Latin America. This potential added value for the EC of Spain's membership was made much of right from the first application filed in 1962. At the same time, Spain stepped up its presence in the region through collaboration with the Latin American Free Trade Association (*Asociación Latinoamericana de Libre Comercio*), the Organization of American States (*Organización de Estados Americanos*) and the United Nations Economic Commission for Latin America (CEPAL - *Comisión Económica para América Latina*) (Powell 1995: 45, see also Lerma Palomares 2004).

At the same time, mainly for political reasons, Spain sought to maintain good relations with the Arab states. This was ironic in that, in the meantime, in some of these countries monarchical governments – with some of which Spain had had friendly relations -had been overthrown. In their place arose populist governments supported by the Soviet Union. In the Middle East conflict, Spain, in contrast to the United States, supported the Palestinians. Castielli's anti-imperial rhetoric did not, however, stop him from making pragmatic decisions. During the Six Day War in 1967, Spain not only agreed to the use of its bases by the Americans, but undertook to protect Jews living in Spain. Economic cooperation agreements were only signed with Arab countries in the 1970s, including with Saudi Arabia, Algeria and Iraq (Powell 1995: 45-46; Pereira 1983: 191-192).

---

[8] On the decolonisation of Spanish territories in Africa, see also Vilar 2000a; Vilar 2000b; Espadas Burgos 1998: 207-220; Oreja Aguirre, del Campo Urbano 2001: 13-25; Salas Larrazábal 1992: 245-320; Ruiz Miguel 1995: 53-165.

2.3. Relations with international economic organizations, the United States and the European Communities

In less than a year after Castiella took office, in January 1958 he managed to gain membership for Spain of the Organization for European Economic Co-operation (OECD) and, in May 1958, of the International Monetary Fund (IMF) and the International Bank for Reconstruction and Development (the World Bank) (in 1963 Spain joined the GATT). Joining these organizations at a time when the Spanish economy was still autarchic in character signalled change. Spain now gained access to the technical and financial assistance needed to open its borders to the flow of capital and goods. The Stabilization Plan of 1959 (*Plan de Estabilización de 1959*) proved highly beneficial for the Spanish economy, this success (a balance of payments surplus) was thanks to the growth of tourism and the influx of capital from Spanish émigrés.

The crowning diplomatic event of the Spanish-American alliance was the visit of President Dwight Eisenhower to Madrid in December 1959. Bilateral relations were good at the time, though strategic differences did exist in the face of the crisis in Ifni. In 1963, Spain and the United States renewed their alliance. The new agreement provide for few changes compared to that of ten years previously. The secret clause providing for procedures for the use of military bases remained in place, the Rota base being transformed into a nuclear zone, and economic compensation for Spain being minimally increased. Important for Spain and for the further developments was the establishment of the consultative committee (*Comité Conjunto Consultivo*) and conclusion of a declaration (*declaración Conjunta*) in which the United States recognized Spain's contribution to shaping the security of the Western bloc. This last event was considered a success by Franco's diplomacy (*España y los Estados Uniodos...*, Calduch 1994: 129).

In relations with the European Communities of Spain stumbled on ideological and political barriers. In accordance with a European Parliament resolution adopted at the request of the German Social Democrat Willy Birkelbach, a country wishing to apply for membership in the EC had to meet geographic, economic and political conditions. In the last of these categories, the *sine qua non* was a government enjoying democratic legitimacy (Powell 1995: 43). This was a precondition that Spain did not fulfil. It is thus no surprise that the letter sent by minister Castielli to the then President of the Council of Ministers of the EC, Maurice Couve de

Murville, declaring Spain's readiness to associate with Communities did not receive a substantive reply.

Spain made its next step towards the Communities in February 1964, when the Count de Casa Miranda, the Spanish representative to the Communities, sent another letter, this time expressing rather more modest expectations. The response from the Communities was positive. Negotiations began and resulted in the signing in 1970 of the so-called "Preferential Agreements" (Calduch 1994: 130-131; Pereira 1983: 191; Huguet 2003: 5-7; see also Contreras 2007: 119-138; Powell 2003; Mizerska-Wrotkowska 2013).

2.4. Relations with the United Kingdom in the context of Gibraltar

One of the most pressing issues of the times, when Castiella was Foreign Minister of Spain, was the problem of Gibraltar. The United Kingdom objected to negotiations on this matter. Spain therefore decided to publicize the "question" in the international forum. In 1963, thanks to its representative to the United Nations, Jaime de Piniésa, Spain managed to put the problem of Gibraltar before a meeting of the UN's decolonization committee. The Committee recommended that the States that were party to the dispute commence bilateral talks, and its view constituted the basis of Resolution 2070 (XX) of the UN General Assembly on 16 December 1965.

Spanish-British negotiations began in May 1966. At the first bilateral meeting Spain presented a draft agreement to supersede the Treaty of Utrecht[9]. The first article of the proposed document determined the matter of Spanish dominion over Gibraltar, but later on the document spoke of far-reaching concessions to the United Kingdom. The UK would be able to maintain a military base in Gibraltar, and Gibraltar and its community to maintain political, social and economic rights. But this proposal did meet with acceptance.

In the face of fruitless negotiations, Spain began to apply certain forms of pressure. In 1965, it imposed restrictions on the movement of people from Gibraltar into Spain, and then obstacles to overland and air travel. At the same time the Spanish government passed a program of social and economic support for the *Campo de Gibraltar* to compensate its nationals working in Gibraltar[10] for the impact of the restrictions.

---

9 The Treaty of Utrecht, concluded in 1713, brought an end to the Spanish war of succession. It was on the basis of this treaty that Great Britain took over Gibraltar from the Spanish.
10 The Spanish district bordering the rocky peninsula.

On the other side of the dispute, the United Kingdom planned a September 1967 referendum on the future of Gibraltar and requested the deployment of international observers. Despite the negative view taken by the decolonization of the Committee on 1 September 1967, a few days later, the UK held a referendum (the majority of participants opting to maintain Gibraltar's relationship with Great Britain). In response, the UN General Assembly in its Resolution 2353 (XXII) found the referendum to be inconsistent with accepted documents and urged the resumption of bilateral talks on the decolonization of Gibraltar.

In the face of silence from the UK, Spain decided to apply tougher sanctions. In 1968, Spain closed the border post, and adopted a practice of not considering Gibraltar residents as foreigners (Huguet 2003: 508). At the same time, the UK adopted a new constitution of Gibraltar (30 May 1968), in which the area was no longer regarded as a colony but as "part of Her Majesty's dominions" (*"parte de los dominios de Su Majestad"*).

A Spanish reaction was not long to follow; in January 1969 Spain expanded its territorial waters, and on 8 June 1969 introduced a total blockade on land communication, then on telegraph and telephone communication with Gibraltar and liquidated the sea crossing to Algeciras. The negative effects were immediate and affected both sides. Almost five thousand Spaniards working every day on Gibraltar lost their jobs. On the other hand, the outflow of labour paralyzed the construction and hotel industries as well as trade (Huguet 2003: 508).

These action, and those to follow in subsequent years, led to a genuine blockade of Gibraltar. However, sanctions and the support for Spain at the UN failed to bring about a resolution to the problem. The fiasco that was Spanish foreign policy on Gibraltar - the flagship strategy of minister Castielli - was one of the reasons for his speedy resignation (Calduch 1994: 132-134; Pereira 1983: 191; Powell 1995: 47, see also Anguita Olmedo 2007: 191-203).

2.5. The end of Castiella time in office

Castiella's last years in office were marked by negotiations for new Spanish-American ties. Talks were held on the one hand in the shadow of the Arab-Israeli conflict of 1967 and the war in Vietnam, and on the other hand, under the pressure of the Spanish public's outrage at the

Palomares air disaster[11]. In addition, at that time there was already palpable tension between the technocrats of Opus Dei (*"tecnócratas"*), supported by Carrero Blanco, and supporters of 'opening' (*"aperturistas"*) of which Castiella was one. In view of the difficulties encountered in the negotiations and the U.S. presidential campaign, it was decided to extend by six months the validity of the existing Spanish-American treaty, in accordance with the provisions of the 1953 deal.

The November 1968 elections in the United States were won by Richard Nixon and a meeting between Franco and the U.S. Secretary of State, Dean Rusek, took place. In June 1969, Castiella and William Rogers (the new Secretary of State) decided to further extend the defence treaty to 26 September 1970.

The conflict between Castielli and Carraro Blanco intensified. The Minister did not see the conclusion of a negotiated treaty. In October 1969 on a wave of scandal over the company MATESA[12], he was removed from the government, along with the Information and Tourism Minister, Manuel Fraga Iribarne (Calduch 1994: 134-136).

3. Spanish foreign policy 1969-75

In 1969 Gregorio López Bravo, an Opus Dei technocrat became the Minister of Foreign Affairs[13]. In many respects he was a continuation of Castielli (concluding deals with the USA and the European Communities). Beyond strengthening the traditional focus of Spanish foreign policy (France, Latin America[14], the Arab states), he initiated work in new areas such as relations with countries of "people's democracy" and the CSCE process.

3.1. *New deal with the USA and Preferential Agreement with the European Communities*

On 6 August 1970 an Agreement on Friendship and Cooperation was signed between Spain and the United States. This agreement introduced a number of political and military modifications beneficial to Spain.

---

11 The air catastrophe at Palomares happened on 17 January 1966. As a result of a mid-air collision between two American aircraft (a strategic bomber and a tanker) during air-to-air refuelling, four thermonuclear bombs fell on the coast causing radioactive contamination.

12 MATESA was an Opus Dei-run business producing textiles machinery. In 1969 the company collapsed amid a scandal over the defrauding of public funds. The scandal triggered a political crisis leading to the reconstruction of the government.

13 À propos the foreign policy of Lópeza Bravo and other foreign affairs ministers of the Franco era, see: Pardo Sanz 2000: 364-369; Espada Burgos 1998: 245-260; Powell 2007: 19-60.

14 See M.J. Henríquez Uzal 2008.

But Spain not get an express U.S. security guarantee or succeed in raising the rank of the agreement, which would have required the approval of the U.S. Senate, which was traditionally unfavourable to Franco (Powell 1995: 49). Under the new deal, Article 34, which permitted the United States to use bases on Spanish soil without first consulting the Spanish government, was cancelled. The system of bilateral consultations on defence matters was strengthened: at the government level and within the framework of the Joint Committee (Article 36). At the same time both sides agreed that their cooperation on defence was a part of the Western system encompassing the Atlantic and the Mediterranean. Also announced in Article 35 was the future regulation of formal relations within the system (which was intended to bring Spain closer to NATO). The new agreement also determined that bilateral cooperation would expand into other areas (Calduch 1994: 136-137; Pereira 1983: 192).

López Bravo, like Castiella, was an advocate of closer cooperation with organizations of European integration. Having once been Minister of Industry (in the years 1962-1968) he knew the importance of economic relations, including trade, with Western Europe. In June 1970, concluded a preferential agreement that was economically favourable to Spain (the Community significantly lowered customs duty on industrial goods in comparison with more moderate cuts by Spain). Nevertheless, the political aspirations of Spain reached much further. In 1973, primarily due to the accession to the Community of Denmark, Ireland and the UK, it was already necessary to modify the deal with Spain. On the basis of the Additional Protocol, these countries were excluded from the operation of the preferential agreement and were in practice treated as third countries (Powell 1995: 48).

3.2. Relations with France, Portugal, Morocco and the Vatican

At the same time as this was happening, the new foreign minister sought to ensure the best possible relations with its neighbours. In the case of France, this worked, in the form of two 1970 agreements, one commercial (for the purchase of 30 Mirage M-3 fighters) and one military. A further breakthrough in bilateral relations took place in the following year, when the French Foreign Minister Maurice Schuman paid a visit to Spain. At the same time, however, certain contentious issues manifested themselves. These included the operations of ETA, the problem of political emigrants, agricultural and financial policy and France's objection to Spain's admission to the EC (Pereira 1983: 192).

Relations with Portugal also saw their own revival of sorts: in May 1970 Franco met Marcelo Caetano, resulting in the signature of the Additional Protocol to the Agreement of 1939 (the "Iberian Pact"). However, when in March 1975, General Antonio de Spínola asked Franco for help, he refused, claiming that the provisions of the Iberian Pact did not apply in the "new circumstances" (i.e. after the military coup) (Powell 1995: 51).

During the discussed period, the Spanish government lost much sleep over the issue of Western Sahara. It turned out that Spain's concession of giving Morocco Sidi Ifni in 1969 had only whetted the appetites of that country and its neighbours, Algeria and Mauritania. At the UN, Spain maintained its position on the self-determination of the people of the territory, but failed to put forward a concrete timetable. At the same time Spain conducted the negotiations with the countries concerned, hoping in this way to divide them by offering beneficial bilateral economic contracts. Mauritania was offered the establishment of a fishing business (thereby establishing IMAPEC, a 51 per cent stake in which Spain gave to Mauritania in 1979). Morocco was offered a financing agreement (finally signed in July of 1970). In summary, the only achievement of the López Bravo administration with respect to the issue of Western Sahara was to prevent armed conflict. The lack of success in pursuing Spanish interests foretold the country's speedy withdrawal from the territory.

The growing conflict between the Spanish episcopacy and the Franco regime led to further defeat for López Bravo - failed negotiations on a new Concordat with the Holy See[15]. The draft, negotiated by diplomats of the regime in 1970, did not meet the expectations of the Spanish Church hierarchy, which had been expecting only minor revisions to the existing Treaty (Calduch 1994: 137-140). The conflict could not be resolved at the meeting of Pope Paul VI with López Bravo in 1973. A year later, in connection with the so-called "Añoveros case" ("*caso Añoveros*"), the Vatican threatened the Arias Navarro government not only with excommunication but also with the severance of diplomatic relations. Conflict was finally resolved, when the contemplated expulsion of the outspoken the Bishop of Bilbao, Antonio Añoveros, was not carried out. Añoveros had been demanding respect for the separate culture and

---

15 It is noteworthy that the sympathetic Franco Pius XII died in 1958. Relations between Spain and the Vatican during the pontificate of his successor, John XXIII, were correct, but chilly (mainly due to the support given by the Pope to Spanish political exiles). Paul VI, in contrast, was openly hostile (Pereira 1983: 192-193).

language of the Basques. Such a forced exile would have been a violation of the Concordat of 1953 (Pereira 1983: 190-194).

3.3. Cooperation with Eastern Europe

A novelty in the foreign policy of López Bravo was the opening of the trade and diplomatic cooperation with the countries of Eastern Europe. The Castiella government established commercial and consular relations with Poland and Romania, and that of López Bravo with Hungary, Bulgaria, Czechoslovakia and Yugoslavia. But the real breakthrough came with the gradual normalization of relations with the Soviet Union. In 1970, the head of Spanish diplomacy met with USSR Minister of Foreign Affairs, Andrei Gromyko. This meeting sparked confidential bilateral negotiations, culminating in the conclusion in September 1972 trading agreement. Even it was not until 1977 that the parties decided to give each other full and complete recognition.

No less surprising was Spain's recognition, in March 1973, of the communist government in Beijing as the sole representative of the Chinese state and its recognition early the next year of the German Democratic Republic. Interestingly, despite the opposition of the United States, Spain also maintained diplomatic and trade relations with Communist Cuba. By the end of López Bravo's time in power, the only communist countries with which Spain did not have relations Albania, North Korea and Vietnam.

3.4. Spain in the CSCE process

A second interesting manifestation of Spanish foreign policy of the period was the nation's participation in the CSCE process. Spain confirmed its willingness to participate in this undertaking in a memorandum addressed to the governments of Hungary and Finland on 13 December 1969. The representatives of the Spanish delegation (Nuño Aguirre de Cárcer, then Miguel Solano) enjoyed decision-making autonomy in spite of the growing crisis of authoritarian rule in Spain.

A key negotiating priority for Spain was security in the Mediterranean basin. Spain advocated maintenance of the territorial *status quo* in Europe (with the exception of Gibraltar), the right of every country to self-determination, and the prohibiting of intervention by other states or organizations in a country's internal affairs. Spain supported a reduction in military presence in Central Europe, though at the same time fearing that the centre of gravity of the prevailing tensions might shift towards the Mediterranean. Spain also advocated dialogue between East and West in areas such as migration, tourism and environmental pollution.

The seal was set on an open up of Spanish foreign policy at the CSCE Summit in Helsinki in the second half of 1975. Prime Minister Arias Navarro used this meeting to establish direct ties with many European leaders. Prince Juan Carlos was also involved in the CSCE process. In his speech at Helsinki he stressed the positive impact that the CSCE had had on Spanish foreign policy (Huguet 2003: 514).

3.5. The end of the "era of Franco"

In 1973, Franco resigned as prime minister, making way for Luis Carrero Blanco, keeping for himself the dignity of head of state and head of the armed forced. This entailed the sacking of the old government and appointment of a new. Laureano López Rodó was appointed Minister of Foreign Affairs, but had held the position for only a few months. In December 1973 Carrero Blanco was killed in an ETA attack. The new Prime Minister was now Carlos Arias Navarro (Pereira 1983: 140-143).

The last foreign minister of the Franco era was professor of international law and former ambassador to Paris, Pedro Cortina Mauri. During his brief, not quite two-year tenure, three problems occupied him: Spain's isolation in the international arena; the decolonization of Western Sahara and the consequences of rising oil prices. Furthermore, during this period anti-Franco opposition made its presence felt and the conflict between Church and government intensified. Spain also lost its close ally on its western border. In April 1974 the "Carnation Revolution" took place in Portugal, leading to the deposing of Marcelo Caetano. The democratization process in Spain's neighbour had begun, and with it a cooling of relations with Spain, as well as suspension of cooperation in the framework of the Iberian bloc.

Relations with the United States underwent a revival. This was due to the American decision that a base must be maintained in Spain at all costs. This decision was affected by the oil crisis in 1973 and the outbreak of the Yom Kippur War. As a consequence, the eastern Mediterranean became one of the least stable regions of the world. Further, in Portugal and Greece pro-American authoritarian regimes had fallen, while in France and Italy support for the Communist Party was on the increase. Spain was now the only country in Western Europe run by an authoritarian government (Pereira 1983: 195).

In this context, in June 1974, the government signed a joint Spanish-American declaration to lay the ground for a further renewal of the 1953 agreement. In this document, the two countries once again acknowledged that cooperation in the field of defence was an important part of Western security. Also adopted was the "Musketeers' rule" in mutual relations in relation to any external attack or threat of attack (see *Texto de la declaración...* 1974). In 1975 Gerard Ford visited Spain President in spite of advice to the contrary from his ambassador in Spain. Neither did the objections of the opposition Democratic Party concern him. A few months later, in October 1975 the Spanish-American preliminary agreement was hurriedly concluded (Powell 1995: 50).

In the summer of 1974 the Spanish government approved a new anti-terrorism law (*Decreto-ley antiterrorista*). In September of the following year the death sentence was carried out on two ETA members and three representatives of FRAP. This provoked a storm of protest, but above all, international isolation, comparable to that of thirty years previously. In protest the European Communities broke off trade negotiations with Spain and NATO's Parliamentary Assembly condemned the sentences and sought to cease all activity the aim of which was to make possible Spain's entry into the organization. At the UN, Mexican President Luis Echeverría requested the removal of Spain from the organization. In all, eighteen countries recalled their ambassadors to Spain "for consultations". All over the world demonstrations and were organized, along with boycotts of anything Spanish. The Soviet Union and the Eastern bloc, and, independently of each other, Pope Paul VI and the International Council of Jurists, condemned the sentences, and the United States broke off negotiations with Spain (Pereira 1983: 195).

The crisis was exploited by Morocco, trying to take from Spain Western Sahara and Ceuta and Melilla. This meant a change of front, since until then all neighbouring countries, Morocco included, had agreed to respect the disputed territory's right to self-determination. In an official letter addressed to the Minister of Cortina dated 23 September 1974, King Hassan II stated his claim to Western Sahara, citing historical evidence and proposing the dispute be resolved by the International Court of Justice. In relation to this claim, the UN General Assembly (in Resolution 3292/XXIX of 3 December 1974) asked two questions of the ICJ: (1) at the time of the Spanish colonization was the Western Sahara a no-man's land (*terra nullius*)?, (2) if not, what are the legal ties between of the territory with the Kingdom of Morocco and the Mauritanian Union? At the same time Resolution 3292, called upon Spain to delay its planned referendum in the Western Sahara pending the final judgment of the ICJ.

In the face of tensions with Morocco, Mauritania and Algeria and its struggle with the Polisario Front, Spain declared its intention to withdraw from the Western Sahara before the ICJ handed down its judgement. This announcement gave rise to the threat of conflict between those neighbours. Spain reiterated its position during the visit of the UN Secretary General in Madrid. Any cancellation of the decision to immediately withdraw would depend on the fulfilment of two postulates: Morocco would have to stop provoking border incidents, and Algeria would have to support the Polisario Front. On 16 October that year the ICJ announced its judgement: that the Western Sahara could not be regarded as having been a no-man's land at the time of its colonization by Spain. However, it judged the links between the nomadic people inhabiting the territory and the states of Morocco and Mauritania to be insufficient to legitimize the sovereignty of these countries over the disputed area.

Hassan II, able to count on the US support, and to some extent that of France, announced that he had no intention of respecting the judgement. In a gesture of protest he organized the so-called "Green March" – and 300 thousand civilians crossed the green border to enter the territory of Western Sahara. Asked by Spain to intervene, the UN Security Council did not decide to take any steps. On 7 November 1975, one week after King Juan Carlos took power from a gravely ill Franco, Morocco's ambassador in Spain put forward a proposed settlement. A week later, Spain, Mauritania and Morocco signed the "Madrid Declaration" (*la declaración de Madrid*). In this document, the last treaty concluded by Spain under the Franco regime, it was agreed that Spain would withdraw from the Western Sahara on 28 February 1976. Until this time Spain would operate a temporary administration in the Sahara in which representatives of Morocco and Mauritania and Yema would participate - an assembly representing the Sahrawi people. The Secretary-General of the United Nations was to be informed of the results of the tripartite negotiations. The law on the decolonization of Western Sahara was adopted by Cortes on 19 November 1975, a day before the death of Franco, which marked the beginning of the transformation process in Spain (Calduch 1994: 144-148; Pereria 1983: 195, see also Oliver 1989; Criado 1977).

4. Conclusions

In summary, the foreign policy of Spain under the dictatorship of Francisco Franco was to a great extent a continuation of previous actions (Powell 1995: 52), although it was closely linked to domestic policies. Franco, joining for the better part of his reign the roles of the head of state and head of government, was formally the prime mover of the country's external actions, but entrusted their implementation to successive foreign ministers, who were for the most part people with ties to the Falange and Opus Dei.

The turning point in Spanish post-war history was the year 1953, when the Concordat with the Holy See was concluded and relations with the US established. By entering into these agreements, which meant many concessions towards its partners, Spain paid a high price for ending its international isolation. Nevertheless, very tangible benefits were achieved by Franco himself: he guaranteed support for his regime from the Head of the Church and the world hegemon (Powell 1995: 40). This compromise enabled a continuation the opening up of Spain's external relations: Spain joined many international organizations, paved the way for its integration with Western security structures and European integration and cultivated bilateral relations with other countries.

Nevertheless, in the period under review, Spain failed to resolve the issue of Gibraltar in its favour, or to keep its North African colonies. The deep crisis in domestic politics, which emerged after the death of Carrero Blanco, left its mark on foreign policy. It only became possible to overcoming the new wave of hostility towards Spain in the international arena after the death of Franco and the establishment of democratic government (Pereira 1983: 196-197)[16].

5. Bibliography

Algora Weber M.D. 1995, *Las relaciones hispano-árabes durante el régimen de Franco. La ruptura del aislamiento internacional (1946-1950)*, Madrid: Ministerio de Asuntos Exteriores.

Anguita Olmedo C. 2007, *La reivindicación de Gibraltar en la transición española*, [in:] *Del autoritarismo a la democracia. Estudios de política exterior española*, ed. by Ch. Powell, J.C. Jimenez, Madrid: Sílex: 191-212.

---

[16] On the subject of Spanish foreign policy under the Franco regime, see also Gil Pecharromán 2008; Halstead 1980; Portero and Pardo 1996. On the balance sheet of Franco's foreign policy see Viñas 1989, Mesa 1988: 17-38. On the political-economic system of the discussed period, see Ruiz Martínez 2013: 43-56.

Areilza de J.M. 1984, *Memorias exteriores 1947-1964*, Barcelona: Espejo de España.

Calduch R. 1994, *La política exterior española durante el franquismo*, [in:] *La política exterior española en el siglo XX*, ed. by R. Calduch, Madrid: Ediciones de las Ciencias Sociales: 107-156.

Contreras D. 2007, *La relaciones de España y la CEE (1962-1979)*, [in:] *Del autoritarismo a la democracia. Estudios de política exterior española*, ed. by Ch. Powell, J.C. Jimenez, Madrid: Sílex: 119-142.

Cortada J.W. 1978, *Two nations over time: Spain and the United States 1776-1977*, Westport (Connecticut): Greenwood Press.

Criado R. 1977, *Sáhara: pasión y muerte de un sueño colonial*, Paris: Ruedo Ibérico, Paris.

Elkin M. 2004, *Franco's last stand: an analysis of Spanish foreign Policy regarding Moroccan independence in 1956*, "International Journal of Iberian Studies" 2(17): 67-86.

Espadas Burgos M. 1998, *Franquismo y política exterior*, Madrid: Rialp.

España y los Estados Uniods, 26 de septiembre de 1963, Madrid: Ediciones de la Oficina de Infomación Diplomática.

Gil Pecharromán J. 2008, *La política exterior del franquismo (1939-1975)*, Barcelona: Ediciones Flor del Vento.

Granell F. 2011, *España y las organizaciones internacionales*, [in:] *Política exterior española: un balance de futuro*, ed. by J.M. Beneyto, J.C. Pereira, Madrid: Instituto Universitario de Estudios Europeos de la Universidad San Pablo-CEU: 1035-1076.

Halstead Ch.R. 1980, *Spanish Foreign Policy, 1936-1978*, [in:] *Spain in the twentieth-century world. Essays on Spanish Diplomacy 1898-1978*, ed. by J.W. Cortada, London-Westport (Connecticut): Aldwych Press-Greenwood Press: 41-96.

Henríquez Uzal M.J. 2008, *El Prestigiio Pragmático: Iberoamérica en la política exterior de Gregorio López Bravo (1969-1973)*, serie: Cuadernos de historia de las relaciones internacionales nr 6, Madrid: Comisión Española de Historia de Relaciones Internacionales.

Huguet M. 2003, *La política exterior del franquismo (1939-1975)*, [in:] *La política exterior de España (1800-2003)*, ed. by J.C. Pereira, Barcelona: Ariel: 495-515.

Laboa J.M. 2000, *La política exterior de Franco: las relaciones con el Vaticano*, [in:] *La política exterior de España en el siglo XX*, ed. by J. Tusell, J. Avilés, R. Pardo, Madrid: UNED: 371-390.

Martínez Lillo P.A. 2000, *La política exterior de España en el marco de la guerra fría: del aislamiento limitado a la integración parcial en la sociedad internacional, 1945-1953*, [in:] *La política exterior de España en el siglo XX*, ed. by J. Tusell, J. Avilés, R. Pardo, Madrid: UNED: 323-340.

Mesa R. 1988, *Democracia y política exterior en España*, Madrid: Eudema: 17-38.

Mizerska-Wrotkowska M. 2013, *Spain's integration with the European Union*, [in:] *Poland and Spain: from Political Transition to European Integration*, ed. by M.Mizerska-Wrotkowska, J.Mª Reniu Vilamala, Barcelona: Huygens Editorial: 173-174.

Oliver P. 1989, *El Sahara Occidental en las Naciones Unidas*, [in:] *Las relaciones internacionales en la España contemporánea*, ed. by J.B. Vilar, Murcia: Universidad de Murcia: 303-315.

Olivié F. 2004, *Memoria e Historia: La política exterior de la España de Franco*, [in:] *Del aislamiento a la apertura: la política exterior de España durante el franquismo*, Madrid: Comisión Española de Historia de Relaciones Internacionales: 15-53.

Oreja Aguirre M., del Campo Urbano S. 2001, *Tres vascos en la política exterior española*, Madrid: Real Academia de Ciencias Morales y Políticas.

Palomares Lerma G. 2004, *La política exterior del franquismo hacia América Latina*, [in:] *Del aislamiento a la apertura: la política exterior de España durante el franquismo*, Madrid: Comisión Española de Historia de Relaciones Internacionales: 55-58.

Pardo Sanz R. 2000, *La etapa Castiella y el final del régimen, 1957-1975*, [in:] *La política exterior de España en el siglo XX*, ed. by J. Tusell, J. Avilés, R. Pardo, Madrid: UNED: 341-369.

Pereira J.C. 1983, *Introducción al estudio de la política exterior de España (siglos XIX y XX)*, Madrid: Akal Editor.

Portero F., Pardo R. 1996, *La política exterior*, [in:] *La época de Franco (1939-1975): política, ejército, Iglesia, economía y administración*, ed. by R. Carr, Madrid: Espasa Calpe: 195-302.

Powell Ch.T 2007, *Estados Unidos y España, de la dictadura a la democracia: el papel de Henry A. Kissinger (1969-1977)*, [in:] *Del autoritarismo a la democracia. Estudios de política exterior española*, ed. by Ch. Powell, J.C. Jimenez, Madrid: Sílex: 19-71.

Powell Ch.T. 2003, *España en Europa: de 1945 a nuestros días*, [in:] *La política exterior de España en el siglo XX*, ed. by F. Portero, Madrid: Ayer-Marcial Pons: 81-119.

Powell Ch.T. 1995, *Las relaciones exteriores de España, 1889-1975*, [in:] *Las relaciones exteriores de la España democrática*, ed. by R. Gillespie, F. Rodrigo, J. Story, Madrid: Alianza Editorial: 25-52.

Río Cisneros del A. 1965, *Viraje Político Español durante la II Guerra mundial 1942-1945. Replica al cerco internacional 1945-1946*, Madrid: Ediciones del Movimiento.

Rocío Piñeiro Álvarez del Mª 2006, *Los convenios hispano-norteamericanos de 1953*, "Historia Actual Online" 11: 175-181.

Rodríguez Nieto J.A. 2007, *Las relaciones España-Santa Sede*, [in:] *Del autoritarismo a la democracia. Estudios de política exterior española*, ed. by Ch. Powell, J.C. Jimenez, Madrid: Sílex: 171-190.

Ruiz Martínez F.J. 2013, *The franquist era, return to democracy, and consolidation of the welfare state in Spain*, [in:] *Poland and Spain: from Political Transition to European Integration*, ed. by M.Mizerska-Wrotkowska, J.Mª Reniu Vilamala, Barcelona: Huygens Editorial: 43-73.

Ruiz Miguel C. 1995, *El Sahara Occidental y España: historia, política y derecho. Analisis crítico de la política exterior española*, Madrid: Dykinson.

Sagredo Santos A. 2004, *Estodos Unidos y el franquismo: de la neutralidad a la cooperación. El pacto de Madrid de 1953*, [in:] *Del aislamiento a la apertura: la política exterior de España durante el franquismo*, Madrid: Comisión Española de Historia de Relaciones Internacionales: 125-129.

Salas Larrazábal R. 1992, *El Protectorado de España en Marruecos*, Madrid: Editorial Mapfre.

Texto de la Declaración de Principios hispano-americana 1974, "Revista de Política Internacional" 133: 346-347.

Vázquez Montalbán M. 1974, *La penetración americana en España*, Madrid: Talleres Gráficos Montaña.

Vilar J.B. 2000a, *La descolonización española en África*, [in:] *La política exterior de España en el siglo XX*, ed. by J. Tusell, J. Avilés, R. Pardo, Madrid: UNED: 391-410.

Vilar J.B. 2000b, *España y la descolonización de Marruecos*, [in:] *Relaciones entre España y Marruecos en le siglo XX*, ed. by J.U. Martínez Carreras, Madrid: A.E.A.: 65-76.

Viñas Á 1989, *La política exterior del franquismo*, [in:] *Las relaciones internacionales en la España contemporánea*, ed. by J.B. Vilar, Murcia: Universidad de Murcia: 115-124.

Viñas Á. 1981, *Los pactos secretos de Franco con Estados Unidos. Bases, ayuda económica, recortes de soberanía*, Barcelona: Ediciones Grijalbo.

Wacławczyk W. 2004, *Dyktatura generała Franco. Opór przeciwko reżimowi i przejście do demokracji*, „Dialogi Polityczne. Polityka – Filozofia – Społeczeństwo - Prawo" 2: 107-125.

Poland's Security Policy after the Second World War

JACEK CZAPUTOWICZ
UNIVERSITY OF WARSAW

In the nineteenth century Poland did not exist on the map of Europe. For 123 years the country was divided between the partitioning powers - Russia, Prussia and Austria. Twenty years after regaining its independence in 1918, Poland became the object of aggression by Nazi Germany and the Communist Soviet Union. During World War II, Poland was a member of the anti-Hitler coalition, but as a result of the Yalta accord fell within the sphere of influence of the USSR, eventually becoming part of the communist bloc. Its boundaries changed, lands in the East being lost and lands in the West being gained. In terms of geographical area and population, Poland now places eighth in Europe.

Understandably given this historical experience, Poland is particularly sensitive to security issues. Security, as for any other country, is dictated by both internal and external factors. The internal factors are geographical location (between Germany and Russia/the USSR), territory, population size and ethnic composition, economic potential, the size and quality of the armed forces, the quality of leadership and society's ability to accept the costs of ensuring security. External factors, in turn, are alliances, the international situation surrounding the country, which includes other countries' interest in the region, the alignment of Polish interests with the interests of other countries and potential for other counties to affect Poland's security (Kuźniar 2002: 34-35; Żurawski vel Grajewski 2012: 396).

This chapter consists of four parts. The first presents Polish security considerations during the Cold War, a period when Poland was in forced alliance with the Soviet Union and belonged to the Warsaw Pact and the Council for Mutual Economic Assistance (CMEA, also known as

Comecon). This part will also examine Polish peace initiatives as well as the impact of the Conference on Security and Cooperation in Europe. The second part will discuss the Polish security policy after 1989 when the Polish geopolitical situation changed radically and the basis for the country's national security became its membership of the North Atlantic Alliance. Poland took up its place alongside the United States in the coalition of states intervening in Iraq. The third part is devoted to Polish position with respect to the European Security and Defence Policy (ESDP) of the European Union. Initially sceptical, this position has changed to one whereby Poland has actively participated in the creation of stabilization missions and battle groups as well as initiating action to strengthen the military capabilities of the European Union. The fourth section looks at Poland's security strategy, including perception of threats and how those threats have been responded to, and reforms related to the armed forces. Section four also presents an analysis of strengths, weaknesses, opportunities and threats relating to the Polish national security system. The chapter ends with conclusions that may be drawn from its four sections.

1. Security policy during the Cold War

During the Cold War Poland was not an entirely sovereign state. Internally, under the auspices of Moscow power was held by the Communist Party. The government did not represent society, the system was undemocratic and the opposition repressed. Externally Poland was a satellite state of the Soviet Union, its foreign policy subordinated to the interests of a foreign power. Poland's dependence was deepened by its membership of Eastern bloc international organizations. In the economic realm 1949 saw the creation of the CMEA.

In the military sphere functioned the Treaty of Friendship, Cooperation and Mutual Assistance, signed in May 1955 and known as the Warsaw Pact. The Warsaw Pact defined itself as a regional organization of collective self-defence in the meaning of the UN Charter. Article 4 provided for immediate assistance in the event of an armed attack, including the use of military force. In accordance with the letter of international law this was a system of collective self-defence, registered with the United Nations and having a clearly defined *casus foederis*, initiating allied operations and joint political and military bodies (Skubiszewski 1959). However, the Warsaw Pact was primarily an instrument to legitimize the stationing of Soviet troops and achieve Soviet interests through forced unity, a doctrine of limited state sovereignty and Russian political, military and diplomatic dictation. It was in fact a military bloc, and not a military alliance of the Western kind, its international legitimacy purely fictitious, and its similarity to NATO superficial.

The main institution was the Political Consultative Committee, comprising Member States' first secretaries of the party, prime ministers and ministers of foreign affairs and defence (Nowak 2011: 51-53). States vied for position within the Pact. For instance, in the 1970s Poland sought to set up a permanent secretariat in Warsaw, an initiative which did not meet with Russian approval. Poland was one of the Northern Group of Forces of the Warsaw Pact, which in the event of war was tasked with attacking the Federal Republic of Germany and Denmark.

The decision making process of the Warsaw Pact was completely centralized. Russians assigned tasks to armed forces of member states, and any opposition was ruled out in the name of socialist internationalism. Poland, like other Warsaw Pact countries, did not have its own security strategy. Military doctrine was completely subordinated to the Soviets. The armed forces were part of a greater whole and as such could act only within the operations undertaken and controlled by the Soviet General Staff. Efforts to achieve independence were harshly punished, as evidenced by the Soviet intervention in Budapest in 1956 and the Warsaw Pact countries 1968 intervention in Prague.

The Polish army, the second-largest among the socialist countries, was focused on offense, in 1980 numbering over 400 thousand soldiers, along with 2800 tanks, 2300 guns and 500 aircraft (Balcerowicz 2001: 440-441). This army took part in the military intervention in Czechoslovakia in 1968 and the suppression of workers› protests in Poland - in June 1956 in Poznan, in December 1970 at the coast in Gdańsk and Szczecin and in December 1981 during martial law.

Poland did, however, put forward significant peace initiatives. At the twelfth session of the General Assembly in 1957, Polish Foreign Minister, Adam Rapacki, announced plans to establish a nuclear-free zone across the Federal Republic of Germany, the German Democratic Republic, Poland and Czechoslovakia (Wandycz 1994, Ozinga 1989). Later, in 1963, the Gomulka plan assumed a nuclear arms freeze on the territory of Poland, Czechoslovakia, and the two German states. These initiatives, inspired by the Soviet Union, were aimed at strengthening the strategic position of the Socialist camp.

Poland also put forward the idea of convening the Conference on Security and Cooperation in Europe. From Poland's perspective, this initiative was to contribute to the affirmation of the Oder-Neisse borders and international recognition of the German Democratic Republic, which would also form a security buffer along the western border of the country. For the USSR, the proposal was propaganda meant to improve its image, especially tarnished by the intervention in Czechoslovakia in 1968.

Adopted in 1976, the Helsinki Final Act of the Conference on Security and Co-operation in Europe, confirmed the borders within Europe and strengthened the territorial *status quo*. The socialist states hoped the CSCE would bring about a détente and greater international cooperation; Western countries saw in the conference an instrument for putting pressure on respect for human rights in Central and Eastern Europe. The CSCE contributed to the crystallisation of the democratic opposition in Poland, the creation of the Workers' Defence Committee, the Human and Civil Rights Protection Movement and, later on, «Solidarity» (Czaputowicz 2013).

In 1989 came a breakthrough as a result of the agreement between the authorities and the opposition in the so-called "Round Table". The Civic Committee, representing the opposition, defined the main objectives of the Polish nation as ensuring sovereignty as well as political and economic independence. Regaining state sovereignty required a suitable alignment of relations between Warsaw Pact allies on the basis of equality and without ideological sigma. National security was to be ensured through a policy of disarmament and reductions in defence spending – a result of the victory over the Cold War division of Europe, the development of international cooperation based on the principles of the UN and OSCE, and a fuller realization of human rights. Within this view the use of force and interference in the internal affairs of other countries are unacceptable (Czaputowicz 2009: 64-65).

2. Security policy after achievement of independence in 1989

During the Cold War Poland bordered the German Democratic Republic in the west, Czechoslovakia in the south and the Soviet Union in the east. After 1989, a united Germany became Poland's neighbour to the west, the Czech Republic and Slovakia to the south, and to the east, Ukraine, Belarus, Lithuania and Russia (Kaliningrad oblast). The primary task of

Polish foreign policy was to regulate relations with all its neighbours via treaty.

The Round Table agreement defined the institutional form of the state, including the division of powers with respect to security policy. Solidarity's leaders recognized the leading role of the Communist Party on foreign policy and security. General Wojciech Jaruzelski was chosen as President by a parliament in wich, thanks to an agreement at the Round Table, the communists and their allies had a guaranteed majority. As such, General Jaruzelski had a wide range of competences in formulating security policy: he was head of the armed forces and had power to appoint ministers of defence, the interior and foreign affairs, which positions were thus filled respectively by Czeslaw Kiszczak, Florian Siwicki and Krzysztof Skubiszewski.

The Polish doctrine of Defence of 21 February 1990 still accepted that an important element of Poland's security is membership Warsaw Pact as well as and bilateral and multilateral alliances, the role of which would change over time as a new European security system was formed. This disregard for the impending and inevitable collapse of the Warsaw Pact meant that the doctrine was outdated even at its adoption. It was also mistakenly assumed that there was a continuing threat to national security from Poland being drawn against her will a conflict between NATO and the Warsaw Pact in which nuclear weapons might be used. Combining the old with the new, this doctrine was a document of the transition period (Koziej 2001: 405-406, Minkina 2011: 623-625).

The strategy of the Ministry of Defence of September 1991 was based on the principles of equal security for all states and avoidance of military alliances. As such, it was an "all-azimuth" strategy assuming the need for defence in all directions (Malendowski 1998: 23). The slow pace of change in Polish security policy was a consequence of the Round Table agreement of leaving the military in the hands of the communist forces and the stationing of Soviet troops on Polish territory (Kuźniar 2001: 36).

It seemed that the Conference on Security and Cooperation in Europe (CSCE) was particularly well-suited to fulfilling the function of collective security, bringing together states on both sides of the Iron Curtain, and possessing a mandate covering both security and economic issues as well as the so-called "human dimension". The strength of the CSCE was the membership of all states from Vancouver to Vladivostok, its weakness its lack of effectiveness. Adopted on 21 November 1990, "the Paris Charter for a New Europe," proclaimed an end to the division of the continent and the start of a new era of democracy, peace and unity. This proclamation soon proved to be wishful thinking (Czaputowicz 1998: 92-95). Nevertheless, the process of institutionalization of the CSCE had begun, and the Treaty on Conventional Armed Forces in Europe (CFE) had been signed. This treaty was to become the basis for the military order on the continent (cf. Żurawski vel Grajewski 1997).

Polish policy towards the Warsaw Pact thus evolved along with the changes in the political situation. First, there was an attempt to transform the character of the Warsaw Pact from military to political. Then there were the so-called "cross-security guarantees" provided by both the Soviet Union and NATO. Finally, along with Hungary and Czechoslovakia, Poland decided to dissolve the Warsaw Pact. This dissolution took place on 1 July 1991, only days after CMEA was disbanded, on 28 June 1991.

In its relations with Germany the government of Tadeusz Mazowiecki sought to conclude a treaty confirming Poland's western border. In relations with Russia, the main goal of Polish foreign policy was to transform the existing relationship of dependence into one of equality and partnership. In September 1990 a postulate to withdraw 64 thousand Soviet troops from Polish soil was made (Menkiszak 2001: 129-130). The withdrawal finally began in April 1991, taking until September 1993. A bone of contention in Polish-Russian relations was Russia's demand for assets remaining at Russian bases to be transferred to Polish-Russian joint venture companies. Ultimately, this issue was resolved in Poland's favour (Kostrzewa-Zorbas 1995). Polish eastern policy was hailed as a two-track policy. This meant simultaneously maintaining good relations with both Moscow, at the heart of the USSR, and the republics (Zielke 1997: 194-196). On 2 December 1991 Poland was the first to recognize the independence of Ukraine, a country crucial to the security of the entire region.

The summit of Polish, Czechoslovakia and Hungary leaders in the Hungarian town of Visegrad in February 1991 gave institutional form to cooperation between the three countries. The Declaration announced the identification of cooperation in political, economic, social and security spheres. Good relations between these countries was proof to western states of their capacity for future cooperation within the structures of an integrating Europe.

NATO was initially seen in Poland and other Central European countries as a Cold War organization that should be dissolved along with the Warsaw Pact and replaced by a pan-European security system set up on the basis of the CSCE. Among the leadership of the Polish Army, trained in the USSR and not speaking English, there were concerns about whether there was a future with the Polish army.

Following NATO's adoption in November 1991 of the New Strategic Concept, the alliance's relations with the former Warsaw Pact countries gradually began to strengthen. Psychological barriers were broken down and an atmosphere of mutual trust built. This helped to establish cooperation, which was deepened through specific ventures. Poland joined the North Atlantic Cooperation Council, which provided a framework for consultation on political and security issues relating to defense planning, strategy, force structure and command and opened a permanent office at NATO headquarters in Brussels and at NATO's Supreme Headquarters Allied Powers Europe near Mons (cf. Kupiecki 2001).

The failed coup of Yanayev in Moscow was a signal that the peaceful development of the situation in the Soviet Union was not a foregone conclusion. A belief grew that the OSCE would not be in a position to ensure security. In the new geopolitical situation the government of Jan Olszewski specified NATO membership as a strategic objective. Poland's road to Europe was to lead via NATO and membership of the alliance was in turn to ensure better terms of membership of the European Union. The North Atlantic Alliance was recognized as an essential element of the European security system (Hyde-Price 1995: 242-244; Cottey 1995; Czaputowicz 1997).

In the defence doctrine of 2 November 1992 a change in the threat assessment took place. Due to the dissolution of the USSR and the collapse of the bi-polar system, the threat of global nuclear war was reduced. Now regional conflicts found themselves in first place (e.g. the Balkans) along with non-military threats[1]. At the same time membership in the North Atlantic Treaty was defined as an essential strategic objective that would ensure continued national security. Speaking in favour of this approach were the strengthening of Poland's ability to defend itself, a high assessment of the deterrent value of the alliance and strengthening of Poland's image as a state of stable and responsible participant in international relations.

Strategic documents from the 1990s emphasise the view that Poland's place is among the family of countries belonging to Western civilization,

---

1 The broad definition of security threat involves action or sequence of events that threaten to short-term quality of life and limit the scope for policy choices by the institutions of a state. The security challenge is a phenomenon which requires the formulation of a response and the undertaking of appropriate action (Czaputowicz 2012: 23).

and that the country was returning to the fold after a half-century of Soviet domination (Siren 2009). Polish aspirations to NATO membership were strongly backed by Germany, seeing for itself enhanced national security and greater stability in its neighbours. In negotiations Poland referred to historical arguments, the necessity of supporting democracy and the norms applying in the alliance, such as the principle of equality and indivisibility of security (Schimmelfenning 2003: 229-236).

For Poland the value of NATO membership was derived from Article 5 of the Washington Treaty - the collective defence of the Member States. However, NATO intervened in 1999 in the former Yugoslavia, which fell outside the scope of the treaty. From Poland's perspective the alliance's participation in expeditionary operations should not be at the expense of its traditional function of defending the territory of its member states. Poland pushed for the even distribution of the defence infrastructure of the alliance and the development of cooperation between NATO and the European Union. American involvement in Europe was seen as a guarantor of security and stability. An important instrument for cementing the partnership with the United States was taking part in foreign missions[2].

From NATO's perspective, Polish membership of alliance increased its potential in terms of both defence and peacekeeping operations around the world, eliminating the "grey zone" of security in Central Europe which formed after the dissolution of the Warsaw Pact and the collapse of the Soviet Union. Poland has contributed extensive knowledge of the issues facing Eastern Europe. As a member of the alliance Poland has consistently advocated an "open-door" policy and supported its eastern neighbours in their efforts to gain membership in the organization (Czaputowicz 1998: 192-197).

Poland took part in the military operations in Iraq in 2003 in order to demonstrate its solidarity within the alliance, thereby strengthening its image as a close ally of the United States. Poland was counted among the states of the "new Europe"; those states striving to maintain close relations with the Americans, in contrast to the "old Europe", those states sceptical of military involvement alongside America[3].

---

2 Poland has had a long tradition of participating in UN peacekeeping operations. In the years 1953 to 2007 over 64 000 Polish troops took part in 66 peacekeeping missions.
3 A benchmark for assessing Polish participation in stabilization missions could be Spain, a demographically similar country, although with a larger economy. In the same way added value from Spain's involvement in Iraq was derived from contingents from Spanish-speaking Latin American countries - the Dominican Republic, Honduras, Nicaragua and El Salvador (Domejko-Kozera 2006: 44-50), so added value might be expected in Polish involvement in the form of the possible participation of the Central European region,

Polish participation in the Iraq operation has been judged as a military success, a political draw and an economic defeat. The Polish military gained valuable experience in logistics, operations and the command of large multinational forces, thus increasing its credibility in the eyes of its allies. Poland's political objectivity and strategic independence have both been strengthened. Action in Iraq brought home the need for a fully professional army and accelerated armed forces reforms. The disparities between countries against the background of intervention in Iraq has shown that NATO is unable to take joint action in the event of differences of interest between members. This has resulted in greater attention being paid to Poland's capacity to act independently in a crisis. At the same time hope that involvement in Iraq alongside the United States would bring a "strategic partnership" between the two countries and increased American presence on Polish soil proved unrealistic. The negative effects include the weakening of NATO's cohesion due to discord among members over the legitimacy of the intervention in Iraq. Neither has Poland achieved its economic goals in the form of contracts for the reconstruction of Iraq (Koziej 2012b: 37-38; Czaputowicz 2004: 20-22).

Concern for the future of NATO has led the Polish authorities to transfer military involvement in Iraq to Afghanistan. The participation of a 1200-strong Polish contingent in the NATO-led operation has been seen as a long-term investment in the country's security. Also noted has been the fact that the Alliance has been involved in operations of a pre-emptive - and so offensive – nature, which from Poland's perspective has been unfavourable, since it has led member states to develop expeditionary capabilities substantially different from the capabilities necessary for collective defence against external aggression (Balcerowicz 2011: 141-14).

3. Poland and the European Security and Defence Policy

At the close of the 1990s and the start of the new century Poles were sceptical about European cooperation in security and defence. In the strategic dimension there was "an instinctive Atlanticism" regardless of which party was in power. Because of its pro-Americanism, Poland has been referred to

---

and so the Baltic States (Lithuania, Latvia, Estonia), the Visegrad countries (Czech Republic, Slovakia, Hungary), Ukraine and Romania (Żurawski vel Grajewski 2010: 131). With regard for its own security, Spain has focused more on developing of its air transport and satellite capabilities. In 2001 Poland purchased from Spain seven medium-sized CASA C-295M transport aircraft.

as the "Trojan horse of America". The intention announced in Helsinki in 1999 to create a European intervention force was met with Polish reserve. It was feared that a European Security and Defence Policy (ESDP) could lead to a weakening of ties between Europe and the United States and undermine NATO. Poland's attitude to the ESDP was also affected by the fact that the country had already been a member of NATO and did not accede to the European Union until 1 May 2004.

Scepticism regarding the European Security and Defence Policy (ESDP) resulted from the weakness of European military institutions and the fear of duplicating NATO structures. Poland proposed strengthening transatlantic ties as an alternative to creating the EU security institutions (Osica 2001: 14; Zaborowski 2004: 18). Polish representatives at the European Convention criticized the creation of a "two-speed Europe" in the field of security, arguing that the ESDP should be part of a broader transatlantic security system, in which NATO played the main role (Miszczak 2007: 17).

From the perspective of Poland the 2003 European Security Strategy was too focused on new security threats which were important for Western countries, at the expense of traditional military threats relevant to the countries of Central Europe. The Poles proposed recognising NATO as the main security institution in continental Europe, and Russia as a potential partner in the cooperation, but also as a potential source of instability. They were sceptical about the possibility of achieving "effective multilateralism", acknowledging that the European Union should be able to conduct operations without the need for UN Security Council authorization, which could be vetoed. Poland proposed to take account of traditional security threats, including the "frozen conflicts" in Eastern Europe. Poland did not agree to the mention of Ukraine alongside Belarus as a potential source of threat (Osica 2004).

Perceptions of European cooperation in the field of security and defence changed after Poland's accession to the European Union. In 2004, 77 per cent of Poles believed that the European Union should have its own military force with which to defend its own interests (Longhurst, Zaborowski 2007: 54). Prime Minister Jaroslaw Kaczynski proposed a one hundred thousand-strong European army, which would work closely with NATO, but this initiative did not meet the approval of other European states (Spinant, Taylor 2006).

In 2008 the transatlantic direction of Polish security policy was still dominant (Madej, Terlikowski 2009: 45-46). A change took place in this respect due to the fall in U.S. engagement in European security, President Obama's announcement of a "reset" policy towards Russia, and difficulties in deployment of the U.S. missile defence shield (cf. Piątkowski 2008: 142-146). However, Russian aggression against Georgia in August 2008 had a significant impact on new Polish thinking about security policy. This aggression was not met with a strong response from the United States or the European Union, who instead wished to avoid jeopardizing relations with Russia. It turned out that Georgia's good relations with the United States and application for NATO membership did nothing to secure it against aggression; in fact the opposite was true: they had magnified the threat (cf. Karagiannis 2013). The credibility of U.S. security guarantees for the states of Central Europe, including Poland had been seriously undermined (Żurawski vel Grajewski 2010: 131). From the energy security perspective, the gas pipeline built by Russia and Germany under the Baltic Sea also had negative effect.

Polish involvement in the development of the European Security and Defence Policy (ESDP) was a result its efforts to extend security guarantees for fear of U.S. withdrawal from Europe (O'Donnell, 2012: 1). As the sixth largest country in the European Union, Poland is ranked fifth in terms of participation in EU operations. Four hundred Polish soldiers took part in the EUFOR mission in Chad and the Central African Republic, the aim of which was to ensure the safety of refugees from Darfur. One hundred and thirty Poles took part in the EUFOR in Congo, 277 in Operation Althea, and 17 in Concordia (Estimates... 2009: 414). By sending troops into conflict zones, Poland ceased to be merely a consumer of security, and became a producer (Longhurst 2003: 50-63). Participation in stabilization missions is also contributing to the modernization of the Polish armed forces, including reform of their structure and organization, professionalization and improving combat readiness (Górka-Winter 2007: 268-270).

During work on the report on implementation of the European Security Strategy in 2008, Poland commented on security challenges originating in Russia, energy security, EU rapid response capability, civilian-military cooperation, the Eastern Partnership, and possible solutions to the Georgian crisis (Chappell 2012: 128-129). Within the framework of the European Defence Agency, Poland co-authored a plan to develop the European Union's defence capabilities as well as strategic documents concerning cooperation in the field of armaments and integration of the European defence industry.

Poland was one of the countries to give direction to the work to establish EU battle groups, whose task it is to face the growing security challenges in the neighbourhood of the European Union. Poland participates in three combat groups. In 2006, a battle group, which saw duty in the first half of 2010, was established under an agreement between Poland, Germany, Slovakia, Lithuania and Latvia. Poland was the so-called "framework nation", with responsibility for the functioning of the group, organization, training and leadership (it was located in Potsdam, Germany). Poland provided 50 per cent of the group in the form the 17th Wielkopolska Mechanized Brigade, which had served in both Iraq and Afghanistan. Germany provided 30 per cent of the force's strength, leading in logistics and medical support. Slovakia and Lithuania contributed 200 personnel and Latvia 60 (Terlikowski 2010: 1).

The "Weimar Battle Group" is a result of the 2006 agreement between France, Germany and Poland. Here Poland is also the framework nation, and provides equipment in the form of a mechanized battalion and operational command. Germany provides logistical support, and France medical. The Weimar Battle Group was activated in mid-2013. There are plans to transform the group into a larger, permanent and more flexible unit with suitable military and civilian capabilities. Logistics support for ESDP operations required the creation of integrated C3 capabilities (command, control and communications) (Dickow, Linnenkamp, Maulny, Terlikowski 2011: 7-8).

Poland is additional a framework nation for the Visegrad Battle Group, formed together with the Czech Republic, Hungary and Slovakia. Central European states share a similar culture and a similar strategic perception of security threats. Earlier Slovakia, the Czech Republic and Poland formed a multi-national brigade (Tarasovič 2011: 70-71). The Polish contingent will number 950 troops, the Czech force 750, while Hungarians and Slovakians will provide 400 each. The group is planned to be operational in the first half of 2016.

The Polish Defence Strategy states that ESDP contributes to peace, stability and prosperity of the Member States of the European Union and its neighbours (Defence Strategy ... 2009). Strengthening the EU's civil and military capabilities was one of the tasks of Poland's Presidency of the Council of Europe in the second half of 2011. Poland sought to improve the instruments for raising forces for a mission, strengthen planning and command structures, create permanent operational headquarters in Brussels (Operational Headquarters - OHQ) and build capacity through pooling and sharing. The strategy also emphasized the need to maintain the integrity of ESDP activities with those of the North Atlantic Alliance as well as the need to develop cooperation with immediate neighbours. From the Polish perspective the weakness of EU security policy is the lack of strategy towards Russia.

4. Poland's security policy in strategic documents

Polish security depends on the situation in the Central and Eastern Europe region. Poland's neighbours to the west and south are stable - Poland shares borders with countries belonging to NATO and the European Union, thus, Germany, the Czech Republic and Slovakia. The challenges to Polish security come from the East. The independence and stability of Ukraine are essential for the safety of Poland and any armed conflict involving this country would constitute a serious challenge. Belarus is heavily dependent on Russia and its undemocratic nature gives cause for concern. The Baltic states, meaning the directly bordering Poland Lithuania as well as Latvia and Estonia, are Poland's allies, members of the European Union and NATO. To the North-East Poland directly borders Russia (the Kaliningrad oblast) whose policy in recent years could constitute a challenge to Polish security. Further away, but still in the vicinity, lie Moldova, Georgia, Azerbaijan and Armenia, an area of frozen conflicts (Transnistria, South Ossetia, Abkhazia, Nagorno-Karabakh), which could spark war. Poland thus has a strong interest in stability and democratization in the region (Żurawski vel Grajewski 2012: 394-402).

The National Security Strategy of 13 November 2007 broadly defines national security to include military, political, social and environmental questions. It was judged that the likelihood of large-scale armed conflict is currently limited. The challenge is, however, the dependence of the Polish economy on imported Russian energy resources. The strategy expressed readiness to send Polish forces to participate in stabilization missions and peacekeeping and humanitarian operations outside Poland's borders (National Security Strategy... 2007: 23). The optimal level of commitment abroad is 3,200 to 3,800 soldiers, which would allow Poland to achieve its objectives without weakening of the country›s defensive capabilities (Strategy of Participation... 2009, Pietrzak 2012: 75).

The Polish army performs defensive and expeditionary roles that are partially complementary and partially competing. The former role requires a sufficient saturation of weapons to effectively combat the tanks and warplanes of Poland's Eastern neighbours. The latter role requires the development of the capacity to respond rapidly in distant conflict zones (patrol vehicles and aircraft transport).

In accordance with *the Program to Professionalize the Armed Forces of the Republic of Poland for the Years 2008-2010*, Poland abandoned national service and converted to an entirely professional army, thereby increasing its capacity to participate in foreign missions. Polish Army is creating a force of one hundred thousand regular troops and 20 thousand reservists. Poland is one of only a few countries that, despite the financial crisis, have maintained their military budget: defence spending in 2010 amounted to USD 8.43 billion (1.8 per cent of GDP), in 2011, USD 9.43 billion (1.82 per cent of GDP) and in 2012, USD 10.43 billion (1.98 per cent of GDP).

According to the *Strategy for the development of the national security system for the years 2012-2022* Polish security environment is determined by four factors: NATO, the European Union, relations with the United States and relations with Russia. NATO remains the chief guarantor of Poland's security; the challenge for Polish security policy is to keep its allies interested in the function of collective defence. A threat to the European Union is the Eurozone financial crisis, and the challenges include the renewal and strengthening of the Common Security and Defence Policy, maintaining U.S. military involvement in Europe and building a system of cooperative security and partnership between NATO and Russia and Poland and Russia. Internally, threat come from the deterioration of Poland's infrastructure and demographics, including the emigration of the young generation of Poles. In terms of energy security, the exploitation of Polish shale gas presents an opportunity (Strategiczny... 2012: 8).

The probability of armed aggression on territory of Poland is small, but the use of force in Poland's neighbourhood cannot be ruled out. The priorities for the modernization of the Polish armed forces that emerge from this assessment are expansion of reconnaissance and command systems, air defence, especially anti-missile capability, and increasing troop mobility by the of helicopters (Aspekty... 2012: 52)[4].

In times of crisis the interests of particular states will prevail over the interests of the Community. The threats that affect Polish national security

---
[4] Poland plans to spend PLN 900 million on modernizing its Navy, giving by 2030 twenty new ships, ten An-28 aircraft, 13 helicopters and six unmanned reconnaissance drones. Some commentators argue that developing the navy based around the Baltic Sea is irrational, as it would be cheaper to combat the enemy ships with aircraft and mainland-based missiles (Żurawski vel Grajewski 2010: 117).

in the twenty-first century include terrorism, proliferation of weapons of mass destruction, threats from cyberspace and organized crime. The United Nations system and arms control regimes may weaken. A serious challenge is posed by the need to ensure that energy supplies remain accessible. A weakness of the Polish security system is the civil defence system and the low defensive capability of Polish society (Strategia... 2012: 10, 32). The strengths and weaknesses of the Polish security system are presented below in a SWOT analysis.

Table 1. SWOT analysis of the Polish national security system

Strengths	Weaknesses
• Active participation and greater effectiveness in achieving Poland's priorities within NATO and the European Union • Professionalization of the Polish Armed Forces • Training of personnel; experience gained in missions abroad • Prestige of military service in Polish society	• A departmentalised approach to security • Insufficient saturation of modern weapons • Only partial interoperability with the forces of allies • Lack of regular military exercises, and inadequate protection of critical infrastructure
Opportunities	Threats
• Confirmation in NATO's strategy of the priority of collective defence and contingency planning • Increase in the presence of allied defence infrastructure • Development of ESDP in order to obtain additional security guarantees • Verification of weaponry during overseas operations • Increase the effectiveness of international law with respect to non-proliferation of WMD	• Persistence of the international threats and challenges • Fall in defence spending in comparison with other countries • Falling societal acceptance of participation in foreign missions • Technological and economic barriers to Polish defence industry limiting the opportunities for cooperation

Source: *Strategia...* 2012: 52.

The strategy puts forward a balance of internationalization and increased Polish independence in security, which *de facto* means a greater than hitherto focus on ensuring defence self-sufficiency and maintaining a state of readiness, ability and determination to independently providing defence for the state against potential external aggression. Of particular importance to a frontier state such as Poland is the ability to counter a surprise attack. The locating of allies' interests in Poland is also important since it increases the probability of obtaining support if the interests of such allies were threatened (Strategiczny... 2012: 6-7).

The best solution from the perspective of Polish security would be to create a defensive union through enhanced European integration. This vision, however, is currently unachievable due to differences of interests among Member States and the lack of a shared European strategic culture. It would be useful to supplement the European Union with NATO to create a synergy effect. The European Union, which has economic instruments at its disposal, could improve its defensive potential while an alliance having military capabilities could perform planning roles and conduct operations (Koziej 2012b: 36-37, 43). It is hard, though, to expect such a division of roles to be approved by all European Union Member States.

5. Conclusions

Polish security policy after the Second World War travelled a road from strategic incapacitation within the Warsaw Pact to strategic independence and equal membership of NATO and the European Union (Koziej 2012a: 30). During the Cold War, Poland was a member of the Warsaw Pact and Comecon. The chief risk was of conflict of NATO, perhaps even nuclear. After 1989, the situation changes diametrically. Poland joined NATO and the European Union and the security challenge become regional conflicts and asymmetric threats coming from the East (see Table 2) [5].

---

[5] Under communism, one third of Poland's trade was with the USSR, one third with other Comecon countries and one third by other countries. At the turn of twenty first century this structure was turned on its head: one third of trade was accounted for by Germany, one third by other EU countries, and one third to other countries (Kuźniar 2002: 33).

Table 2. Instruments of Polish security policy

	"Cold War"	End of Twentieth Century/ Beginning of Twentieth Century
Military alliance	Warsaw Pact	NATO
Economic organisation	Comecon	European Union
Threats	Conflict between NATO and the Warsaw Pact	Diffuse and asymmetric regional conflicts
Origin of threats	from the West	from the East

Source: author's own work.

In the 90s Poland achieved strategic independence. This required a break with its previous role as executor of tasks coming from outside, and basing strategic culture on its own national interests. The Polish republic's political and strategic defence directive was implemented and ties between Poland and the Soviet Union broken. The Warsaw Pact was dissolved, as was Comecon. Relations with Germany, Russia and other neighbours have been regulated through treaties and the previous hierarchical relations between Moscow and its satellites were replaced by horizontal relations between the states of Central Europe.

Poland advocated the creation of a collective security system, an expression of which was the transformation of doctrine from one of war to one of self-defence. Immediately after 1989, it seemed that the organization on which the international order would rest would be the CSCE. Then, the main objective of the Polish security policy was NATO membership and of the European Union (respectively happening in 1999 and 2004).

Polish security policy at the beginning of the twenty-first century was affected by the changes in the international environment after the terrorist attacks of 11 September 2001. Poland earned its own strategic subjectivity and consolidated its strategic position in the security structures of NATO and the European Union. Reform of the armed forces and the security system took place, adapting them to NATO and the European Union standards (Koziej 2012a: 19-20; Koziej 2012b: 19). Poland took a pro-American stance, took part in resolving the conflict in Iraq, reinforcing its image as a close ally of the United States.

Initially Poland was sceptical of the ESDP. This scepticism arose from fears that the ESDP would lead to a weakening and duplication of NATO structures. The country advocated maintaining a contingency planning and conducting regular military exercises. After joining the European Union in 2004 Poland saw that the ESDP could in fact contribute to the nation's security, especially as U.S. involvement on the continent was shrinking. Poland actively participated in missions to solve crises in Africa and in the creation of the EU battle groups. During its Presidency of the European Union in the second half of 2011, it initiated a talks on strengthening the ESDP by creating a planning and command structures. Strengthening the ESDP is considered by Poland as an additional guarantee of its security.

Involvement in stabilization missions contributed to the modernization and professionalization of the Polish armed forces. The defence budget, unlike that of other European Union member states, has not been significantly hit by the financial crisis. From the Polish perspective the best solution would be to build the EU's crisis resolution capacity while maintaining NATO's responsibility defending members of the alliance against military aggression.

As a frontier state of NATO and the European Union, Poland is particularly sensitive to threats from the East, a region where democracy is not deeply rooted, and conflicts are frozen (Transnistria, Abkhazia, South Ossetia, Nagorno-Karabakh). Russia's actions in the immediate vicinity, such as the war with Georgia in August 2008 and the gas blackmail against Ukraine in 2009, cause disquiet in Poland and led to a Polish focus on developing self-defence capabilities. This focus may constrain Poland's involvement on expeditionary operations beyond its borders.

6. Bibliography

Aspekty bezpieczeństwa militarnego w ujęciu Strategicznego Przeglądu Bezpieczeństwa Narodowego 2012, „Bezpieczeństwo Narodowe" nr 23-24: 37-54.

Balcerowicz B. 2011, *Poland' involvement in Euro-Atlantic Security*, [in:] *Poland's foreign Policy in the 21st Century*, ed. by St. Bieleń, Warsaw: Difin: 136-150.

Balcerowicz B. 2001, *Armed Forces in Polish Defense Policy*, [in:] *Poland's Security Policy 1989-2000*, ed. by R. Kuźniar, Warsaw: SCHOLAR: 439-465.

Chappell L. 2012, *Germany, Poland and the Common Security and Defence Polity. Converging Security and Defence Perspectives in an Enlarged EU*, New York: Palgrave Macmillan.

Cottey A. 1999 (ed.), *Subregional Cooperation in the New Europy. Boulding Security, Prosperity and Solidarity from the Barents to Black Sea*, London and New York: MacMillan Press and St. Martin's Press.

Czaputowicz J. 2013, *Multilateral Diplomats of Central European States Before and After 1989*, [in:] *Routledge Handbook of International Organizations*, ed. by B. Reinalda, New York: Routledge: 244-256.

Czaputowicz J. 2012, *Bezpieczeństwo międzynarodowe. Współczesne koncepcje*, Warszawa: Wydawnictwo Naukowe PWN.

Czaputowicz J. 2009, *Foreign Policy in Opposition Activities Before 1989*, "The Polish Quarterly of International Affairs", 3(18): 40-66.

Czaputowicz J. 2004, *Zaangażowanie w Iraku a polska polityka europejska*, „Polska w Europie" 3 (47): 17-24.

Czaputowicz J. 1999, *Review of Poland's Foreign Policy and Foreign Ministry Activity in 1997*, "Yearbook of Polish Foreign Policy 1998", Warsaw: Ministry of Foreign Affairs: 13-34.

Czaputowicz J. 1998, *System czy nieład? Bezpieczeństwo europejskie u progu XXI wieku*, Warszawa: Wydawnictwo Naukowe PWN.

Czaputowicz J. 1997, *Poland's International Security*, "Yearbook of Polish Foreign Policy 1997", Warsaw: Ministry of Foreign Affairs: 23-33.

Defense Strategy of The Republic of Poland. Sector Strategy of the National Security Strategy of the Republic of Poland 2009.

Dickow M., Linnenkamp H., Maulny J-P., Terlikowski M. 2011, *Weimar Defence Cooperation - Projects to Respond to the European Imperative*, Warsaw: The Polish Institute of International Affairs.

Domejko-Kozera P. 2006, *Polityka bezpieczeństwa Hiszpanii w latach 1992-2004*, Warszawa: Wydawnictwo Naukowe „Semper".

Estimates of Member States' contributions to military ESDP operations, 2009, [in:] *European Security and Defence Policy: The First ten Years (1999-2009)*, ed. by G. Grevi, D. Helly, D. Keohane, Paris: EUIIS: 414.

Górka-Winter B. 2007, *Poland in Peacekeeping and Stabilization Operations*, "Yearbook of Polish Foreign Policy 2007", Warsaw: 67-76.

Grajewski J. 2001, *Regionalism in Poland's Defence Policy*, [in:] *Poland's Security Policy 1989-2000*, ed. by R. Kuźniar, *Poland's Security Policy*, Warszawa: SCHOLAR: 194-226.

Grevi G., Keohane D. 2009, *ESDP Resources*, [in:] *European Security and Defence Policy: The First ten Years (1999-2009)*, ed. by G. Grevi, D. Helly, D. Keohane, Paris: EUIIS: 67-114.

Hyde-Price A. 1995, *The International Politics of Eastern Europe*, Manchester: Manchester University Press.

Karagiannis E. 2013, *The 2008 Russian-Georgian war via the lens of Offensive Realism*, European Security 22 (1): 74-93.

Kostrzewa-Zorbas G. 1995, *The Russian Troops Withdrawal from Poland*, [in:] *The Diplomatic Record 1992-1993*, ed. by A.E. Goodman, Boulder: Wesrview Press.

Koziej St. 2012a, *Obronność Polski w warunkach samodzielności strategicznej lat 90. XX wieku*, „Bezpieczeństwo Narodowe" 21: 19-30.

Koziej St. 2012b, *Pierwsza dekada funkcjonowania w strukturach bezpieczeństwa NATO i UE – strategiczne doświadczenia Polski*, „Bezpieczeństwo Narodowe" 22: 19-45.

Koziej St. 2001, *Polish Defence Policy Evolution*, [in:] *Poland's Security Policy1989-2000*, ed. by R. Kuźniar, Warsaw: SCHOLAR: 403-438.

Kupiecki R. 2001, *Atlaticism in Post-1989 Polish Foreign Policy*, [in:] *Poland's Security Policy 1989-2000*, ed. by R. Kuźniar, Warsaw: SCHOLAR: 229-285.

Kuźniar R. 2009, *Poland's Foreign Policy after 1989*, Warsaw: SCHOLAR.

Kuźniar R. 2002, *Wewnętrzne uwarunkowania polskiej polityki zagranicznej*, [in:] *Polityka zagraniczna RP 1989-2002*, ed. by R. Kuźniar, K. Szczepanik, Warszawa: Wydawnictwo ASKON, Fundacja Studiów Międzynarodowych: 31-49.

Kuźniar R. 2001, *Security Policy in Polish Foreign Policy*, [in:] *Poland's Security Policy 1989-2000*, ed. by R. Kuźniar (ed.), Warsaw: SCHOLAR: 19-91.

Longhurst K. 2003, *From Security Consumer to Security Provider*, [in:] *Poland – A New Power in Transatlantic Security*, ed. by M. Zaborowski and D. H. Dunn, London: Frank Cass: 50-62.

Longhurst K., Zaborowski M. 2007, *The New Atlanticist: Poland's Foreign and Security Policy Priorities*, London: The Royal Institute of International Affairs, Chatham House.

Madej M., Terlikowski M. 2009, *The Political and Military Aspects of Poland's Security Policy in 2008*, „Yearbook of Polish Foreign Policy", Warsaw: 41-64.

Malendowski W. 1998, *Nowe uwarunkowania i cele polityki zagranicznej Polski po 1989 r.*, [in:] ed. by B. Łomnicki, M. Stolarczyk, *Polska i jej sąsiedzi w latach dziewięćdziesiątych. Polityczne i ekonomiczne aspekty współpracy i integracji*, Katowice: Wydawnictwo Uniwersytetu Śląskiego.

Meyer Ch.O., Strickmann E. 2011, *Solidifying Constructivism: How material and Ideational Factors Interact in European Defence*, "Journal of Common Market Studies" 49 (1): 61-81.

Menkiszak M. 2001, *Difficult Neighborhood. The Security Questions in Polish Relations with the Soviet Union and Russia*, [in:] *Poland's Security Policy 1989-2000*, ed. by R. Kuźniar (ed.), Warsaw: SCHOLAR:125-170.

Minkina M. 2011, Evolution of the Perception of Threats to the Security of the Republic of Poland in Polish Strategic Documents, "Journal of Slavic Military Studies" 24: 621-647.

Miszczak K. 2007, *Poland and the Development of the European Security and Defence Policy*, "The Polish Quarterly of International Affairs", 16(3): 10-31.

National Security Strategy of the Republic of Poland 2007, Warsaw.

Nowak J.M. 2011, *Od hegemonii do agonii. Upadek Układu Warszawskiego – polska perspektywa* [*From Hegemony to Agony: The Fall of Warsaw Pact – Polish Perspective*], Warszawa: Bellona.

O'Donnell C.M. 2012, *Poland's U-turn on European defence: A missed opportunity?*, Policy Brief, London: Centre for European Reform.

Osica O. 2010, *Transformation through Expeditonary Warfare: Military Change in Poland*, [in:] *A Transformation Gap? American Innovations and European military change*, ed. by T. Terriff, F. Osinga, T. Farrell, Stanford: Stanford University Press:167-186.

Osica O. 2004, *Poland's Role in CFSP/CESDP: Added Value or a Trouble Maker?*, [in:] *The European Security Strategy. Paper Tiger Or Catalyst for Joint Action?, Perspectives from Italy, Poland, Austria and Finland*, Part II, Newsletter 5 (14), ed. by M. Overhaus, H.W. Maull, S. Harnisch, Trier: deutshe.aussenpolitik.de: 9-15.

Osica O. 2001, *CESDP as Seen by Poland*, "Reports and Analyses" Center for International Relations (Warsaw) 5.

Ozinga J.R. 1989, *The Rapacki Plan, The 1957 Proposal to denuclearize Central Europe and Analysis of its Rejection*, McFarland, London: Jefferson.

Piątkowski K. 2008, *Tarcza antyrakietowa - opcje strategicznego wyboru*, [in:] Polityka zagraniczna Polski. Unia Europejska - Stan Zjednoczone - Sąsiedzi, ed. by J. Czaputowicz, Warszawa: Polski Instytut Spraw Międzynarodowych: 131-150.

Pietrzak P. 2012, *Armed Forces of the Republic of Poland in International Operations– Legal Grounds, Strategic Considerations, and Practical Implemen-*

tation, Polish Ukrainian Bulletin, Warsaw: National Security Bureau (Poland), National Security and Defence Council of Ukraine.

Schimmelfenning F. 2003, *The EU, NATO and the Integration of Europe. Rules and Rhetoric*, Cambridge: Cambridge University Press.

Siren T. 2009, *State Agent, Identity and the New World Order. Reconstructing Polish Defense Identity after the Cold War Era*, Lambert Academic Publishing, 2009.

Skubiszewski K. 1959, *The Postwar Alliances of Poland and the United Nations Charter*, "The American Journal of International Law", 51(3): 613-634.

Spinant D., Taylor S. 2006, *Polish premier: EU should be military power*, „European Voice", 31 August, http://www.europeanvoice.com/article/imported/polish-premier-eu-should-be-military-power/55494.aspx (30.06.2013)

Strategia udziału sił zbrojnych Rzeczpospolitej Polskiej w operacjach międzynarodowych 2009.

Strategiczny Przegląd Bezpieczeństwa Narodowego. Główne wnioski i rekomendacje dla Polski 2012, Warszawa: Biuro Bezpieczeństwa Narodowego.

Strategia rozwoju systemu bezpieczeństwa narodowego RP 2012-2022 (2012).

Szczerski K. 2009, *Analiza Neogeopolityczna (neo-geo)*, [in:] *Podmiotowość geopolityczna. Studnia nad polska polityka zagraniczną*, ed. by K. Szczerski, Warszawa: KSAP: 7-58.

Tarasovič V. 2011, *The possibilities for cooperation of the Visegrad countries and their Eastern Neighbours in the development of security and defence policy in the EU and beyond: the Slovakian perspective*, [in:] *Visegrad cooperation within NATO and CSDP*, V4 Papers Warsaw No. 2, ed. by C. Törö, Warszawa: The Polish Institute Of International Affairs: 69-72.

Terlikowski M. 2010, *Polish-led EU Battle Group*, "Bulletin PISM" 3 (79): 1-2.

Wandycz P. 1994, *Adam Rapacki and the Search for European Security*, [in:] *The Diplomats*, ed. by G.A. Craigs, F.J. Loewenheim, Princeton – New York: Princeton University Press – Chichester: 289 – 317.

Zaborowski M. 2004, *From America's protégée to constructive European. Polish security policy in the XXI century*, ISS Occasional Paper no 56, Paris: 1-28..

Zaborowski M., Longhurst K. 2003, *America's protégé in the East? The emergence of Poland as a regional leader*, "International Affairs" 5(79): 1009-1028.

Zielke K. 1997, *Polska droga do NATO*, [in:] *Bezpieczeństwo europejskie. Koncepcje, instytucje, implikacje dla* Polski, ed. by J. Czaputowicz, Warszawa: Ararat: 191-209.

Zięba R. 2001, *The CSCE/OSCE in Polish Security Policy*, [in:] Poland's Security Policy1989-2000, ed. by R. Kuźniar, Warsaw: SCHOLAR: 321-346.

Żurawski vel Grajewski P. 2012, *Bezpieczeństwo międzynarodowe. Wymiar militarny*, Warszawa: Wydawnictwo Naukowe PWN.

Żurawski vel Grajewski P. 2010, *Geopolityka – siła- wola. Rzeczypospolitej zmagania z losem*, Kraków: Ośrodek Myśli Politycznej.

Żurawski vel Grajewski P. 1997, *Traktat CFE a bezpieczeństwo Polski*, [in:] *Bezpieczeństwo europejskie. Koncepcje, instytucje, implikacje dla* Polski, ed. by J. Czaputowicz, Warszawa: Ararat: 239-264.

Defence Policy and Safety Perceptions in Franco's Spain

JUAN CARLOS JIMÉNEZ REDONDO
CEU SAN PABLO UNIVERSITY

1. The basis of the safety and defence policy in Spain 1945-1975

1.1. Arrangement and safety with respect to the Cold War

Historically, the international society has been characterized by some order criteria derived from the coexistence of the independent and sovereign units and the absence of centralized organs of power. The insufficient global regulators supposed to the contrary to what was happening inside the States, where prevailed the idea of the social pact, the international system remained embedded in the Hobbes' state of nature. After the First World War constitution of the League of Nations was the attempt to mitigate the anarchic framework through the principles of international dialogue and cooperation, as well as the collective safety. However, the evident failure of the Assembly did not prevent from establishing in 1945, based on the same principles, a new organization called the United Nations, this time, however, this time, well shaded in - as all the matters related to solving problems referred to international peace and safety were ceded to this unique governing body consisting of five other, worldwide organs. As happened in the interwar period, these new principles of the collective safety were not able capable to guarantee and assure a peaceful international order, so that the United Nations had to continue to meet their safety needs by their own means and power politics, although this time the only possible way to do so was the formation of defensive alliances, given the radical changes and transformations that the world power structure had experienced because of the emergence of the Soviet Union as a new global superpower and the unprecedented expansive force of the world communism.

The months immediately following the end of the World War had been marked by a certain expectations of cooperation, however, soon faded when the communist parties of the Eastern European countries liberated by the Red Army were liquidating the just established governments upon national agreement to impose so-called "democracies"; that is the homogeneous, communist governments dependent on Moscow. Also, in Eastern Europe, the communist parties that had capitalized the resistance in Albania and Yugoslavia ended up with imposing, almost without any opposition, their ultimate power and influence on any, other political forces. Outside Europe, the communism was eligible to succeed within the civil war broken out in China, had seized the opportunity to win the power in North Korea and Mongolia and struggled to win in Malaysia, the Philippines and throughout Indochina. Moreover, the communist parties had a very extraordinary strength in France, Italy and especially, in Greece and Turkey, where they held, respectively, very favourable positions in the civil conflicts, facing them directly, as well as the conservative monarchist forces and the nationalist successors of the Turkish Youth Movement, whose resilience relied on the help and support received from the British government.

In 1947, this powerful expansion of the communism convinced the U.S. government to adopt a very strong policy of its containment, which supposed the following: firstly, to give up any idea of cooperation or direct negotiation with the Soviet Union, and secondly, to launch a massive support program and help to discourage the popular fame and appeal of the communist parties, especially in Europe, and, thirdly, undertake a very active policy of containment aimed at creating a defence system to ensure the safety of the western world, because they considered that only through a effective power politics international peace there would ensured.

Ultimately, the international system assumed, starting from 1947, the form of a cold war, that is, a kind of confrontation between the two superpowers in all areas of power, except the direct military, since the possibility of mutual destruction exerted a very notable influence acting as deterrent. The mutual nuclear terror, fixed from 1949, became a very important element of the Cold War rationalization, limiting the chances that both superpowers were facing against each other, but to the contrary, that helped even more to prevent from getting an indirect character of this permanent and ongoing conflict and moving it to any potential conflict scenario. The Cold War and nuclear terror led to something, what may be called the safety dilemma, whereby the superpowers built their own safety blocks forming their own safety and increasing their military arsenals and capabilities hoping that in such a way, they might deter the rivals from initiating an attack or aggression (Glaser 1997: 172-173). However, what the superpowers really managed to achieve was only a permanent armaments race, as well as the permanent need and demand to incorporate new countries to join their respective power blocs, thus depriving and reducing their neutral status to a minimum.

The Cold War system integrated the world geostrategically, as the bipolar logic exerted its tremendous globalization pressure on the whole set, at the same time imposing some various, rigid criteria of the hierarchical organization and structure tailored to form and structure two systems based on their own principles, a logic of power and some specific institutions. Thus, the Soviet Union gathered its satellites swirled under strict geopolitical surveillance criteria applied by the communist orthodoxy by means of the frequent interventions, although it was unable to suppress some dissents coming from Yugoslavia or China, which strengthen even more the control and supervision held over other countries in the eastern European zone of influence. Also, it was established a powerful geo-economic control mechanism of their block by imposing centrally planned economy as the alternative to the free-market capitalism. In turn, the United States built-up its block according to the its hegemony principles of consensual hegemony, cooperation and market freedom introducing various directive and administration criteria that allowed to assure its primacy and hegemonic position without resorting to any costly interventions, except the proximate area of Latin America.

In summary, a new geostrategic scene of the Cold War based on the bipolarity experienced in each of the blocks an accelerated process of institutionalization, with the creation of the numerous organizations aimed at regulating, constituting and structuring each block within their military dimensions, economies and policies. The safety was no longer a pure national factor, except for each of the two superpowers, it converted into a collective safety mechanism. That is, in this particular context of confrontation, which took place between the blocs, no state, except the Soviet Union and the United States, was already able to meet their safety needs individually, as they had to do so only through the agreed and arranged mechanisms that would allow to move all the available and sufficient resources to deal with the threat provoked by the existence of the systemic enemy of two dimensions: quantitative, that is, the amount of power that could be accumulated as well by this particular state [*nation*] as its block of origin or membership, and qualitative, that is, the ability to plan and organize enough power for deterrence, defence or war purposes. And this resource coordination should be performed in their three core dimensions, such as, political - military, economic-financial and, eventually, the cultural-ideological dimensions.

In conclusion, during the first decade of the Cold War there existed a general, however, vague belief that the new war would break out in Europe. The blockade in Berlin carried out by the Soviets in 1948 was interpreted by all European governments as a clear sign that the war might have remained a close reality, so there was no other solution than to establish a defence system that could deal with the new and formidable enemy represented, this time, by the Soviet Union and its entire block of influence.

1.2. *El franquismo y España: ostracismo político y valor geoestratégico*

The context of the cold war and the confrontation existed between the blocks challenged all European states with the new safety requirements. Firstly, the obligation to define their accommodation within one of the two presented blocks, as there was no neutrality, except the one which was recognized by both superpowers, and which was, in the case of Spain, simply not possible. Secondly, the objective need to find a cooperative safety environment to get incorporated, as it was impossible that a single state could ensure its own national safety means, which in the case of Spain could not be anything more than the internal western formed and built up by the United States. Thirdly, within the scope of the general conflict, the safety became a very considerable factor of the national interests of the United States. This meant that regardless of the authoritarian political regime, being then in force in Spain, the state itself, faced the needs of applying defence and safety measures which were a kind of must to be met and fulfilled by any means possible.

The authoritarian character of the regime of General Franco was a real problem for Spain, which represented a kind of a structural impediment to any potential direct and full incorporation of the country willing to get allied within the institutional Western bloc configuration (Portero 1989: 35). However, it should be noted that the Spanish ostracism did not owe its authoritarian nature to the general political regime, but to the highly symbolic load that the civil war was still waking up in the good part of the Europe. The evidence of the aforesaid was conclusive when Spain got secluded from all the international organizations that had emerged since the mid-forties and early fifties, Salazar's new State of Portugal itself could do it, despite representing and being also such a repressive and authoritarian regime. The reason for this asymmetry is that Franco was always spreading and fuelling around and among the European democracies the memory of the defeated fascism, and not only because of having been supported by the German and Italian military troops during the civil war, but also of having been situated so clearly in favour of the fascist powers during the world war. Franco was always seen as a military leader comparable to Hitler or Mussolini, unlike, for example, the Portuguese dictator, who was always considered to be a teacher who had been running the government of orders aimed at getting Portugal out of its chronic and continuous political instability and economic backwardness.

Therefore, in such an environment, still full and dominated by war suffer, by the Nazi death camps horrific discoveries revealed by the allied troops, and the memory of the figure of the fascist dictators, the Francoism eventually suffered from a strong campaign of international discredit, loss of prestige and repudiation that commenced during the Potsdam Conference, whose final communication contained the allies' refusal to admit to UN a government of such Spanish features. The international, official condemnation of the repression enacted by the government of General Franco's regime crystallized and materialized ending up with the adoption, in December 194, of the resolution 39 (I) of the General Assembly, which excluded the Spanish regime from participating in the international organizations and conferences dependent on these organizations, at the same time, recommending their members to revoke the ambassadors and ministers plenipotentiary in Madrid (Lleonart 1978: 386-388). The withdrawal of the ambassadors left the Spanish regime internationally isolated and unable to perform any manoeuvres to participate actively in the re-composition and restructuring of international society, which forced the Franco government to undertake a reactive policy aimed at saving the situation of the international condemnation in which it was found to be[1].

---

[1] The priority in overcoming Spanish separation appears in numerous circulars sent by the Ministry Artajo, in which he authorized the diplomatic representatives to invest all the necessary credits, while asking them to treat this issue as the priority. ARCHIVO GENERAL DE LA ADMINISTRACIÓN (AGA) Caja 6672. Circulares 14 a 16. s.f.

The Franco's government was aware, a long time before the war ended, of the difficulties that would be faced by the new international society dominated by the allies, so that, from late 1942, he established an accommodation strategy which has its relation axis with the Portugal support (Doussinague 1949: 124). Thus, the idea of the Iberian Block intended to highlight the idea of neutrality and the political component of the Peninsula acting as a supportive space of peace that had stayed out of the war and being put on the sidelines and overcoming the pressures exerted by Germany (Jiménez 2009: 181). This strategy had been maintained upon the conclusion of a secret agreement with the U.S., in late 1944, according to which Spain allowed the American to benefit from its air facilities adopting at the same time some various internal reforms which permitted to erase and remove the most significant features of the Spanish fascist regime. Besides, a course of the external actions was triggered which was also benefited by Portugal and used as an axis between the Spanish relations, firstly to encourage Great Britain to adopt a more favourable pro-regime approach, which was only a question of good will by providing this particular country some significant economic and commercial benefits, and secondly, linking the Iberian Block line with the pro-allied line meant a corresponding secularization of the Luso-British alliance. Additionally, Portugal should serve as a connection link with France and act as a facilitator to get the Spanish Mediterranean approximation with Great Britain and Italy[2]. Finally, the benefits received from the collaboration with Portugal should be used to reassess the strategic role of the Iberian Peninsula, trying to highlight the importance of this particular factor to ensure that Spain does not stay out of the institutional system that began to get adopted and articulated in the European defence system Europe applied against the Soviet Union.

This initial planning had to be modified in the light of the negative attitude of the European countries toward Spain, although Franco was always aware that the international condemnation was limited somehow, with respect to maintain the regime itself. That is, the Spanish government was relatively sure that even if Spain continued to be subjected to the acute isolation process, the future of the regime would not be a real risk, so he thought that the major, western powers would never decide to introduce any regime change in Spain due to the lack of confidence in the

---

2 ARCHIVO MINISTERIO ASUNTOS EXTERIORES DE ESPAÑA (AMAE). Leg. 1374. Exp. 10. *Instrucciones para el embajador de España en Londres*. 1 de diciembre de 1945. *Carta Martín Artajo a embajador en Londres*. 3 de diciembre de 1945. Leg. 1374. Exp. 2. *Instrucciones para el embajador de España en Roma*. 7 de enero de 1946.

stability of a new government that were not strong enough supported by the army. And at this point, the Madrid government was absolutely right, as the major European countries showed very little confidence of theirs in the former republican leaders, as the restoration of the republic might have ended up with a new civil war, while the monarchist option represented by Juan de Borbón was also seen with serious reluctance, as it did not get too much support from the military forces and army, a kind of the cornerstone which was believed by all to be rotated to trigger a possible change of the Spanish regime. Without this particular guarantee of the stability, both the UK and France or even the United States preferred the continuity of Franco power and regime[3].

This relative safety made the Spanish government's policy respond to the United Nations imposed condemnation using the slogan engraved by Luis Carrero Blanco about "the order, unity, tolerance and endurance"[4], which was translated as: firstly, analyse in detail the character of anticommunist regime and use the Catholic dimension as the flag of the international legitimacy of the dictatorship, and, secondly, establish as new foreign policy objectives a deep analysis of the relations held with Portugal, the Vatican , the Arabian and Latin American countries which are so ideologically[5] y and, first of all, focus your attention on the United States aiming at incorporating Spain into the occidental defence system, which would definitely bring many unquestionable advantages and strategic, added value to the Iberian Peninsula. So, even if Spain were a semiperipheral country representing the European South it would constitute a communications bridge between the African continent and Europe and assuming a key, geostrategic and fundamental role related to the centre focusing two lines and high-value communication: the first one- vertical, euroafricana, and another one, the horizontal, mediterranean. Additionally, its atlantic position would allow to play a significant role within another line of very strategic and important communication: the one which would unify America, Africa and the Indian Ocean (Munilla 1984: 51-82; Alonso Baquer 1988: 89-102).

---

3 PUBLIC RECORD OFFICE, FOREIGN OFFICE, (PRO.FO) 371/60446. *O'Malley to Ernst Bevin*. Lisbon, March 7th, 1946.
4 The lines which constitute the classical vectors of the Spanish external policy. It is possible to continue to call them, as it did Fernando Morán, mere policies of substitution. In the case of the author, it was so obvious, that the dictatorship was not able to develop the regular external policy, as it was only possible to performed within the democracy (see Morán 1980). However, it seems less logical to keep maintaining uncritically the idea of the substitution policy. Eloquent diplomatic documentation available at De la Torre 2011: 61 y ss.
5 Appearance of Carrero in the Spanish international situation in AMAE. Leg. 1911. Exp. 22. *Notas sobre la situación política*. Madrid, 29 de julio de 1945.

In turn, for the government of the United States it was important to incorporate Spain to the western defense system, both for the strategic advantage reasons that could provide them by obtaining the military bases in Spain and considering the Peninsula as a bridgehead where a Soviet attack may be directed to. This means that, not seeing any possibilities to stop the first Soviet Union military initiative undertaken in the territory of the continent, Spain, Italy and the UK were considered to be the first and basic points of withdrawal from which it could be possible to apply the attack response strategy. In any case, the key point is to search any safety space used against any Soviet threat did not represent any simply instrumental feature, that is to say that, it was not only directed to overcome the isolation and thereby, ensure the survival of the dictatorship, but also had a structural dimension. It was the dimension shared by the rest of the Western Europe countries which had to ensure its defence system to be apply against the Soviet threat collectively and closely linked with the United States, the only country that could ensure and guarantee an effective response to the hypothetical attack of the Red Army.

1.3. Spanish incorporation into the western defence system: from the Iberian Pact to the agreement signed with the United States

In the face of the Soviet expansionism, the American politics admitted the idea of establishing some stable footholds in the countries considered to be strategically important, regardless of their applied democratic or authoritarian regime. For the United States, the Spanish problem did not have a pure political nature, but, what really mattered, was first of all, the safety. The militant anticommunism was just replaced, according to the US public opinion, for the previous anti-fascism, so that the Spanish question was not practically the subject of its interest, any more (Ordaz 1993: 425). In this particular situation, the way of reaching the bilateral agreement was open and the road ahead to culminate it depended only on the removal process of the international ostracism presented in Spain. For Washington, Franco - Spain became to be considered as a potential ally, reprehensible in many, various aspects, but stable enough to play a significant role in the global US defense strategy (Portero 1989: 278). However, it was not only the United States which informed about this favorable approach. There were also some other Western Europe and American countries which expressed their support and positive approach in this particular matter. The given evidence of the matter aforesaid constitutes the gradual reduction of the countries which turned to be against Spain: of 36 countries in 1947 to only 15 in May 1949, and conversely, supports got increased of only five in 1947 till the 26th May 1949. This favourable environment led to the adoption of the resolution 386 (V) by the General Assembly, on November 4th, 1950 that finally brought to an end the Spanish matters facilitating the integration of this country with the international organizations and the return of the ambassadors to Madrid[6].

Within the framework of the Western defence system, the Iberian Peninsula presented not only the well- integrated defensive set, but also a welcome accordance with the ideological line applied by their governments, which also became very supportive. In this sense, there existed a key concept which demonstrated that the Pyrenean border was a great defensive and fortified bastion used against the Soviet invasion, and even, according to the Spanish geostrategic discourse, the Pyrenees were considered to present a natural barrier hardly passable for tanks or airborne forces, and serve as natural guarantee and protection against a Soviet nuclear attack (Losada 1990: 192). This highly regarded geostrategy explains that the half of the Spanish troops were located in the Pyrenees and there, most of the Spanish military efforts converged. Although, there was also another key reason for this high concentration of troops was related with the internal safety needs within the regime system raised due to the powerful movement of guerrilla infiltration operating, since 1944, in the northeast part of Spain. The intention related to a coordinated, peninsular defence policy was explicitly confirmed by signing, in September 1948, the II Additional Protocol to the Treaty of Friendship and Non-Aggression of 1939. However, the constitution of the North Atlantic Treaty Organization (NATO), which by including Portugal as its founding member, left still Spain even more isolated, tried to nullify the idea of joint peninsular defense assumed by both Madrid and Lisbon. Therefore, the Portuguese government always highlighted in any negotiation process of the Alliance that the absence of Spain was a fundamental error within their planning approach[7], as according to their opinion,

---

[6] Diplomatic relation normalization continued to be performed in the accelerated form. The US ambassador comes to Spain in March 1951 and, the European states were represented by: Island, November 1949; Ireland, October 1950, Greece, February 1951, Belgium, February 1951; Holland, February 1951, Luxemburg, March de 1951; Norway, March 1951; Sweden, March 1951; Great Britain, March de 1951; Italy, April 1951; Denmark , April 1951; Turkey, October 1951; France, December 1951; Federal Republic of Germany, November 1952.
[7] ARQUIVO DO MINISTÉRIO DOS NEGÓCIOS ESTRANGEIROS DE PORTUGAL (MNE). PEA, 309. *Projecto de resposta ao promemória de 6 de ocutubr*. Lisboa, s.f.

in the event of any Soviet attack forced to leave Europe Therefore, the Portuguese government always highlighted in any negotiation process of the Alliance that the absence of Spain was a fundamental error within their planning approach, in the event that any Soviet attack would force to leave Europe, the Peninsula should be the basis from which the reconquest should be initiated. It was, therefore, so necessary to have these two peninsular states adopted the same policy and have them united within the same defensive alliance. However, the strong antipathy surrounded Franco's Spain and expressed by the majority of the European partners made even the intention of the Spanish possible integration useless. The Franco's government, knowing that their margination situation[8], trying even to threaten to denounce the Iberian Pact which bounded military Spain with Portugal, coming forward with the arguments that in case of war, the obligations of Portugal as a member of NATO and the military assistance provided by Spain to Portugal could drag inexorably Spain into unwanted war in which it would not rely on any guarantees upon mutual military assistance that stipulated the Atlantic Pact[9].

However, the Spanish claims were not directed to obstruct Portugal join the NATO, they aimed at highlighting, first of all, to the U.S. government, the inconsistency of the defence supposed to be incorporated into the western part of the Peninsula, leaving the eastern country aside, as well as expose the need to find any satisfactory solutions that would allow to remediate and deal with the arisen exclusion problem (Brundu 1990: 141). There were, basically, three key suggested alternatives: the first one represented a defence axis which would link the United States with Spain embracing subsequently Ireland and Portugal, and the second one represented a Mediterranean pact that would be incorporated as complementary to NATO, and the last one represented a bilateral pact with the United States which then would embrace Portugal (Marquina 1986: 354-397).

The obstructionist positions disappeared when having checked the willingness and positive approach of the U.S. government to conclude any agreement of this type[10] and just because Portugal was playing a vital and important role as a diplomatic intermediary representing the

---

8 AMAE. Leg. 3372. Exp. 22. *Informe 582-E, Agregado de prensa a subsecretario de Educación Popular*. Lisboa, 21 de marzo de 1949.
9 AMAE, Leg. 3372. Exp. 22 Telegrama ministro Asuntos Exteriores a encargado de negocios en Washington. Madrid, 25 de marzo de 1949. AMAE, Leg. 3372, exp. 22. *Memorándum de la conversación mantenida entre Nicolás Franco y Caeiro da Mata*, 21 de marzo de 1949. Tlgra. *encargado de negocios de España en Washington a ministro de asuntos exteriores*, 25 de marzo de1949.
10 AMAE. Leg. 3448. Exp. *Nota para su Excelencia*. Madrid, 20 de marzo de 1951.

Franco's government. Hence the idea of tripartite pact represented the Spanish-Portuguese joint strategy, whose main principles had been born during the meetings between Franco and Salazar in La Coruña and Ciudad Rodrigo, from 1950 to 1952 respectively, and, especially, during the plenar Atlantic organization conference held in Lisbon in 1952, in which the Portuguese ministry first presented in public the idea of a defense agreement between Spain, Portugal and the United States, which provoked strong opposition expressed by the governments of Great Britain and France (Jiménez 1999: 105). In the first case, it was London to fell that the growing link between Spain and Portugal could diminish reduce its traditional influence over Lisbon, and in the second, the French government believed that while the U.S. was determined to rearm Spain, ignoring all the political conditioned constrains, and thinking that Europe could not be defended on the French side of the Pyrenees, which could obviously expose the country to a new invasion as the response campaign would be generated in the Iberian Peninsula[11].

The process of incorporating Spain into the Western defence system was, therefore, held in the indirect way and upon the bilateral agreements signed with the United States and subsequently joined by Portugal. The agreements of 1953 did not present any form of a mutual safety agreement signed in the absence of any commitment to defend Spain by the United States. Thus, Spain was being integrated into the European defence system assuming at the same time, all risks arising from its status as a U.S. ally, but without any guarantees of defence stipulated in the agreements signed by the United States with other countries.. Moreover, in case of any Soviet aggression, the United States reserved the right to use the bases upon one simple notification relating to their scope and intentions, but without any authorization received from the Spanish government. In turn, the United States agreed to provide economic and military aid to Spain that would allow the Spanish Armed Forces to meet the objectives assigned to defend, together with the Portuguese Armed Forces, the Iberian Peninsula as it was stipulated upon the agreement signed by three parties in 1956 (Viñas 2003; Jarque 1998; Termis 2005).

Evidently, the Portuguese reaction on the signing of these aforementioned agreements seemed to be very positive, although the country expressed his strong objections to the supposedly secret clauses that stipu-

---

11 MNA. P. 2, A. 48. M. 267. *Conversa com o encarregado de negócios de Grã Bretanha*. Lisboa, 28 de setembro de 1950. PRO. F.O. 371/89424. *Paul Grey to Clement Attlee*. Lisbon, September 26th, 1950. PRO. F.O. 371/101958. *B.A.B. Borrows to N. J.A. Cheetham*. Washington, May, 5th, 1952.

lated the terms and conditions of use of the U.S. bases without knowledge and permission of the Spanish government, which they thought they might have dragged Spain into a war without being previously warned. In fact, the Portuguese Ministry of Foreign Affairs advised the Spanish government to enclose a restrictive clause, upon which in the event the United States enter the war they would not be authorized to use the Spanish bases by the time they are given by the Spanish government aforementioned approval[12]. did not grant approval. But obviously, such a recommendation escaped out of the real possibilities of the Spanish government.

Having signed the agreements, there was only thing left to do, establish the form of engagement and the role to be played by Portugal in executing the terms of the aforementioned agreements. The negotiations performed upon the agreement of 1956 turned out to have been fruitful providing some specific missions to be assumed by the Armed Forces originating from each country. The Spanish Ground (terrestrial) Army would have to defend Pyrenean steps, considering especially, the support provided by the Portuguese army. The Spanish Navy would focus on the defence of the national territorial waters and communications lines, while the Portuguese navy, in addition to the inspection of their specific national missions, would also participate in the missions addressed to defend all the peninsula. The peninsular airspace would be defended jointly by both Air Force. Finally, it was remembered to limit the responsibilities within defending the territory of the mainland, so the defence of the Spanish and Portuguese archipelagos would constitute an exclusively national responsibility (Marquina 1986: 636-637).

Moreover, the military chiefs of the both countries had establish the way of periodic and institutional contact via regular conferences organised for the Major Peninsular States, which were launched in 1954 and gathered the representatives of the three branches of the armed forces focusing their work on studying various aspects of the joint defence provided on the Iberian Peninsula. (Tiscar 2011: 88-105).

The agreement of 1953 was possibly the only one that could be signed by the Spanish government, however, this did not mean that the Francoist authorities considered it fully satisfactory, especially because of the absence of the control that Spain could wield over the American bases settled on national territory. Therefore, starting from 1957, the Spanish

---

12 ARCHIVO DE LA JEFATURA DEL ESTADO (AJE). Leg. 16, 4, 1. *Embajador en París a ministro Asuntos Exteriores.* París, 27 de abril de 1953.

government was permanently trying to incorporate its modification and ratification taking into consideration the fact that the circumstances had changed in the following four years, since that time. Firstly, just because the general threat of the Soviet communism was still alive, however its intensity had decreased significantly, in the light of the new concept of the peaceful coexistence. And, secondly, because some new sources of conflict and new, even more intermediate and proximal threats were included into the generic risk war against communism, especially those which come from the North Africa: Morocco's independence, the situation of the enclaves in the Spanish colonial territories which still had been out of the war and, in particular, the situation of instability and conflict erupted in Algeria after the outbreak of the colonial war. Spain, in fact, no longer feared of both, the general war and the appearance of a set of any hot spots and any other tensions which may affect their interests, given the geographical proximity of the African continent.

Considering these new circumstances of a general nature, it is also necessary to add that the Spanish diplomatic sources expected to face more than one predictable change within the relation that the U.S. government had with Spain, given the new conditions of peaceful coexistence. The bases could lose their importance and if that happened, it would also be likely that the U.S. government lack the sufficient incentives to maintain granted economic and military aid. Within this particular scope, the objective addressed to the Ministry of Foreign Affairs was clear: Spain had to find a new formula of the reconciliation and agreement held with the United States based on the following idea of "basis of economic aid exchange", and for that, Spain was available to strengthen its negotiations to prove the U.S. government and convince it to apply for the provision of the long-term economic credits to maintain the recognised in their military bases extraterritorial status which may get changed significantly in case of any lack of the financial resources.

However, this negotiating strategy maintained by the Ministry of Foreign Affairs had always relied on a powerful internal brake: the military general staff supported by Franco, had the impression, that once signed the defence relationship agreement with the United States would be a kind of irrevocable decision that on no account could be ever jeopardized. These two ways of performance were becoming less and less compatible with each other, so that finally they were ended up with the dismissal of the ministry. Despite the fact that the assessment of the root cause problem and the suggested solutions were much more realistic and accurate to those offered by the military officials, it was evident that the level of risk assumed by Spain was not in any way compensated by the enormously limited economic and military aid received by this country. Between 1946 and 1960 the military aid offered to Spain was of only 456.6 million dollars, less than it was dispensed and granted to all other Western European countries except Portugal, while the financial donations were, in the same period, of 1.013,7 million dollars, which also presented the lowest sum than the donation receive by e.g. Luxembourg, Norway, Denmark and Portugal.

As referred to the strategic scope, the position of the Ministry of Foreign Affairs was also absolutely reasonable and justified once the President Eisenhower administration had defined a new strategy which was based on the new concepts of flexibility and mobility to deal with any possible aggression from the Soviet bloc. The basic idea was to have the organization divided into smaller units, equipped with tactical nuclear weapon, which would carry all the load of the military operations, excluding the military ground operations performed at a large scale, at least in the initial stage of any war in Europe. This new vision diminished the importance of the strategic recognition of the Iberian Peninsula in general, and Spain in particular, where was a withdrawal zone assigned for the land armies, though still relevant in terms of its use as a base for naval and air support in the South Europe, and especially, the use of the Rota base for U.S. nuclear submarines.

Y tan importante como esta revisión estratégica era la situación económica que comenzaba a atravesar el país, con crecientes déficits presupuestarios que empujaban hacia necesarios recortes de las ayudas exteriores, especialmente en aquellos países no absolutamente esenciales en la definición de los intereses nacionales estadounidenses. And as important as this strategic review was the economic situation began to cross the country, with growing budget deficits necessary pushing toward foreign aid cuts, especially in those countries not absolutely essential in the definition of U.S. national interests.

The support provided by the Spanish military officials to the U.S. entrenched their intransigence positions in case of any modification of the agreements. Of course, they never intended to force any attempt related to the Spanish integration in the NATO while there were some other European countries which protested in more or less decisive way, however, the never accepted any fundamental change of the provisions contained in the agreements of 1953. For this reason, the negotiations performed in

1963, when the ten-year period covered by the agreements of Madrid, Spain was met and Spain had to give up its claim to set up and sign new agreements having to accept their ratification spanning only five years in exchange for a kind of additional help donated in form of the financial aid of the one hundred million dollars and fifty more in the form of the financial loan to purchase U.S. military equipment. The only gesture that the U.S. administration did toward the Franco government was to accept a joint public statement in which the U.S. government reaffirmed the importance of Spain to assure the safety on the Atlantic and Mediterranean coastline. But it was, once again, a very simple declaration, that contained neither legal commitments nor mutual defence agreement.

Four years later, in November 1967, at the beginning of new the negotiations performed to in order to renew the agreements, the positions were still located at the same points. In turn, the Spanish part, saw the need to balance the Spanish situation through its integration with the NATO organisation and the need to increase significantly the amount of the received aid; as far as the United States is concerned, its government admitted its desirability of renewing the agreements, but without any additional increase in financial aid, taking into account the war in Vietnam ate up large amount of the available resources and that Spain had had to entered a phase of the rapid economic development. The progress of the negotiations was slow and very difficult, as the majority of the democrats in the Congress objected to any possible direct defence commitments that the U.S. government might have wanted to conclude with Spain, or for any increase of the funds allocated for economic and military related aid or assistance. Finally, in August 1970 a new Agreement of Friendship and Cooperation was concluded for the duration of five years and will be renewable for another five. This agreement contained, contained this time, a much longer than the previous text preciously describing, in its opening chapters, an extensive cooperation between these two countries in the scope of education and culture, scientific and technical cooperation, urban development and environment protection, agricultural and economic cooperation, and information media. Only the eighth chapter referred to the military cooperation, and stipulated that the bases would be transmitted to the Spanish government, ended with the secret clause of 1953 which authorized the unilateral use of the aforementioned bases. Now, in the event of any external threat the actions related to any response would be subject to consultation held between the two governments and would be resolved upon a joint resolution adopted by the Joint Committee that was constituted with the aim of coordinating defence issues and problems that may arise during the validity of the agreement. The service compensation was reduced to one hundred and twenty million dollars in form of the loan perceived for the purchase of U.S. military equipment and the military equipment delivery to the ground army. A very novel aspect referred to the ban received in the scope of the chemical and bacteriological weapons storage, although there was no reference at all to any nuclear weapons.

Despite its undoubted progress, the new agreement still did not contain any defence- related commitments to be assumed by the U.S. government, which only declared its readiness and availability to support the Spanish defensive effort. Only after the death of the General Franco, in January 1976, the U.S. government decided to transform the nature of the agreements changing it, according to the concept of a real relationship and defensive relation constitution, although it was still not clearly specified, in the view of the reciprocity and equality in connection with safety plans existing in NATO. From this time period, there will be always lots of political and ideological differences that would affect the integration of Spain into the NATO, and no conditions of the international rejection, the result of authoritarian political system that lasted for almost forty years. While closing the agreements renewal with the United States, the Spanish and Portuguese government initiated the procedure of explicit renewal of the Iberian Pact, which had not been done for the previous twenty years. A new protocol provided more specific things, such as the establishment of the political consultations hold between the foreign affairs ministers twice a year; in addition to establish the basic principles needed to increase the cooperation within four potential areas: economy, trade, science and technology and fishing. The result obtain in the view of the extraordinary historical modesty represented by the economic, commercial and financial bilateral relation was very partially positive, however letting perform some certain improvements within the trade relations, which, for the first time, began to generate the minimally significant data. Moreover, both governments agreed to enhance their cooperation on improving the internal safety, as they were perfectly aware of the importance of the Iberian policy that would ensure effective Iberian border safety in the territories of these two regions. This political collaboration police was aimed at fighting against *"the communists and other fellow travellers, in a coordinated manner as any victory of these enemies in the territory of one of these aforesaid countries would be detrimental to the other".* The agreement reached in 1970 established, firstly, that the direct delivery performed by one police to another of any suspected or convicted individuals *"who seek refuge in one of these two countries. The measure shall be documented applying the formula covering an expulsion out of the territory, although it is convenient to have this measure adopted generally without any publicity. "* Secondly, some mechanisms to prevent illegal emigration of the Portuguese citizens to Spain, also the Spanish citizens to Portugal were stipulated and adopted. Also, there was established a regulated procedure referred to the list of the people who *"should be forbidden the entry into the neighbouring country, all this, for the purpose of avoiding any of the two nations is converted into the conspiracy base acting against the other"*. Finally, it was a linking mechanism created of the *"direct and immediate character which may be applied at all levels of the police organs"*[13].

2. Potential sources of thread

The safety policy's main purpose is to mobilize and activate the resources necessary to ensure the integrity and independence of the national territory and assure the tranquillity of its citizens and basic public institutions. In turn, the national defence policy embraces the set of tools and instruments, resources and measures which the state has to develop to avoid any perceived threats. Therefore, the national safety could be threatened from both, the internal side, that is, in case when the constitutional national order of the state is violated or infringed; and the outer side, when any other states or international groups threaten the integrity, violate welfare or any other values respected within the particular state.

This dual internal and external dimension of the safety is independent of the political regime effective in the state, which means, that in case of the authoritarian regimes, whose safety features are inseparable from the established political regime preservation, so the safety and defence policies acquire a dual and inseparable, external safety function of the state and the internal preservation of authoritarian institutions. In other words, it is quite obvious to say that Franco established his own safety and defence policy to maintain the dictatorship, because logically considering, with a long lasting system and effective permanence and stability criteria - designed to last at least until General Franco lives - the defence of the state and the defence of the regime became the concurrent

---
13 ARCHIVO GENERAL DE LA ADMINISTRACIÓN (AGA). Caja 6636. *Normas de colaboración entre las policías portuguesa y española*. Lisboa, 27/5/1970.

objectives. In other words, for forty years, an essential part of the national safety was hopelessly confused with the political safety authoritarian Franco regime. A different thing is the discussion held on the legitimacy of the regime and evidence if there were any Spanish citizens, for example the Spanish refugees, for whom the franquists and Spain represented totally different realities. This intimate connection between the internal and external safety and between regime and the state made the sources of threads perceived by Francoism were represented essentially by two types: the first one, the traditional, external threat of the national interests represented by the states qualified as the "enemies" and the other one, the thread that resulted from the ideological or material origin and threatened the regime's domestic tranquillity.

The classic goals of the national safety, aimed at preventing or rejecting the military threats caused by other states, were clearly determined by the civil war and the change of the alliances that Franco's Spain tested during the first phase of the Second World War. The link with Germany and Italy granted the Franquism the status of "enemy" in respect to all the allies, especially to France and Britain. France, due to its triple status as a rival in the Spanish historical power and to a large extent, was the cause, in the eyes of the *Franquist* nationalism, of the "shrinking" process of the country considered to be a potential European power; and secondly, has the character of a border country, where it could be prepared a ground military invasion directed to other countries, it represents the point of arrival of a significant number of republican refugees who could benefit from the war to reorganize themselves and launch guerrilla offensives spread out over Spain. Do not forget about the Franco-Spanish competition to inspect and control the northern part of Africa, especially, Morocco, where the *Franquist* nationalism was considered to have enough space for the natural expansion of Spain.

The British case was more complex, as for a long time it had been set in the symbolic universe of the Spanish conservative and reactionary nationalism as the great enemy of the greatness existing outside the country. The „Perfidious Albion" presented, for this particular nationalism, a very essential support for the American independences and it was, in fact, the obstacle that prevented from making the old dream of the Iberian Union come true. In addition, the Portuguese dependency on London was seen as a clear threat, firstly, in practical and concrete terms, as Portugal could serve as a support to the British forces which were penetrating the peninsula, and secondly, in symbolic terms, as the initial

Franquist nationalism always believed that it should play a leading role in the politics applied to the whole peninsula. And of course, representing such power the British government maintained the responsibility for the colony located on foreign, Spanish soil: Gibraltar, what that aforementioned nationalism always interpreted as a permanent humiliation of the Spain county as the international power.

All these aforementioned elements made the early *Franquism* defense policy establish the following, four, main goals: prevention of any invasion to the territory coming from France, any potential occupation of Morocco, the annexation of Portugal and recovery of Gibraltar (Morcillo 2010: 230-232). It seems to be certain that General Franco was seriously thinking about the intervention of Spain in the World War, although his performance would be very limited, restricted and circumscribed to very specific targets, such as Gibraltar, North Africa and Gibraltar, and directed always to the clear and limited phase of the conflict. But that wish of his has never been fulfilled. The unquestionable historical fact proves that those expectations related to belligerence have never exceeded the pure planning phase, except for one case of his sending a small contingent to the eastern front to fight with the Soviet Union troops. This dual reality has exposed a profound historiographical debate held between those who prevailed over the interventional and circumstantial evidence, and therefore, assume that the *Franquism* adopted a position of the pre-belligerence that was not created only by the accumulation of different circumstances that prevented the dictatorship from reaching its goals, but also those who attested that Franco's government had never thought of any effective military intervention, but had to take certain pro-German positions as a way to preserve their neutral position on this stormy stage.

This interpretative scope, seemingly irreconcilable, acquires a new light coming from the analysis of the relations existed between Franco's Spain and Oliveira Salazar's Portugal, as there is no possibility to understand the politics of these both countries outside the peninsular dimension which transcended both of them wrapping them up in the determinant and common scenario. In fact, it can be stated that although the Spanish neutrality cannot be only explained by the Portuguese mutual neutrality, in any way that had been possible to take over and adopt by Salazar a different position which was then followed by him. In other words, the *Franquism* ambiguity and clear Franco's perceptible shifts within its position in the event of any conflict were only possible just because Portugal maintained its neutrality, as well as the rest of the peninsular set.

Obviously, it is worth to use the same statement to understand the Portuguese politics, so if Spain had participated in the war, Portugal would not have had any chance of remaining neutral. It was something that both dictators were always aware of: to conclude, the binomial neutrality/intervention has never been a strictly national option, but it covered the peninsular unavoidable dimension. So, Franco knew that any Spanish intervention attempt could be an explicit invitation sent to the allied British troops to come to the Portuguese ports, the possibility that turned to be lethal to the permanence of the emerging and incipient dictatorship; and Salazar, who started from the premise that a strong Spanish alignment with the axis Spain will inexorably provoke the German troops to come to the territory of the peninsula making inevitable the Portuguese participation in the war alongside the allies. This mutual fear forced both regimes to take a very cautious maneuver, however unmistakable.

The path followed to mitigate this common feeling of insafety and fear forced the parties to sign the Friendship and Non-Aggression Pact of 1939, a legal instrument lax enough to let both signatory parts to maintain considerable freedom of the future movements and, at the same time, explicit enough to highlight to the others, that the undertaken path of neutrality was the most satisfying for all. An equivocal nature which reveals the facts related to the background of some different, political strategy that moved these two governments, at the time of reaching the agreement. During the Portuguese mainland soil neutralization there was a kind of the permanent policy option used by the Franco regime as a visible attempt to attract Portugal to its orbit in order to replace the traditional British influence with a new position of the Spanish hegemony. It was a very ambitious but unachievable for the *Franquism* objective, especially at the stage of implementation, so that it had to accept resignedly a Portuguese refusal to consider any slightest initiative that would give the sensation of progressing in that particular direction.

Both the *Franquism* as Salazarism faced the beginning of the war from a position of their instrumental neutrality which in any way, conceal the failure of the partnership caused by the conflict that had occurred in the peninsular soil. While Portugal remained strongly anchored to the old British alliance and, therefore, structurally hooked on allies, in Spain, the commitment to get integrated with the Nazi-fascist, evident since 1938, continued to grow. This basic divergence and the fear that certain unilateral initiatives of one of two countries inevitably involve any other country in a interventional spiral constituted real moderation and prudence factors that did not even hamper any rupture moments, generally they reaffirmed the positions of their neutrality. The major break came at the beginning of the spring/summer of 1940, when the overwhelming march of the German armies troops was seen, which had ended the resistance of some, small countries, such as Denmark, Norway, Holland and Belgium, defeating also the French resistance (Ros 2009: 17). Nazi Germany had not only acquired practically absolute continental domain, but also it managed to divide France into two parts: the France resistant and the France collaborationist, with Marshal Petain to lead it, who some months earlier, became the first French ambassador based in Franco's Spain.

This new European scenario seemed to be based more than ever on the inevitability of the new fascist order that only Britain could escape, but certainly not for a long time. Hence, the regimes, such as Italian or Spanish re-adapted its positions in view of the increasing conflict with the Nazi Germany: Mussolini taking the final step toward belligerence; Franco adopting the legal non-belligerency equivocal position. The Portuguese regime that stayed middle patch not wanting to abandon its traditional pro-British line, inaugurated a new tactic so- called "variable geometry". What all these regimes were doing, in summary, was only a pure review of the terms and their possibilities of their incorporation, participation and co-existence in this new order of the German hegemony that seemed to became dominant and command on the continent. The basic difference is that while Salazar was revising a new formula of the coexistence, Franco opted for the insertion, although getting dependent on the compromise which allowed him to gain material, territorial and substantive benefits. As much as the Spanish officials plan the military occupation of the French Morocco, it seemed to be always conditional and depended on the Nazi regime approval, something that had never happened.

In any case, any unilateral decision was not able to stop predicting peninsular dimension, which forced the Franquism to take a new step toward neutralization of the British influence in the neighboring country. Serrano Suñer himself, pointed it out to the Portuguese ambassador in Madrid during their meeting held in June, 26th saying that Portugal should fear a German attack if it continued to act as the ally of Great Britain. According to Serrano opinion, this possibility, which could provoke the entry of the German troops to Spain, could not have been accepted by the Spanish government. But since Spain seemed to support the German victory, and since the government, as it was stressed by the minister, was not willing to give up the great opportunities that Hitler could offer to Spain, Spain could be forced, somehow, to take over the operation. Summing it up, the Spanish minister's argument was very clear: the Spanish military intervention together with the German would basically obtain the peninsular dimension, although that military action would have been avoided if the neighboring country had agreed to abandon its alliance with Britain and accept the military and political hegemony of Spainy[14].

This maximalist approach represented by Serrano Suñer was quickly abandoned. Salazar did not accept the proposed change of the alliances and the Franco's government had again to settle for what he had and signing the additional, ambiguous protocol, which guaranteed only the confident opposition and objection of the Portuguese government in case their territory is used by the allied troops, accepting at the same time, the equal commitment of Spain toward Germany[15]. The additional protocol of 1940 proved two things: one, that Franco could not think of participating in war if Portugal remained loyal to the British alliance, hence he had the attack plans of the invasion of the neighboring country, and the second, that his wish related to the intervention presented, in fact, too many obstacles to make it true (Ros 2002: 34). In fact, there was no sufficient internal consensus, the economic situation was stifling, the British were getting too strong and the possibilities that Germany would take over an important part of the Spanish costs were practically void.

Besides, the plans related to Portugal, the Franco's military regime drew up the military plans how to regain Gibraltar and set Tangier military occupation. In the case of Gibraltar and Portugal, the existence of the plans did not mean that any final political decisions had been taken. Not at all. Actually, the poor means available to the Spanish Armed Forces did not allow, in fact, to think and imagine more objective than the aforesaid, additionally, they had to be approved by the Germans, which also was very doubtful that it happened at all. Different was the case of Tangier. As the French collapse made both the British and French government accept the Spanish action, which was performed on a temporary

---

14 *Correspondência...* vol. III. (1990: 297-323).
15 *Correspondência...*vol. II, (1990: 64-65); *Dez anos de política externa...*vol VII (1971: 247-249) *Dez anos de política externa...* vol. VII, (1971: 322-323). Salazar rejected the Spanish initiative aimed at confirming the Spanish primacy: meetings celebrations between State -Major. *Correspondência...* vol II. (1990: 77-78).

basis and to ensure only the neutrality of the Moroccan city, although it was important for the allies that the Spanish action moved away Italy from Morocco.

The opening of the Russian front and the U.S. entry into the war again changed to date positions. The gradual return to more clear neutralist policy brought again closed the Iberian dictatorships. This time it happened in more definitive way. Lisbon, in a symbolic way opened its door to the allies that the Franco regime had not benefited of. In February 1942, Franco and Salazar met for the first time to symbolize this new entente peninsular whose final step embraced the presentation of the Lisbon rhetorical proclamation, in December 1942, the constitution of the "Iberian block" in the clear and defensive dimension, as the risks perceived by both dictators were the same: they had to do something to prevent any possible allied landing in France or in the north of Africa and their reaching the peninsula that may put at risk the continuity of their own, authoritarian regimes.

After the World War, the rapid evolution of the international system toward a bipolar configuration focused the enemy in the Soviet Union. In general, within the communism, a concept that hold a strong internal load was used mainly by the dictatorship to classify all those who expressed their strong opposition to the regime. However, since the mid-fifties, the generic reference to the communist threat began to progress and focus on a the new potential sources of the conflict: the north of Africa. Ifni war of 1957, which shaped a new enemy: the newly independent Morocco, which aspired to control the northern part of the Spanish colony, even the western part of Sahara and also defined the limits of the military pacts that Spain maintained with the United States, as in fact, the American country did not hesitate to support the Moroccan King Mohamed V. Franco was always aware that the U.S. and French support of Morocco would prevent him from assuming a major offensive action which could result in a possible, open war with Alawite, for which, in fact, he also lacked the sufficient military resources. Therefore, he set the goal to preserve the town of Sidi Ifni considering its acceptable cession to Morocco governance with entire, surrounding area, including the so--called Protectorate South, located in the north of the Western Sahara.

The concentration of the North African conflict became chronic when Algeria became independent in 1962, and became an essential place that concentrated an important part of the political opposition to *Franquism*, the one that was supported by the new Algerian leaders assumed that the defeat of *Franquism* -Salazarism- had to proceed through the armed struggle. However, the high risk to the *Franquism* safety had taken a clear and definitive internal dimension with the emergence of Catalan independence movements and, above all, the Basque, as in this particular case, the independence fueled a terrorist spiral that constitute even the greater internal risk not only to the stability of the authoritarian regime, but also essentially, to all political transition projects, which since the late sixties began to imagine what it would be Spain like after the death of General Franco.

3. Methods and instruments of the safety policy

3.1. Franco armed forces: symbolic elements and material shortage

One may argue whether the Franco dictatorship was a military dictatorship in its strict sense or not, since the soldiers did not occupy the entire power (Muñoz Bolaños 2010: 15-16), however, this dictatorship of a soldier should not be the objective of any discussion, as that military status turned to be decisive in the way of exercising power, and as the military officials constituted a fundamental base of support within this dictatorship (Bolaños Muñoz 2010: 15-16). The military officials turned to be very essential to maintain a regime based, until the fifties, on a purely ideological legitimacy derived from the victory in the civil war. That is, civil war defined a specific military mentality and also, established a permanent commitment of the officials on maintaining the military regime that emerged in 1939 and embedded its own self-awareness of the social legitimacy to proceed with the depuration and repression of all elements recognized as hostile to this particular system.

The dichotomy of the winners/losers was instrumental in defining the military mentality based on conservative and reactive principles of a large part of the Spanish middle class. A fairly homogeneous mentality that changed relatively a little, over the time, within the scope of isolation of the educational system applied to the military education was maintained definitive around three core principles. Firstly, the mystical cult of the nation, the homeland, based, of course, on unity and indivisibility. Therefore, the patriotism did not get the character of a simple value that should be exalted, it was also considered to be a kind of obligation to be assumed by all Spanish citizens. Conversely, nothing was more abhorrent to the Francoist military than having his/her unity with the nation, somehow, questioned. The second basic principle attributed to such military mentality outlines the catholic approach, since the vast majority of the fights undertaken in 1936 had been a kind of crusade. This made that the Catholicism acquire a totalizing nature of faith, which in terms of homeland defense turned to be the defense of the altar. In another sense, the Francoist military was convinced that his/her surveillance work of the society and defense of the regime had a quasi-sacred legitimacy form originated from this intrinsic alliance from the civil war. Finally, the third characteristic feature was related to his/her belief of being one of the guarantors of the social and political order established in 1936, the result of the conservative and politically reactive vision. The Franco military internalized deeply that the Franco regime had returned to Spain all their purest essentials. The army should, therefore, act as a political actor responsible for double functions: to ensure the maintenance of the regime essentials and suppress any attempt to subvert the established order.

Furthermore, considering themselves as the important representatives of the moral perfection and acting as efficacy guarantors, their political functions should be comprehensive enough to allow them to transmit to the society their own virtues. Hence, until the sixties, they assumed, in addition to the typical functions and responsibilities within the internal and external-safety scope -and defense, a leading role in managing the economic policy, foreign policy, in their pure educational scope, as well as they took various important positions related to the civil public administration. However, this highly symbolic and social model granted to the military officials always contrasted with the military hypertrophied structure and major shortage of material resources. Indeed, the material limits of all kinds of resources led to the spiritualization of the military virtues, including the idealization of war considered as an expression of courage, honor and supreme virtue (Cardona 2003: 186).

At the end of the civil war, the victorious army had a strength that exceeded the million troops. The rapid demobilization conducted from the beginning of 1939 reached the approximately number of 300,000 soldiers that, anyway, seem to be enormous with respect to their maintenance and costs, as until the end of World War I the military cost consumed more than a quarter of the entire state budget. These structural and organizational problems limited the military role and importance during the time of the Second World War to strictly political –related issues, so it was the only period when a relative failure of military cohesion around the

Franco's leadership arouse. An important part of the general officials and leaders were questioning in public the leaders' maintenance costs wising Juan de Bourbon monarchy exit while the others took strong positions as germanophfils, fond of all is German which definitely provoked, undoubtedly, the continuous fascism process within the dictatorship. However, Franco demonstrated his undoubted leadership skills to manage such differences, as his opposition did not even protest when dissatisfied generals received some important destinations served as the base to even stronger military unification around Franco, thus avoiding any serious, internal collapse (Martínez Roda 2012; Cardona 2001; Alonso Baquer 2005).

The end of world war. The material military shortage that oversized the army demand and need got more than evident (Cardona 2003: 186). Unable to assume his guarantor's duties within the State's foreign safety, he focused on internal safety making, from 1944, incursions of the anti-Franco leaders who were penetrating the French border and were going to centralize the state's repressive apparatus. However, from the late forties, the needs of the system integration with the Western defense pact was forcing an accelerated restructuring process within the military resources and infrastructure. In order to perform it, it was necessary to reduce the army that could perform some of the planned outside the state safety missions, at a minimal level of their efficiency, as well as, some rejuvenate the scale of their operations and modernize available weapon. These objectives could be met starting from 1953 thanks to the financial aid and loan provided by U.S. government. The financial aid allowed not only to perform a considerable improvement of the material resources available to the Spanish army, it also allowed do perform the undeniable tactic strategic and even ideological modernization and refresh of the Spanish military resources, which was mainly achieved by implementing various training courses addressed to the officers. This initiative helped a lot to give a slow but visible birth to the new army, new military mentality, which possessed the basic parameters described above, if a new, more professional, technical and less ideologically radical perspective was being incorporated progressively abandoning the reference to the civil war treated as the only and exclusive source of the social legitimacy (Barrachina 2007: 126; Escrigas 2010: 297).

3.2. *The military forces as the instrument of the internal safety of the regime*

As the regime left a bloody civil war, Francoism began its walk convinced of the need to apply the policy of extensive prophylaxis. This sort of war extension was legally regulated by the law related to political responsibilities issued in1939, also the law for the repression of Freemasonry and Communism and state safety issued in 1940, which outlines some, various peculiarities based on the retroactivity principle of the criminal law applying to all those who had been defending the republican constitutional order and which also identified the concept of rebellion together with the particular defense concept. Moreover, starting from 1943, any violations to the public order laws have been treated as military rebellion and all accused are now within the military jurisdiction. In the Spain of Franco the basic functions of the political repression were carried out by upon the responsibility of the special the francoist political police division called *Brigada político-social* upon the Safety Directorate which has always been led by a military (Muñoz Bolaños 2000: 53). In fact, the formula used that Francoism to ensure absolute fidelity of its Safety Forces or the police, as the Civil Guard was reorganized to be military body –as there were lots of soldiers present in its ranks (Aguilar Olivencia 1999: 57 ff; Soto 2010: 380 ff). In addition, the military jurisdiction was responsible for implementing the repressive and penalty laws to punish any crime of subversion by the time it was taken over by the Public Order Tribunal, however five years later it was reintroduced into the military jurisdiction system together with some decrees on banditry and terrorism.

Since, with the exception of Ramon Serrano, all the ministers of Franco governance were always represented by the military officials, and the Army appeared as the main safety regime guarantor institution acting against any interior enemy. The army took over the leading role within the management of the victory in 1939.

3.3. State progressive bureaucratization and the loss political centrality of the armed forces

As a military dictatorship, Francoism had been always attributing, since its birth, a special importance to the military elements, both within the nation' government and its particular departments. The military officials held not only three military positions reserved only for them, although there was no legal provision to do so, but also they carried out their civil duties within such important departments as Governance, External Affairs, Industry and above of all, the governmental presidency, the most powerful and decision making body and instance of the regime, just after Franco, himself (Tusell 1993). This pre-eminence situation of the military within the state apparatus was always obvious and evident, though it never became so dominant no to allow to appear or emerge any other political class within the regime responsible for carrying out the management of the public affairs.

Surely, the most surprising thing, which referred to this wide range of the military functions was its practical monopoly of the industrial and economic policy and generally, the economy maintained by the late fifties (San Román 1999; Olmeda 1988: 106-107). The military officials were directly responsible for this archaic, autarchic dream Francoism had in the first years of its existence, and that the great conflicts wars might have been justified, after their completion and their only defensive argument was based on the ideological assumptions of this particular nationalist conservatism illiberal, so typical for such barracks mentality. Moreover, during the World War, the industrialization trials was being developed with the assistance and participation in the German industrial developmentalism, upon a general belief, that the Nazi Germany was interested in integration economy which served as the locomotive for the Spanish development. Obviously, it was not true at all, as the German claim referred to the fact that the small Spanish industry was offered and used by the German war economy, without providing any formal transfer of the technology or any other, most appreciated and positive synergy with the national economy.

The autarchic experiment turned to be a resounding failure, without any remedy or palliative therapy, which forced Franco to look for a new development model that could, somehow, led by the military officials. This new model of integration in its common core of the developed capitalism carried with a significant technical complexity within its implementation, however, it was not the only thing that triggered a deep reform of the public, general administration, as a whole. The technical competence was replaced by the selection criteria of the Francoist elite limited only to mere organic fidelity, which relocated the military to the more expanded areas of the military power, especially those, who were directly related to the governing body of the economic policy, and which woke its growing opposition toward these new technocrats accused of a certain desviacionism openness with respect to the essential principles of the National Movement for the excessive capitalist modernization.

In any case, the fact is that, starting from the change of the economic model, the Franco regime civilian faced a very strong civilian process. The military continued to occupy numerous, important positions within the state power hierarchy, which at the same time, created a more professional military profile, as well as they were moved to some management positions, affected even more by the bureaucratized complex forms and limited by the scope of management performed by the three military departments.

Summing it up, the evolution of the authoritarian state generated a process of demilitarization of its fundamental structures. If the military base of the authoritarian regime and the absence of a strong single party made the political component supplied by military personnel overrepresented in the key areas of the state control weakened, since the sixties, then, the evolution of the regime toward increasing bureaucratization meant a corresponding primacy of the civilians over the military personnel. The consolidation of the dictatorship turned to reduce a political role of the armed forces. The proof of this was represented by the gradual reduction in the military presence in the Franco government, especially in the final moments of the regime when its institutional and organizational base became, in its major part, already civilian.

The gradual demilitarization of the dictatorship run in parallel, together with the increasing differentiation between the state and the regime. During the early years of the dictatorship, it was hardly possible to establish this differentiation, so the state and its key institutions were defined as barracks state. However, the distinction between regime and state was getting more and more accentuated over the time, mainly due to the new economic and social policies of developmentalism that brought a remarkable growth of the state, both in terms of its actual delivery as its presence in the economic and public services. The proof of this was represented by the fact that military expenditures started to be in sharp decline in relation to total state expenditure, from the 25% in the fifties to only 14% in the late sixties. In parallel, the components of the sanitary, education and social expenditure presented in the general state budget started to consume nearly half of all public financial resources.

4. Conclusions

As it might be a difficult concept to be precisely defined, it is clear that any state, in its national interest, has to adopt their own safety system, which is understood in terms of its the territorial integrity, defense of its basic institutional framework provoked by any externally driven change.

For this reason, Francoist developed a defense policy directed to seek any guarantee for the state security, which would work, in permanent risk scenario represented by the international bipolarity system and the Cold War. For this reason, all the states developed a defense policy directed to ensure the safety needs, especially in a permanent risk scenario was the international system of bipolarity and the Cold War. And, of course, this defense policy should also involved the need to preserve the core regime institutions constituted in 1939. A ridiculous thing is that the Spanish government of the dictatorship had adopted a totally different policy. As the regime was determined to survive, so it had never established any difference between itself and Spain. It means that for the Francoist, there was only one Spain, anti t was the Spain ruled by General Franco. by General Franco. The idea of different Spain, Spain of the defeated, the Spain of exile or antifranco activists was always a pipe dream, an imaginative dream, which was, somehow a bit real and tangible.

Ultimately, safety constitutes an inherent element of every state, regardless of who manages it. Anyway, Francoist had to seek it in terms of the international repudiation. A very specific ostracism referred, although it did not represented any dictatorial nature of the political regime imposed in 1939, to the assimilation performed by Franco with the fascist leaders defeated in the civil war and, above all, to the highly symbolic content that the civil war still was wakening in a big part of the European and American public opinion. In all cases, the international siege was established, Francoist was skilled enough to recover the clasical vectors of the Spanish - Portuguese foreign policy, as well as the Ibero-American world - to which, a new line of friendship and relationship with the Arabian countries was added based on, in many situations, the good image that the regime was creating in many of these countries acting as a potential political model. In all cases, it is obvious that Francoist managed to show a war strategy used to defeat and combat with international marginalization, that must on the other hand, rated as partially successful.

Undoubtedly, much of this success was based not only on incorporating Portugal into this project, but also on the real and tangible idea of having the Iberian Peninsula strategically united, indivisible and tangible. Therefore, in such reality, the U.S. government did not stop to face some strange situations that took place after having incorporated one part of the Peninsula, Portugal into the Atlantic Alliance, and the absence of the state that occupies almost 80% of thereof. This is the reason why, it agreed to undertake a direct line of incorporating Spain into the western defense system prioritizing this particular policy over some other open possibilities, such as the Mediterranean Pact. In addition, if the cost/benefit analysis of this particular line of the direct agreement signed with Spain were to be established, the result clearly pushed to its conclusion: there was the possibility of establishing military bases in unrestricted Spanish territory. It was something more than a pure advantage. It was a superior advantage of the public opinion inconvenience, yet very limited, and the opposition expressed by some European countries belonged to NATO.

Therefore, from the mid-fifties, the situation of Franco government had changed substantially. The country began to implement a process of international recognition, and its launch was ok thanks to the transformation of the development model implemented together with the government change performed in 1957, economic and social modernization of such intensity that, of course, interfered the balance of power which dictatorship was based on. Until then, Francoist represented the military dictatorship that had adopted the form of barracks state. The military had taken over enormous territories of the power and managed the country upon their self-sufficiency in the scope of industrialization performed by the import substitution of the zero efficiency. The absolute failure of the model forced an accelerated modernization, for which, it was necessary to have a new political elite that would ensure the efficient and more complex management of economy and a society. This was the thing which moved the military officials from the broad areas of power to get them progressively focus on the external, public safety functions, as well as on the internal. The aforesaid functions were taken over starting from the launch of the dictatorship. In fact, the progressive bureaucratization and modernization of the system resulted in a progressive and increasingly clear separation held between the regime and the state. For example, the general administration of State became much more operative and functional, the education and health systems got expanded and, in general, the government management of the expenditure got substantially modern. However, a strong presence of the military who assumed the safety-related positions made the public, at the end of this dictatorship, consider this military institution as a principal defense bastion which existed also when the National Movement was launch, as well as it was perceived as the major obstacle to the state democratization.

However, the fact is that the military had also changed a lot. Surely, it was a slow process, which also deteriorated their separation from the rest of society, and in the manner more individual, rather than collective. However, in any case, this vivid change was promoting, for some decades, this autoconvinced institution to be the best guarantor of the principles, values and ideological schemes so well linked to the regime of General Franco, that took over the democratic transition process started after the General Franco death in 1975.

5. Bibliography

Aguilar Olivencia M. 1999, *El ejército español durante el franquismo: un juicio desde dentro*. Madrid: Akal.

Alonso Baquer M. 1996, *La función política de las Fuerzas Armadas en el último tercio del general Franco*, [in:] *Fuerzas Armadas y poder político en el s. XX de Portugal y de España*, ed. by. H. de la Torre, Mérida: UNED: 167-182.

Alonso Baquer M. 1995, *Franco y sus generales*, Madrid: Taurus.

Alonso Baquer M. 1988, *Estrategia para la defensa. Los elementos de la situación militar en España*, Madrid: Instituto de Estudios Económicos.

Barrachina Lisón C. 2007, *La participación política de los militares en la transición española. Influencias, evoluciones y consecuencias*, Barcelona: Pomares.

Barrachina Lisón C. 2002, El regreso a los cuarteles, militares y cambio político en España, 1976-1981, Universidad de Barcelona, www.resdal.org/Archivo/d0000195.htm.

Busquets Bragulat J. 1984, *El militar de carrera en España. Estudio de sociología militar*, Barcelona: Ariel.

Brundu Olla P. 1990, *L'anello mancante: il problema della spagna franchista e l'organizzazione della difesa occidentale (1947-1950)*, Sassari: Università degli Studi di Sassari.

Cardona G. 2006, *El poder militar en el franquismo*, Barcelona: Flor del Viento.

Cardona G. 2003, *El gigante descalzo. El ejército de Franco*, Madrid: Aguilar.

Cardona G. 2001, *Franco y sus generales. La manicura del tigre:* Madrid: Temas de Hoy.

Cardona G. 1990, El *problema militar en España*, Madrid, Historia 16.

Correspondência de Pedro Teotónio Pereira para Oliveira Salazar (1987-1991), 4 vols., Lisboa: Comissão do LIvro Negro sobre o Regime Fascista/Presidencia do Conselho de Ministros.

Dez Anos de Política Externa, 1936-1947, *A Nação portuguesa e a Segunda Guerra Mundial.* (1964-1980), 11 vols., Lisboa: Imprensa Nacional.

Doussinague J.M. 1949, *España tenía razón*, Madrid: Espasa-Calpe.

Escrigas Rodríguez J. 2010, *Los pactos de Madrid y la transformación de la doctrina en las Fuerzas Armadas: el caso de la Armada,* [in:] *Los ejércitos del franquismo, 1939-1975*, ed. by F. Puell de la Villa F., S. Alda Mejías, Madrid: IUGM/UNED: 297-321.

Glaser Ch.L. 1997, *The Security Dilemma Revisited,* "World Politics" 50(1): 171-201.

Jarque Íñiguez A. 1998, *Queremos esas bases. El acercamiento de Estados Unidos a la España de Franco,* Alcalá de Henares: Universidad de Alcalá/Centro de Estudios Norteamericanos.

Jiménez Redondo J.C. 2009, *España y Portugal en Transición. Los caminos a la democracia en la Península Ibérica:* Madrid: Silex.

Jiménez Redondo J.C. 1999, *Portugal, Espanha e a formação da NATO,* "Política Internacional" 3(19), Monográfico: Os 50 anos da Aliança Atlântica: 97-111.

Losada Malvárez, J.C. 1990, *Ideología del Ejército franquista, 1939-1959,* Madrid: Istmo.

Lleixá J. 1986, *Cien años de militarismo en España. Funciones estatales confiadas al Ejército en la Restauración y el franquismo,* Barcelona, Anagrama.

Lleonart i Ansélem A. 1978-2002: *España y ONU.* 6 vols. Madrid: CSIC.

Marquina A. 1986, *España en la política de seguridad occidental (1939-1986),* Madrid: EME.

Martínez Roda F. 2012, *Varela: el general antifascista de Franco,* Madrid: Esfera de los Libros.

Morán F. 1980, *Una política exterior para España,* Barcelona: Planeta.

Morcillo Sánchez E. 2010, *Planes militares frente al exterior durante el primer franquismo,* [in:] *Los ejércitos del franquismo, 1939-1975,* ed. by F. Puell de la Villa y S. Alda Mejías, Madrid: IUGM/UNED: 209-242.

Munilla Gómez E. 1984, *Introducción a la estrategia militar española,* Madrid: Servicio de Publicaciones del EME.

Muñoz Bolaños R. 2010, *La institución militar en la posguerra, 1939-1945,* [in:] *Los ejércitos del franquismo, 1939-1975,* ed. by F. Puell de la Villa y S. Alda Mejías, Madrid: IUGM/UNED: 15-54.

Muñoz Bolaños R. 2000, *Fuerzas y Cuerpos de Seguridad en España, 1900-1945,* Madrid: Serga.

Olmeda Gómez J. A. 1988, *Las Fuerzas Armadas en el Estado franquista,* Madrid: El Arquero.

Ordaz Romay M. A. 1993, *La imagen de España y el régimen de Franco a través de la prensa anglosajona de Estados Unidos entre 1945 y 1950*, [in:] *El régimen de Franco (1936-1975)*, 2 vols. Madrid: UNED. vol. II: 415-427.

Portero F. 1989, *Franco aislado, la cuestión española 1945-1950*, Madrid: Aguilar.

Puell de la Villa F. 2010, *El devenir del Ejército de Tierra, 1945-1975*, [in:] *Los ejércitos del franquismo, 1939-1975*, ed. by F. Puell de la Villa y S. Alda Mejías, Madrid: IUGM/UNED: 63-96.

Puell de la Villa F. 2005, *Historia del ejército en España*, Madrid: Alianza.

Puell de la Villa F. 1997, *Gutiérrez Mellado: un militar del siglo XX*, Madrid: Biblioteca Nueva.

Ros Agudo M. 2009, *Franco/Hitler 1940: de la gran tentación al gran engaño*, Madrid, ArcoLibros.

Ros Agudo M. 2002, *La guerra secreta de Franco*, Barcelona: Crítica.

Seco Serrano C. 1984, *Militarismo y civilismo en la España contemporánea*, Madrid: Instituto de Estudios Económicos.

Serra N. 2008, *La Transición Militar. Reflexiones en torno a la reforma democrática de las Fuerzas Armadas*, Barcelona: Debate.

Soto A. 2010, *Militares en la política en la España Franquista, Los ejércitos del franquismo, 1939-1975*, ed. by F. Puell de la Villa y S. Alda Mejías, Madrid: IUGM/UNED: 365-384.

Termis Soto F. 2005, *"Renunciando a todo". El régimen franquista y los Estados Unidos desde 1945 hasta 1963*, Madrid: UNED.

Tiscar M.J. 2011, *La ayuda española a Portugal durante la guerra delas colonias de África, 1961-1974*, Tesis Doctoral inédita. Fac. Geografía e Historia, UNED.

Torre, H. de la (ed.) 2011, *España desde el exterior: la mirada de los otros*, Madrid: Editorial Universitaria Ramón Areces.

Tusell J. 1993, *Carrero. La eminencia gris del franquismo*, Madrid: Temas de Hoy.

Viñas Á. 2003, *En las garras del Águila. Los Pactos con Estados Unidos, de Franco a Felipe González, 1945-1995*, Barcelona: Crítica.

Danubian and Polish Exile in Contemporary Spain

JOSÉ LUIS ORELLA
CEU San Pablo University

Relations between Spain and Poland have always been scarce and distant. However, when in Spain the sun never set, there was a beginning of relationship between two countries, which concurred in their golden centuries. The Habsburg and Vasa families looked the possibility of forming an alliance against the Protestant powers of the time (Fontan, Axer 1994; Skowron 2008). Afterwards it would be a bitter experience due to the Polish presence in the Napoleonic armies invading Spain. Wojciech Kossak's paintings on the battle of Somosierra or Jan Potocki's novel *The Manuscript found in Saragossa* helped, along with the visit of some famous Polish writers in exile, to contemplate an exotic and "oriental" Spain. But it will be the Spanish Civil War that will mark the next period, when it became the war of all, and the Poles participated fighting on both sides. After the end of the Spanish Civil War, Spain, with its neutrality, would become the obligatory transit place for hundreds of Poles in their *odyssey* to allied countries.

With respect to the Iberian country, nationalist Spain had formed a new right-wing authoritarian State, although not revolutionary-fascist. The Spanish right side was rooted in strong traditionalism inherited from the ideological origin of the leading intellectuals of the second half of the last century, like Balmes, Donoso Cortés, Menéndez y Pelayo, Vázquez de Mella and Pradera, and in liberal conservatism that had radicalized towards authoritarian positions as a result of fear of the revolutionary left. Under this influence and that of the Catholic Church, through the primate of Toledo, Cardinal Isidro Gomá, who had stated in his pastoral letter "Christianity and Homeland," which key points should the new State keep in mind:
- The family established upon indissoluble marriage.

- Smooth collaboration between Church and State, as the Catholicism is the nation's religion.
- Submission of the laws to moral principles, which constitute the framework of natural human rights.
- Deep sense of justice and love of neighbor, without which social peace is impossible.

The Church with this announcement intended to avoid, as much as possible, totalitarian influences from the German National Socialist friend. The re-Christianization was the only way to achieve peace, around the religious unity. This profile of a Spain that remained neutral in the conflict of the Second World War, but belligerent towards communism, will become after the military confrontation an attractive haven for thousands of refugees from Central and Eastern Europe. After the war and at the beginning of the Cold War, the conservative and anticommunist profile will be reinforcing at the expense of Falangist aesthetics, so similar to Italian fascism.

1. Spain and Central European delegations

1.1. Diplomatic presence in Spain

The progressive occupation of Eastern and Central Europe by the Soviet armies will cause the overthrow of the upstream regimes and that their surrogates, under pressure from the USSR, recognize as Spain's representatives, Republican delegations sent by the exile in Mexico (Ciechanowski 2007: 49-79). With regard to the Spain of Franco, diplomatic prerogatives of free delegations were kept. The Hungarian, under the authority of Ferenc Marossy, was maintained from March 4, 1949 until October 20, 1969. A career diplomat, he was his country's ambassador in Finland, which he left in the direction of Spain. In our country he will live on his professorship of international law at the Central University of Madrid (later Complutense), and represent the Hungarian National Council of New York. His job was to receive refugees, to obtain radio emissions in his language, and transfer of the Hungarian legation (Eiroa 2001: 110-111). Hungary will live in the monitored regime until 1947, when the Communists blatantly take over the power (Horthy 1955; Mindszenty 2009).

As for Czechoslovakia, its representation disappeared together with the country. Slovakia as an independent state, had its representation in

Spain, but the Czech side was occupied by the Third Reich. After the communist coup of 1948, the new Czechoslovakia recognized the republic in exile, and Spain recognized Zdenko Formanek, a former ambassador of his country in Spain, as unofficial representative of the Czechoslovak National Committee in London. His role was to organize and support hundred Czechoslovak refugees in Spain, and integrate some of those young people in the Spanish Legion, for military training. The Slovak ambassador Jozef Cieker lost his representation with the occupation of his country. His new task since 1948 will be directing Colegio Mayor Santiago Apóstol [St. James the Apostle University Residence], but also helping his compatriots, celebrating the 14th of March (Independence Day) and representing the Slovak National Council in New York.

The Polish diplomatic representatives remained in Spain, but in the absence of relations with the People's Republic of Poland, the Count Potocki will be installed on behalf of the Polish Government in London. A man close to the General Anders, whom he will bring to visit Spain, will coordinate the activity of the Polish colony in Spain, around 500 people. As for the Balkan world, Lyoubicha Vichatzky will maintain royal representation of Yugoslavia, recognized by the small Serbian group, and will represent the Yugoslav Committee in London. However, when the King Peter sent Lukovic as a substitute, the predecessor remained in absentia. To complicate matters, most of the Balkan refugees were Croats, and felt better represented by Srechko Dragitchevich, charge d'affaires of the former diplomatic representation of independent Croatia. The Croatian diplomat was best man at the wedding of some Balkan exiles, like the one of Branco Opic Lovrinac with Carmen Yañez Monjardín (ABC 30/11/1955).

The majority of the exiles in Spain were refugees coming from Munich and the villages of northern Italy (Brajnovic 2001: 14; Orlandis 1992: 117; Orlandis 1995: 152; Arteaga 1989: 295-297). Finally, the Romanians were a small group, but of high intellectual quality due to the number of students and professors (Eliade 2001). Three quarters of them were legionaries of the Iron Guard, although with the presence of other groups. Spain kept informal recognition of the Romanian ambassador until 1944, Nicolás Dimitrescu, which was contested especially by the Romanian National Committee in Washington, loyal to the monarch Miguel von Hohenzollern. However, the Romanian community was addicted to Horia Sima, the last president of the Romanian government in exile and leader of the Iron Guard (Veiga 1989: 219).

The European exile communities were very small, in December 1947 the census gave overall figures of residents and transients: 434 Hungarians, 49 Baltics, 118 Romanians, 35 Russians and 119 Yugoslavs (VVAA 1948). The uncited rest was composed of other nationalities. But almost ten years later, the numbers were similar. With residents only: 293 Hungarians, 329 Poles, 106 Romanians, 7 Russians, 92 Yugoslavs and 139 Chineses (VVAA 1956). Spain was still a land of passage and training, from which one could go to the longed America.

1.2. *Pax Romana*

Pax Romana had emerged in Freiburg, in July 1921, with the mission to continue the work done by *Auxilium Studiorum* during the First World War. The goal was to create a free space of coexistence among European Catholic students, belligerent or neutral in the previous conflict, and to promote personal relationships between them to prevent future wars. In 1939, at its XVII International Congress, held in Washington, the Spaniard Joaquín Ruiz Giménez was elected international president. The election was caused by the force that supposed to grant the presidency to someone coming from the last country where religious persecution with thousands murdered took place. From June 21 to July 4, 1946, Ruiz Giménez could celebrate the XIX International Congress in Spain. For our country it was an event of great importance, since the defeat of the Axis powers in 1945 had caused the progressive international isolation. On February 9, 1946 the UN General Assembly condemned the Spanish regime, and on 28 of the same month the border with France was closed.

Spain had to survive its isolation and gain favor with the Anglo-Saxon powers, when the expected rupture with the Soviet Union was formalized. For this purpose, Falangist aesthetics, so similar to fascism, should disappear and the Catholic and anticommunist image should be strengthened. The *Pax Romana* congress offered the chance to show the new face of Spain and make contact with Catholic representatives from different countries, who could in a short future become leaders of Hispanophilic pressure groups in their countries.

The XIX congress was attended by 129 delegates, mostly from the Hispanic world. On behalf of Europe under the Soviets, came representatives of the exile communities from Spain, Belgium and England: Two Croats, Branko Kadich and Kazimir Vrljicak; two Hungarians, Georges Kibedi and Emma Kleer; three Poles, Bogdan

Korsak, Piotr Czartoryski and Jan Kazimierz Tarnowski; and five Ukrainians, Maxime Hermaniuk, Jorge Karmanin, André Kichka, Petro Krasnojarskyj, Roman Kryzanowskij (Anonymous 1946: 153-177).

One of the congress objectives was to commit Catholic student federations to help university students that were war victims, refugees or persecuted because of their faith. For this, the Catholic Action and Spanish Catholic university associations had engaged in founding a Catholic Project for University Assistance (Obra Católica de Asistencia Universitaria - OCAU) The OCAU committee had engaged in managing a University Residence close to the university area of Madrid where persecuted academics, with scholarships raised by OCAU, could finish their studies. After that, they asked Hispanic federations to help as much as possible in installing permanently those cadres of university students formed in Spain in their respective countries.

Only on the part of Polish university students, there were figures of around six thousand refugees in various camps in Germany, Italy or England (Anonymous 1946:126-131). Before this offer made by a country that recently overcame civil war, Jan Kazimierz Tarnowski expressed himself this way: "My mind and heart converge in affection and admiration for this heroic Spain that received us so generously and with such heart. We know how much this nation loves us, and we have come here, in return, to drink at the fountain of the same Catholicism. We've come dominated by the strength of Spanish Catholicism, and here we have been given so many guidelines and teachings as we needed. We have seen the soul of Spain; we have seen the heart of Spain, dejected in some moments of its history; to resurge powerful the undeniable catholicity of this nation that was able to maintain its millenary traditions against the current modernism. Everything is history in this nation, faith and Christianity" (Anonymous 1946:132-146).

2. Colegio Mayor Santiago Apóstol

On May 2, 1947 Colegio Mayor Santiago Apóstol (St. James the Apostle Hall of Residence) was inaugurated, located at calle Donoso Cortés, 63 - Madrid, very close to the university area of Moncloa, as a result of collaboration of the Ministry of Foreign Affairs (Alberto Martín Artajo) and National Education (José Ibáñez Martín). The founding decree said: "The National State always inspired by the principles of respect for the human person and service to the permanent values of Christianity, has decided to cooperate effectively with so generous enterprise, erecting within the framework of the University of Madrid, heir to the glorious Complutense University, in which thinkers of all nationalities made some day appointment, Colegio Mayor for foreign university students that, placed under the patronage of St. James, patron of Spain, will constitute home where students, graduates and professors who arrive at the open Spanish soil will find respect for their ideas, understanding for their patriotic traditions and means to rehabilitate their current and future life" (VVAA 1946).

The Minister of Education, José Ibáñez Martín was responsible for financing Colegio Mayor for foreigners, within the rules of other halls of residence. The new residence, with capacity for 118 residents, remained under the direct responsibility of OCAU. One of the first contributions came from the U.S. Catholic university students, to which contributions from other countries were added. But in Spain Cardinal of Toledo, Enrique Plá y Daniel and the Archbishop of Madrid-Alcalá, Casimiro Morcillo were personally involved in helping young refugees. José María Otero Navascués, president of OCAU, was the man who knew how to catalyze the wishes expressed by Joaquín Ruiz Giménez at the Congress of *Pax Romana*. Otero Navascués was a lieutenant colonel of Armada, a naval engineer and one of the pioneers of research in Spain, as director and founder of the CSIC Institute of Optics, perpetual secretary of the Royal Academy of Sciences and long-time president of the Nuclear Energy Board (LORA 1988).

With regard to official studies, Spanish authorities agreed to recognize the studies conducted previously in their places of origin, especially engineering technical schools. At the conclusion of the course, when they graduated, in order to practice in Spain they had to make a revalidation enabling them to practice professionally. In relation to this the Government issued a special decree on October 6, 1954. The permit would be valid for 10 years and with the possibility of extension for another 10 years. Although one of the projects was to give them education for their subsequent rootage in Latin American countries, in need of professional cadres with higher education (Perez 1947).

Students from refugee camps in Italy began their march to Spain. By Christmas of 1946 came the first foreigners, 18 Ukrainians that would form the first contingent of the future residence (ABC 31/12/1946). In Italy about 300 youths, ex-college alumni, and former soldiers of the 14th division had been installed. From August 7, 1945, thanks to the leadership of the non-commissioned officer, Dmitro Maslo, and with the support of Ukrainian priests of Rome, they managed to organize some courses for about 150 people. The studies lasted one year but gained official recognition in the Vatican and they received diplomas. On December 23, 1946 the first group of 18 students departed from Genoa on the Spanish ship "Valencia" and two days later entered the port of Barcelona. In February 1947 another 7 Ukrainian students joined them (Yarimovich 1997).

On August 14, the press echoed the arrival of four Hungarians and one Croat (ABC 14/8/1947), although the first residents were Ukrainians and almost equal contingent of Poles. Curiously enough, a small group of 28 Polish children, who had been saved from the war in our country, left Spain at that time. The youngsters were collected by Mr Piskorski, delegate of the Polish-American Society (ABC 30/10/1947). Soon, HRH the princess Mercedes de Baviera y Borbón will host a party in honor of European students residing in Colegio Mayor Santiago Apóstol (ABC 16/12/1947). In that year, Ruiz Giménez had offered ten scholarships to Pavao Tijan, in his capacity as President of the Croatian Catholic Action (Juez 1997:281).

The main events were the opening and closing ceremonies of the academic year. In July there was a closing ceremony, in which the principal responsible participated; OCAU president, José María Otero Navascués; director of St. James University Residence, Jozef Cieker; Bishop of Madrid Alcalá, Monsignor Casimiro Morcillo; titular bishop of Eresso and Catholic Action chaplain, Monsignor Zacarías de Vizcarra; National Education undersecretary Mr Rubio, on behalf of Minister José Ibáñez Martín. The last event was in 1949, a conference on "The spiritual situation of European students in Spain" given by Alfredo Sánchez Bella, Director of the Institute of Hispanic Culture (ABC 1/6/1949). In the same way, when the course in October was inaugurated, the format of events, including the personalities, was similar. In 1949, the same people were there, but chaired by the rector of the Central University of Madrid, Pío Zabala, and the speaker was Professor Antonio de Luna, who gave the theme: "Catholics in exile". At the opening of the course, Colegio Mayor granted honorary scholarships to its main sponsors, in that year: Bishops Morcillo, Souto Vizoso and Vizcarra; rector Pío Zabala, OCAU president, José María Otero and Ambassador of Spain to the Vatican, and President of *Pax Romana*, Joaquín Ruiz Giménez. Then fifteen scholarships were given to rewarded foreign residents (ABC 9-11/10/1949).

2.1. Cultural activities conducted in St. James University Residence

During the course, St. James University Residence was the center of cultural activities undertaken by various communities persecuted by communism, and also its residents, receptive part of Catholic education that the Spanish government wanted to emphasize: Father Dabaria OP: "Catholic Spain, response to the world"; Luis Morales Oliver: "Popularism and education in the Spanish Holy Week"; Antonio Dering: "Rebuilding sovietized Europe"; Brother Marosy: "Political problems of reconstruction in global perspective"; José María Otero: "Role of Catholic intellectuals in spiritual and material reconstruction of the countries liberated from communist tyranny"; Pedro Lain Entralgo: "Denouncing the madness of Europe: Luis Vives, Andrés Laguna and Saavedra Fajardo"; Adolfo Muñoz Alonso: "The reasons for our hope"; Gregorio Rodríguez de Yurre: "Theology of social systems"; José Costa Grau: "Luís Vives"; Gabriela Makowicta: "Poland's contribution to culture"; González de Mendoza: "Modern wars"; Dauphin Meunier: "The Church and economic structures of the world"; Claramunt López: "Psychopathology of the sense of guilt"; Santiago Montero Díaz: "Américo Castro and his interpretation of Spain"; Santiago Montero Díaz: "Claudio Sánchez Albornoz, figure of medieval history"; Alberto Martín Artajo: "Moral bases of European unity"; José Luis Gómez Tello: "Berlin and Europe"; Andrés Avelino Esteban: "The upcoming Second Vatican Council viewed by separated Christians"; José María García Escudero: "Christianity and technology"; Luís Morales: "The Passion of Christ in Spanish literature"; Rosendo Cato Hernández: "Will the communism succeed in dominating the Caribbean?"; Ramiro Santamaría: "Africa, the third Soviet front"; Eugenio Beitia: "Christian equilibrium in defense of the person"; Cirilo Pasterk: "Intellectual ideology"; José Luis Sanpedro: "Most recent transformations of global economy"; Joaquín Ruiz Giménez: "Spain and the Hispanic world"; Marqués de Valdeiglesias: "Spain in the face of the global crisis posed by communism"; Marqués de Lozoya: "Spanish art and its universal projection"; Germán Borregales: "Latin America faces communism"; José Luis Gómez Tello: "The truth about Angola"; José Filipovich: "Man as a human being in the Soviet economy"; Luís de Sosa: "Summary of the History of Spain"; Osvaldo Marquet: "The spiritual life and today's world"; José María Mohedano: "Professional education and economic development"; Adolfo Muñoz Alonso: "The man before God and nothingness"; Luis de Sosa: "Reasons for Europe"; Isidoro Martín:

"The Church's relations with Spain from 1936 to the Concordat in force"; Juan Roger: "The political-economic problems of Asia"; Carlos Castro: "Ecumenical movement"; Fernando Fernández: "The plan of Spanish economic and social development"; Cirilo Popovici: "Trends in modern art"; Luis Morales: "The divine election of the Cross"; Antonio Gómez: "The poetry of Unamuno and Machado"; Marqués de Lozoya: "The Road to Santiago"; Jorge Uscatescu: "Adventures of freedom"; F. Juan Alonso Vega: "The principle of totality in medicine" (ABC 22/I/1951 to ABC 9/III/1967).

In addition to these conferences, thematic weeks were also organized such as the one organized by the Student Federation of Ukrainian Catholics "Obnova", that with the cooperation of the Ukrainian Free University in Munich, focused on the man and the community (ABC 9/9/1951). At the same time, they were visited by personalities like George Uscatescu (ABC 5/2/1952); General Anders (ABC 7/6/1955); Chinese Archbishop of Nanjing, Monsignor Paul Yu-Pin (ABC 11/11/1955) and the metropolitan Archbishop of Ukrainian Catholics in Canada, Makaym Hermaniúk (ABC 27/10/1957).

Another of the activities most renowned for residents was the celebration of their national holidays, turning the hall into the center of the small national community based in Spain. The Polish colony, composed at the time of 500 people, half of whom were of recent settlement, celebrated on 3 May (first constitution of the country) with their representative, Count Potocki (ABC 5/5/1950), and in November the Independence Day, together with other personalities like Professor Antonio Deryng, former dean of KUL (Catholic University of Lublin) and regular guest at the residence (ABC 12/11/1952). In a complementary manner, pilgrimages to places of deep religiosity were also organized, as was the participation of the first 120 students in 1947 to Santiago de Compostela, to make an offering to the patron of Colegio Mayor, or the one that led, years later, 31 Polish residents on a pilgrimage to Our Lady of the Pillar of Zaragoza (ABC 11/10/1956).

Similarly, the Slovaks celebrated their independence day on 14 March, chaired by Paul Cablk, former secretary of the embassy, and Jozef Cieker, former ambassador and current director of Colegio Mayor (ABC 14/3/1954) and (ABC 14/3/1954). Even the small representation of Chinese students, coming from Formosa (now Taiwan), celebrated their day of freedom around their ambassador, Dr. Yu Tsene-Chi (ABC 23/1/1955). Though, the day of St. Michael, Patron of Ukraine, was the most spectacular due to performance of the Ukrainian choir "Obnova" who played popular songs from their country (ABC 11/11/1951). The love of music of Ukrainians, even led to sponsor some of their activities, like the piano concert of the resident Lubomyr Hornytzkyj (ABC 12/3/1955). On the part of Hungarians, in addition to their national celebrations, they also organized the VIII Assembly of the Catholic Federation of Hungarian Students Abroad, chaired by its secretary general, Otto Taberzki, who led the Netherlands' group (ABC 24/09/1955). And on the Croatian side, under the chairmanship of the Apostolic Nuncio, Monsignor Antoniutti, they celebrated in the Basilica of St. Francis the Great a Mass for ten years of captivity of Cardinal Stepinac, Primate of Croatia (ABC 11/10/1956).

However, those events did not happen unnoticed by the people of Madrid. In the Holy Week of 1955, the Cardinal Primate and the Bishop of Madrid-Alcalá decided to celebrate Masses in all churches for the Church of Silence, as those suffering domination behind the Iron Curtain were demonized, that culminated in a grand peregrination praying the rosary of Penance for the Persecuted Church, which gathered 120.000 inhabitants of Madrid, and featured St. James' residents as representatives of their national communities, and the special presence of diplomats from occupied nations such as Count Potocki (Poland), Marosy (Hungary), Kamus (Latvia) and Cieker (Slovakia). The latter, director of Colegio Mayor (ABC 29/03/1955). The Day of the Persecuted Church, which took place on April 25, was a day of sad remembrance, but converted residents in the center of attention of the Spanish public opinion.

Later the events of Hungarian revolt, would add adhesions to students, and spur demand for information on those countries. The school of journalism invited to report on the situation Jozef Cieker, director of the hall but also the Polish journalist Jozef Łobodowski and the Hungarian journalist and former player of Real Madrid, Jorge Nemes, exiled in Spain (ABC 17/11/1956). Closer attention was also paid to the red book of the persecuted church, written by Albert Galter and presented by the canon of Freiburg, Henry Marmier (ABC 26-27/4/1957). The extensive work, over 600 pages, detailed the situation of persecution of the church in those countries, and anticipated events of the tenth anniversary of the foundation of the hall. On the playful side, dance groups formed by the Poles and Ukrainians entertained OCAU administration by performing folk dances of their lands and the singing of the Ukrainian choir (ABC 5/5/1957). Regarding the conferences, chaired by the

Cardinal Plá y Daniel, the Bishop of Madrid-Alcalá, Eijo y Garay and the apostolic nuncio Monsignor Antoniutti, who accompanied the director of the Institute of Hispanic Culture, Blas Piñar López, who spoke of the yoke that gripped those nations without freedom (ABC 3/5/1957). In the course of those ten years 423 students had passed by St. James' hall, who by origin were two Albanians, one Palestinian, six Belarusians, two Bulgarians, fifty-five Croats, twelve Czechs, twenty-nine Chineses, twenty-one Slovaks, forty-eight Slovenians, five Estonians, eight Georgians, forty-two Hungarians, nine Latvians, three Lithuanians, eighty-five Poles, twenty-one Romanians, four Russians, five Serbs and sixty-five Ukrainians (Jiménez 1959).

Among the curiosities is perhaps the arrival of Chinese students. They did not arrive in the first rounds, but in 1949. There were six students from Anhui Province, and sent by Spanish Jesuit missionaries. In 1950 they founded the Association of Students from the Republic of China and *Yangguang* magazine. In 1952 the first 30 lucky bursars arrived who were directed to Comillas University and Central University of Madrid. In 1953 relations with the Nationalist Republic of China (Taiwan) were established. The success of St. James the Apostle Hall of Residence with Eastern Europeans, where the Chinese were staying, was taken as an example to repeat the operation exclusively with students from Asia. In 1954 St. Francis Xavier Hall of Residence started its activity, which in 1955 would host 13 Chinese scholars and in 1956 - 31. Between 1954 and 1965 arrived 74 Chinese students to study in Spain, who received additional support from the Vatican (BORAO 1994:193).

2.2. List of the first residents

One of the major problems was to know exactly who were those students that passed by St. James' hall. The documentation disappeared when OCAU transferred the direction of the hall to Complutense and the current authorities have no information about what happened more than four decades ago. However, the General Archive of Administration retained academic records which those students sent to the Minister of Education, José Ibáñez Martín, in order to validate the studies they had in their countries, before enrolling in the Central University of Madrid. One of the most notable cases is that of Dr. Ciril Rozman Borsnar, Slovenian, who studied in Barcelona and became a professor of Pathology and Medical Clinic in Salamanca in 1967, and two years later in Barcelona. Currently, he is a professor emeritus at the University of Barcelona and one of the leading worldwide experts on blood diseases (PARAULA 24/10/2010). In conclusion, one can say that reception of exiles from Eastern Europe, helped the regime to try to break its international isolation, reinforcing its Catholic and anticommunist image. This new face will introduce it into French, Italian, British and German conservative circles of the new Europe.

Below there is a list of residents who came to St. James' hall from May 1947 until April 1949. The transcribed data are the name, surname, nationality and course in which they enrolled: Stane Ziherl (Slovenian) Civil Engineering. Antonija Janja Zuzek Novak (Slovenian) medicine. Janczur Stanislaw (Pole) medicine. Lew Martiuk (Ukrainian) medicine. Rostyslaw Levykij (Ukrainian) medicine. Jaroslav Petruscak (Ukrainian) medicine. Anatol Skorobohatyj (Ukrainian) medicine. Stepan Hladun (Ukrainian) medicine. Roman Bucok (Ukrainian) medicine. Miroslaw Sokolowski (Pole) medicine. Zdislaw Ryndak (Pole) medicine. Adam Wlodarczyk (Pole) medicine. Mieczyslaw Pawlak (Pole) medicine. Ryszard Dulinski (Pole) medicine. Tadeusz Malinovski (Pole) medicine. Jurij Drozdowskyj (Ukrainian) pharmacy. Stanislaw Borucinski (Pole) medicine. Jerzy Krasinski (Pole) medicine. Wladyslaw Pajor (Pole) economics. Bohdan Lotyczewski (Pole) chemistry. Gustaw Wysocki (Pole) chemistry. Jurij Kekisz (Ukrainian) chemistry. Zygmunt Dynowski (Pole) chemistry. Tadeusz Wyka (Pole) industrial engineering. Zbigniew Jankowski (Pole) industrial engineering. Vladimiro Blawackyj (Ukrainian) veterinary science. Jaroslaw Rudawskyj (Ukrainian) medicine. Irena Hulak (Pole) medicine. Romana Lempicka (Pole) Philosophy and Literature. Roman Wojciech (Ukrainian) pharmacy. Jadwiga Jaworka (Pole) political and economic sciences. Marian Dawydko (Ukrainian) veterinary science. Boleslaw Drozak (Pole) economics. Joanna Rozycka (Pole) intern. Zofia Oliera (Pole) intern. Bohdan Plaskatch (Ukrainian) Romance philology. Andrés Lystok (Ukrainian) Modern History. Simon Fediuk (Pole) political and economic sciences. Wladyslaw Gawron (Pole) medicine. Teodorg Barabash (Ukrainian) Mining Engineering. Isidoro Zaplatynskyj (Pole) architecture. Sczpan Praszlowicz (Pole) chemistry. Wladyslaw Bobrek (Pole) chemistry. Dmytro Maslij (Ukrainian) Mining Engineering. Antin Wynnychyj (Ukrainian) marine engineering. Zbigniew Jankowski (Pole) industrial engineering. Uhryn Lublomyr (Ukrainian) forestry. Roman Wawriw (Ukrainian) forestry. Tadeusz Wojnarski (Pole) architecture. Jurij Akulow (Ukrainian) architecture. Marko Miletich (Croat) political and economic sciences. Jan Ptaszynski (Pole) forestry. Ivan Ljevakovic (Croat) law. José Franich (Croat) political and economic sciences. Pero Vukota (Croat) political and economic sciences. Ante Berislav Fulgosikaic (Croat) medicine. Piotr Wrobleski (Pole) Fine arts. Nestor Romanik (Ukrainian) forestry. Wladyslaw Ribkowski (Pole) architecture. Kazimierz Tylko (Pole) political and economic sciences. Miguel Hycka (Ukrainian) agronomic engineering. Alexander Byluk (Ukrainian) agronomic engineering. Peter Klopcic (Slovenian) political and economic sciences. Josef Kolmajer (Slovenian) political and economic sciences. Luka Brajnovic (Croat) Philosophy and Literature. Ivan Madirazza (Croat) architecture. Jaroslav Flys (Ukrainian) Philosophy and Literature. Cornelio Rotaru (Romanian) medicine. Mircea Rahmistriuc (Romanian) medicine. Vladimir Stnkovic (Serb) political and economic sciences. Francisco Porovne (Slovenian) medicine. Zdzislaw Grudzinski (Pole) marine engineering. Cvetka Jakus (Slovenian) chemistry. Francisca Zeljko (Slovenian) pharmacy. José Bernik (Slovenian) law. Gustaw Reepka (Pole) political and economic sciences. Stefan Zywczak (Pole) political and economic sciences. Antonio Gajda (Pole) exact sciences. Jerzy Chmielewski (Pole) physical sciences. Orest Prypchan (Ukrainian) architecture. Yolanda Frey (Ukrainian) architecture. Zdenko Dsanazz (Slovenian) philosophy. Boris Soroki (Croat) political and economic sciences. Eduard Moscovic (Slovak) medicine. Marijan Brandsteter (Slovenian) medicine. Marbete Mazovec (Slovenian) medicine. Marija Serle (Slovenian) Philosophy and Literature. Vanja Velikonja (Slovenian) law. Bohdan Preselj (Slovenian) chemistry. Villam Kona (Slovak) law. Oscar Boria (Slovenian) law. Zdravo Ducmelic (Croat) fine arts. Tomislav Kuraja (Croat) forestry. Miroslav Batucic (Croat) law. Roman Wasniowski (Pole) medicine. Janko Zebre (Slovenian) chemistry. Tadeo Maciejczyk (Pole) medicine. Ismar Walter Winheim Hoppe (Guatemalan) chemistry. Frantisek Chajma (Slovak) philosophy. M Luisa Krocker (Croat) medicine. Dragutn Maric (Croat) political and economic sciences. Adan Milczynski (Pole) architecture. José Santa (Hungarian) Contemporary history. Jan Paczkowski (Pole) political and economic sciences. Milos Vuckovich Yankovich (Yugoslav) political and economic sciences. Cojno Kremenic (Croat) chemistry. Franc Pepevnac (Slovenian) veterinary science. Francisco Koren (Slovenian) political science. Miguel Kresar (Slovenian) veterinary science. Llija Stevanovich (Serb) economics. Valerio Turgal (Romanian) medicine. Arturo Struic (Croat) medicine. José Franic (Croat) economics. Ivan Sifrer (Slovenian) veterinary science.

Constantin Zulukidre (Georgian) economics. Norbert Schady (German) medicine. Ivan Madirazza (Croat) pharmacy. Bohdan Pestotnik (Slovenian) veterinary science. Milan Tuna (Slovenian) medicine. Matija Pavcic (Slovenian) medicine. Franjo Opic (Croat) veterinary science. Zvonomir Putra (Croat) medicine. Janez Gostingar (Slovenian) agronomic engineering. Marijan Gec (Croat) political science. Eduardo Magy (Croat) political science. Dusko Jelavic (Croat) medicine. Zdravo Ducmenic (Croat) fine arts. Wasyl Kostrubiak (Ukrainian) medicine. Guillermo Mihalovic (Slovak) economics. Pierre Andre (Frenchman) Philosophy and Literature. Veljko deum (Croat) Philosophy and Literature. Slobodan Petrovic (Serb) engineering. Merala Marjan (Slovenian) veterinary science. Mladen Zigrovic (Croat) Philosophy and Literature. Branimir Turkovic (Croat) marine engineering. Zlatko Azinovic (Croat) political and economic sciences. Miroslav Batusic (Croat) political and economic sciences. Krasimir Pandzic (Croat) political and economic sciences. Hroje Struic (Croat) chemistry. Antolin Viktor (Slovenian) law. Stanislav Domoslawski (Pole) political and economic sciences. Grga Raspudic (Croat) Philosophy and Literature. Tomislav Tijan (Croat) chemistry. Srecko Pregels (Slovenian) medicine. Ludvik Drobnic (Slovenian) medicine. José Filipovic (Croat) political and economic sciences. Ciril Rozman (Slovenian) medicine. Wladimimyro Pastuszczuk (Ukrainian) medicine. Leopoldo Seme (Slovenian) medicine. Meter Markes (Slovenian) law. Stanislav Ziherl (Slovenian) industrial engineering. Peter Tsao Han-Chao (Chinese) Philosophy and Literature in 1953[1].

2.3. Cultural activities organized in Spain

Romanians had an outstanding presence in culture, through the "Romanian School of Madrid", of whom Vintila Horia should be noted, *The Goncourt Prize* for Literature in 1960, who had written *The rebellion of Soviet writers*, and was a member of LANC (National Christian League); Aron Cotrus, poet and author of *Iberian rhapsody*; Alejandro Busuioceanu, poet and professor at the University of Madrid, participated in the Brief Academy of Art criticism founded by Eugenio D´Ors; Horia Stamatu; George Uscatescu, author of *Prophets of Europe, Seneca, our contemporary, Spanish-Romanian cultural relations, Romania: People, history and culture*;

---

[1] The names have been transcribed as they appear in the documentation deposited in the General Archive of the Administration AGA (05) 001.016 Leg. 20046 TOP. 32/66 and in the Archive of the Ministry of Foreign Affairs AMAE, R.4435-21, 301/54. 8 June 1954. Czechoslovak residents.

Aurelio Rauta, philologist and author of the first Romanian-Spanish grammar, soul of the magazine *Works and days* of Salamanca; Cirilo Popovici, art critic and author of *Two essays on contemporary art* (ABC 1/6/1966).

Other qualified group will be Croatian. Luka Brajnovic was already a mature and married man when he came to Spain, and soon he began working as a journalist in Spain, without losing his relationship with the Croatian community in Munich. His brother-in-law Pavao Tijan, also came in 1947, invited by CSIC, with the task of organizing Slavic Studies in the newly founded International Department of Modern Cultures. In 1954 he became an associate professor of the "Miguel de Cervantes" Institute of Spanish philology. In 1955 he manages to reunite his family (his wife, professor Nedjeljka Luetic, and his daughter). Tijan worked hand in hand with Florentino Pérez Embid in Rialp, *Arbor, Revista general de investigación y cultura* (General magazine of research and culture) of CSIC and publications of the Croatian emigration like *Osoba i Duh, Hrvatska Revija, Sloboda, Glas sv. Antuna* and *Studia Croatica* (Juez 1997:281) and (Brajnovic 2001:190). Brajnovic and his friend Anton Wurster will be later professors of the first institute of the future University of Navarra.

With regard to the Polish group, Juliusz Babecki, delegate of the Polish Red Cross in Spain, ran *Polonia* magazine, which intended to be as *Kultura*, its equivalent in Paris. The magazine that existed from 1955 to 1969, issued 99 numbers, with the participation of Jozef Potocki, ambassador of Free Government in London, Karolina Babecka, Juliusz Babecki, Kazimierz Tylko, Tadeusz Norwid, Miroslaw Sokolowski and Jozef Łobodowski (Mielczarek 2003:125-134). The latter brought his vision of Polish and Ukrainian literature (Bak 2006:229-241). Resident in Spain since 1943, he was held in Figueres, where he wrote his *Listy hiszpanskie (Spanish letters).*

Another important activity carried out by the colony of European exiles was collaborating on *Spanish National Radio* with broadcasts in their respective languages, which contained news of the country, anticommunist speeches, Catholic view of life, and a positive vision of Spain in its Christian solidarity work. There were retransmissions in Hungarian, Slovak, Polish, Czech, Croatian and Romanian. Broadcasts, intended to repeat from Spanish soil the experience of Radio Free Europe, were also sensitive to various political disagreements arising within the fragmented exile (EIROA 2001: 152-156). Pavao Tijan was responsible for emissions in Croatian, who since 1956 until his retirement in 1981 worked in *Spanish Radio and Television*. From the Polish side, Karol "Wagner" Pienkowski will assume the direction in the first period; who had a poet Jozef Łobodowski as the main contributor, Miroslaw Sokolowski and Karolina Babecka as announcers and Kazimierz Tylko as an editor and translator. The religious references were the responsibility of Father Marian Walorek, from the Polish Catholic Mission (Bogdan 2011:153-176).

Another effective tool, but less mediatic was the *Bulletin of Nations Oppressed by Communism*, as an organ of Oppressed Nations' Committee, founded in October 1948 by unofficial representatives in Spain of the countries occupied by Soviet forces. Among them were Boyadjeff from Bulgaria, Dragitchevich from Croatia, Marossy from Hungary, Szumlakowski from Poland, Cieker from Slovakia and Enescu from Romania, who were joined by Nemec from Czechoslovakia, Pusta from Estonia and Kampus from Latvia.

2.4. Sport activities in Spain

The presence of top athletes among the exiles, turned them into the best known faces of their communities. Although in Spain they did not have the misfortune of Lutz Eigendorf, a fugitive from the German Democratic Republic, who joined Kaiserlaurten, and ended up killed in an accident caused by the Stasi in the FRG. The most striking case was that of Hungary, a team formed by Ferdinand Daučík with Hungarian fugitives from their country after World War II. From among them stood out Ladislav Kubala, a Hungarian player, but of Slovak origin, who during the conflict had landed in Bratislava, and then had returned to his native country. Along with other players he took shelter in Austria, where he began a stateless tour by Italy, where he played in ProPatria, until finally reaching Spain. In our country, Real Madrid refused to take care of his brother-in-law, so he was about to leave for Colombia, glimpsed by the technical director of FC Barcelona, José Samitier, was recruited by the club, becoming one of its biggest stars.

In 1953 the Hungarian team was one of the best in the world, having Zoltán Czibor, Ferenc Puskás, Sándor Kocsis and József Bozsik who played in the army team, Honvéd. But the outbreak of the revolt of 1956 caught them playing in Brussels, from where the legendary Kocsis, Puskás and Czibor went to Spain. Except for Puskas who joined Real Madrid, the rest were persuaded by Kubala to form with him, the Hungarian core of FC Barcelona.

Similarly, the exiles enriched with their presence the appearance of new unknown sports in Spain, such as volleyball. Polish and Ukrainian students residing in St. James' hall were those who fed that scarce activity which was enriched later with the arrival of the Spanish from the USSR (former war children), enthusiasts of this sport. Caribbeans from the scholarship programs of the Institute of Hispanic Culture also joined. The Poles, Swieboski, Bogdan, Tylko, Simonovir and Wonzönuwics became the core of Real Madrid, who took advantage of this specialty until 1982, winning twelve cups and seven leagues. The Serb Miroslav Vorgic joined them later.

3. The new emigration to democratic Spain

Spain was never one of the favorite destinations of Polish exile, Great Britain, the United States, France and Germany being places of concentration of several thousand Polish citizens who could maintain sufficient critical mass to sustain their national identity. But the eighties will foster a strong increase in departures from Poland. The severe economic crisis and implementation of the martial law on December 13, 1981, will cause exit toward the West in the eighties of nearly three hundred thousand people, officially. Of whom in 1991 about 7800 Poles would be found in Spain (Arnal 1998: 2006). The Asylum Law passed in 1984 with the socialists, allowed that during the period of processing of asylum claim, it could enjoy a series of aids given by public institutions and NGOs (Rodríguez Rodríguez 1995: 529). But with the fall of the wall, in the early nineties, the Anglo-Saxon countries (USA, Canada and Australia), usual places of the Polish exile, increased restrictions on the arrival of Poles living in Spain. That fact coincided with a small growth of the Spanish economy, protected by the construction sector, closely linked to tourism, true survivor engine of the Spanish economy, and to illegal financing of political parties. That industry demanded plenty of unskilled workforce. According to the municipal census, the Poles passed from being 8.164 in 2000 to 61.218 in 2007 (Stanek 2008: 171) During that period Poland joined the EU as a full member in 2004.

With a stable quantitative mass, the first organization of Polish immigrants called "White Eagle" (Orzeł Biały) could arise in Alcalá de Henares. Among its objectives, what underlines the importance given by Polish families to maintaining their cultural roots, was the birth of a Polish school for their children born in Spain. The goal achieved in 1994. The next year "Polish House" was taking shape, as an association specialized in promoting cultural activities in the group, and weekly collaboration in a special supplement in the local newspaper "Diario de Alcalá". At the same time, the Spanish-Polish Association "Forum" and "Our House" (*Stowarzyszenie Polaków w Hiszpanii Nasz Dom*) emerged in Madrid with objectives similar to those of their neighbors in Alcalá. While the first promotes Polish culture in the Spanish world, the second does that primarily among members of its own community. Among the undertaken activities there is formation of football teams.

One of aspects to note about the Polish organizational process is the importance of Polish chaplaincies. Since the XIX century, when the maintenance of Polish identity was safeguarded by Catholic Church. Diaspora communities kept their unique national identity due to the presence of some clerics with them. The growth of the Polish community in Spain has led to a couple of chaplaincies acting in Madrid and Alcalá de Henares, although the services of priests attached to them, partly from The Society of Christ, are scattered around different parishes offering religious services in the Polish language. But these points of confluence are well used for association, consultation and legal assistance on employment or other (Stanek 2008: 215-237).

In 1961 at the Complutense University, Gabriela Makowiecka will be the pioneer of Polish studies in the Spanish university. A course of Slavic Cultures was attempted, coordinated by María Sánchez Puig, as part of the Institute for Oriental and African Studies. Where collaborated Urszula Aszyk and Kazimierz Sabik. At the same time, in the Autonomous University of Madrid, the pioneer was Janusz Kucharczyk. However, that first experience wasn't firmly established until 1983, in the form of its own title, and two years later as an official title of Slavic Philology. Under the coordination of Julia Mendoza Tuñón, and later Fernando Presa González. The latter, author of the first handbook and the first Polish grammar published in Spain, is responsible for a department divided into four sections: Bulgarian philology, Slovak philology, Russian philology and Polish philology. Notable in the latter are Agnieska Matyjasszczyk, Grzegorz Bak, Clara Angelica Pasiecznik and Fernando Otero (Bak 2005: 259-266). The students, in addition to being interested in the Slavonic culture, were also Spanish with some ancestor from those countries, so they didn't want to lose their family's cultural roots.

4. Bibliography

Anónimo 1946, *XIX Congreso Mundial de Pax Romana*, Madrid: Pax Romana.
Arnal M. D. 1998, *Inmigrantes polacos en España. El camino como concepto teórico para el estudio de la adaptación*, Madrid: Universidad Complutense de Madrid.
Arteaga J. 1989, *Carta a los hombres*, Madrid: Rialp.
Bak G. 2006, *Aproximación a una bibliografía de Jozef Łobodowski*, "Eslavística Complutense" 6: 229-241.
Bak G. 2005, *Los estudios de lengua y literatura polaca en Madrid*, [in:] *España y Polonia: Los encuentros*, ed. by E. González, M. Nalewajko, Madrid: CSIC: 259-266.
Bogdan M. 2011, *Radio Madryt 1949-1955*, Warszawa, LTV-UKSW.
Borao J.E. 1994, *España y China 1927-1967*, Taipei: Central Book Publiching Company.
Brajnovic L. 2001, *Despedidas y encuentros*, Pamplona: Eunsa.
Ciechanowski J.S. 2007, *Las relaciones entre la Polonia comunista y la República española en el exilio. Razones políticas de la misión de Manuel Sánchez Arcas en Varsovia (1946-1950)*, "AYER" 67: 49-79.
Eiroa M. 2001, *Las relaciones de Franco con Europa Centro-Oriental*, Barcelona: Ariel.
Eliade M 2001, *Diario Portugués (1941-1945)*, Barcelona: Editorial Kairós.
Fontan A., Axer J. 1994, *Españoles y polacos en la corte de Carlos V*, Madrid: Alianza Editorial.
Juez F. J. 1997, *In Memoriam Pablo Tijan*, "Studia Croatica" 135: 281.
Matyjaszczyk A., Presa F. (eds.) 2001, *Viajeros polacos en España: (a caballo de los siglos XIX y XX)*, Madrid: Huerga y Fierro.
Mielczarek A. 2003, *Información y propaganda en "Polonia, Revista ilustrada" (1955-1969), publicación periódica de la colonia polaca en España*, "Estudios Hispánicos" 11: 125-134.
Mindszenty J. 2009, *Memorias*, Madrid: Palabra.
Orlandis J. 1992, *Memorias de Roma en Guerra, 1942-1945*, Madrid: Rialp.
Orlandis J. 1992, *Mis Recuerdos*, Madrid: Rialp.
Ramírez Goicoechea E. 2002, *La comunidad polaca en España. Un colectivo particular*, "REIS", 102: 63-92.
Rodríguez V. 1995. *Los polacos en España. De refugiados a inmigrantes*, "Estudios Geográficos" LV 220: 521-527.
Skowron R. 2008, *Olivares, los Vasa y el Báltico. Polonia en la política internacional de España en los años 1621-1632*, Varsovia: Wydawnictwo-Dig.

Stanek M. 2008, *Los inmigrantes polacos en la comunidad de Madrid y su inserción laboral*, Madrid: UCM (Tesis doctoral).

Veiga F. 1989, *La mística del ultranacionalismo*, Barcelona: Universidad Autónoma de Barcelona.

Von Horthy, N. 1955, *Memorias*, Barcelona: AHR.

VVAA 1946, *Decreto del 6 de Diciembre de 1946*, "BOE" 348: 8736.

VVAA 1948, *Anuario del Instituto Nacional de Estadística. Extranjeros residentes y transeúntes*, Madrid: Instituto Nacional de Estadística.

VVAA 1956, *Anuario del Instituto Nacional de Estadística. Extranjeros residentes y transeúntes*, Madrid: Instituto Nacional de Estadística.

Yarimovich V., Bilyc A., Volinsky N. 1997, *Breve historia de la organización estudiantil y de la colonia ucraniana en España: 1946-1996*, Philadelphia-Madrid: NVF.

The Spanish Exile in Poland (1939-1955)

CRISTINA BARREIRO
CEU San Pablo University

The Spanish Civil War forced the exile of thousands of people coming from the losers camp. In the circumstances marked by the international determinants resulting from the Second World War, Europe received the waves of Republicans who started to follow a path. Having entered and stayed on French territory- where anti-communism policies with the "cold war" generated another mass exodus, some of them started a new life in the socialist countries of the Central and East Europe: Poland, converted after 1945 in the state subordinated to the Soviet political interests, was one of them.

1. Spain 1939: starting point to the exodus

The Civil War, divided Spain into two irreconcilable camps, which had different ways of understanding the evolution of the state. The Republic of 1931, that woke so much hope in its proclamation, created by the combination of many ground between ideological blocs which were vivid under different policies, secular and reformist implemented by the leftist governments. The issue of religion, social instability and violence, a controversial land reform policy, statutory radicalization of the extremist political groups, resulted in formal confrontation held in July 1936, led the Spanish to the War. On the one hand, the rebels, the military and the radical right sectors were supported by the majority of the right-wing groups and the conservative Catholic bases. On the other, the heirs of the Popular Front government that after having won the elections in February General lost parliamentary control: Left and Republican Union, moderate liberal tradition intellectuals, socialists, communists, poumistas, anarchists, Basque and Catalan nationalists and in addition, the trade unions. It was a real conglomeration of disparate and ideological interests faced by each of the aforesaid group, for whom the purpose of the conflict was not clearly defined: win the war?, ¿organize the Revolution? These discrepancies, in which the backdrop of Stalinism/Trotskyism duality was a kind of reality, which become the main cause for the final defeat[1].

Even some months before the War ended, some of the Republic prominent personalities had already left Spain - among them, Manuel Azaña himself, who crossed the border in February 1939 – as well as some other politicians, fighters and journalists were leaving the country. This massive political exodus of individuals and families was not for the official reasons of the general hostility, they left their country for the fear of the Franco regime. Political emigrants, refugees and evacuees left Spain facing an uncertain future (see Samper 2005). The data indicated that there were more than 680,000 Spanish who left the country as a direct result of the war evacuations. This particular group should be joined by nearly 50,000 people, who were carrying the asylum granted by the embassies and consulates and those who passed the border illegally (Rubio 1977, as a synthesis, see Soldevilla Oria 2001 as reference). France was, in the first moment, the destination for thousands of Spanish: the number of 430,000 of the initial hours dropped to 140,000 as a result of the repatriation, re-emigration to other countries and natural losses due to their poor life conditions in which they arrived, the conditions of shelters and refugees and the development of the Second World War.

Europe in 1939 was a kind of powder keg ready to explode. The entry of German troops into Poland on September 1, 1939, accelerated the turn of the events. There started the years of national socialist rule, in which the old continent would have to bow to Nazi terror. The Spanish who came to France of Eduard Daladier were welcomed and received as a result of gender, age and condition. Women, children and elderly were distributed by various French departments located away from the border, while the most seriously wounded were evacuated to various hospitals. The men were grouped in so-called "refugee camps" and soon moved into "concentration camps" establish during the occupation[2]. Some like Argelès-sur-Mer or Saint Cyprien responded to the based on improvisation policy created by the government and addressed to such a large emigration, while their living conditions were so precarious. Within Agde,

---
1 To understand the reasons of the Civil War from the ideological perspective: Bolloten 2004; Southworth 1963. See more aspects in: Payene 1995 y para cuestiones internacionales de la guerra de España: Moradiellos 2001.
2 Reference work related to exile in France: Dreyfus-Armand 2000.

The Spanish Exile in Poland (1939-1955)

Septfonds, Bram o Gurs, the were–initially – classified by categories (Catalans, skilled workers, intellectuals or fighters). As the exiles, they were provided with four possibilities to exit the country: return to Spain, a new immigration – history record and asylum found in the USSR, the contract in the external field or the military isolation. However, the French authorities who welcomed the Spanish mass exodus, not always recognized their "refugee status" (officially they will not do it by 1945), what in the Vichy government will cause some serious consequences. During the occupation, thousands of Spanish exiles are sent, as political deported to the concentration camps of tragic fame, such as Mauthausen, Dachau, Auschwitz and Bergen-Belsen. After having liberated France and finished the Second World War, more than 100,000 Spanish refugees applied for their refugee status. They are joined by their families and illegal immigration-which constitutes a total of approximate 50,000 people, who arrive to France at that time escaping from the Franco regime.

But in addition to France, also the Soviet Union welcomed the first, large number of the Spanish exiles: the evacuated children, Spanish marine boat crew which were close to the USSR when the war ended, student pilots who were going to take studies in the Soviet aviation schools and also, the political exiles. But Stalin did not want to let mass immigration merge the Soviet Union as it could cause some "political deviationism problems"[3]. Thus, for many Spanish who had arrived in the Soviet Union this place was not the final destination and many of them, as they will be seen, were sent to other satellite countries, among them, in addition to Czechoslovakia, Hungary and the GDR, there was also Poland.

After the Second World War, in a continent ravaged by the loss of human life, economy, geographical and urban devastation, many europea, including Spanish political exiles launched a new, "re-migration" wave to America, where, they thought, they would be provides more suitable level of the life conditions. Thus, the Evacuation Authorites of the Spanish Refugees (SERE) created by the Republican Government Negrin took the responsibility for organizing the official immigration service in Mexico, a country that admitted the largest number of the Spanish immigrants. No obstante, fue también destacable el número de españoles que decidieron fijar su residencia en Europa, con destinos vinculados a las circunstancias sociopolíticas derivadas de las conferencias de paz.

---

[3] Pethö 2008 (PhD thesis no edited). There are the gaps related to the number of the Spanish communist who came to the Soviet Union, but any other estimation do not exist in relation to 2.000 people. See Alted Vigil 2002.

However, it the number of Spanish who decided to take up the residence in Europe was also remarkable, getting linked to the socio-political circumstances arising from peace conferences. It soon became clear that among the winners, there existed two opposing ideological blocs: capitalism versus communism. Poland was linked to the second orbit being strongly depended on the Soviet sector, which, according to the words of Professor Stanislaw Ciechanowski, was used by the Russians "to strengthen direct ties between the communism, submissive Moscow forces, the real democracy enemies (Ciechanowski 2007; see also Egido Leon, Eiroa San Francisco 2004). Poland was practically given in terms of its democratic power, to Stalin losing its own sovereignty in favour of this totalitarian country, decreasing, at the same time, its own cultural and economic potential level. In a country so much ravaged, decimated and internally divided society, the Soviet occupation regime was eventually and successfully established.

2. The Spanish government in exile and the Central and Eastern Europe: the Polish legacy

After the Second World War, the *Government* of the *Spanish* Republic in *exile* was established and led by José Giral, the leader of the Republican Left, and formed by the socialists, republicans representing small bourgeois parties, regionalist, anarchists unaffiliated who became, starting from the 31 March 1946, the communists. This "government of the hope" was recognised in 1945 by four Latin American countries, Mexico included as the Spanish Left was recognized. In February 1946, the Government was moved to Paris in order to get more official government support in Europe. Some months later, it managed to be recognized by some new European communist dictatorships (Cabeza Sánchez-Albornoz 1997). The first to do so was Poland, on April 4, 1946, as a direct result of the entrance of the communist, Santiago Carrillo, who was acting as the ministry of the "Republic"[4]. Then, Yugoslavia (April 17, 1946), Romania (June 4, 1946), Czechoslovakia and Hungary (August 22, 1946), Albania (October 29, 1946) and Bulgaria (November 29, 1946) were the following countries. The Republican leaders the hopes of the future recognition provided by the western democracies – please, remember

---

[4] Polish ambassador - communist based in París - Stanislaw Skrzeszewski delivered a document to the Spanish government in exile of the 10th, in which he reports that on the 4 April, the Polish government decided to perform "national unity" and constitute the relations between these two countries "the funs of democracy" (see Ciechanowski 2007).

about the UN official decision, upon which, it was recommended to end up with any diplomatic relations with Madrid having Spain, at the same time, excluded from any international conferences -, the situation, which of course had never come to be. The outbreak of the Cold War, the struggle between the free world and the communist totalitarianism was for the Franco regime a big chance to avoid dangerous threats.

El representante de la legación republicana en Polonia, Manuel Sánchez Arcas llegó a la capital, Varsovia, en julio de 1946. The representative of the Republican delegation in Poland, Mr. Manuel Sánchez Arcas arrived in the Warsaw capital, in July 1946. He was accompanied by a Spanish delegation composed of, among the others, the communist generals, Juan Modesto, Enrique Lister and Rafael Sánchez Guerra, who acted as the "ministry" of the Government of the Government Republic based in Paris and was invited by the Polish-Spanish Friendship Association (AAPE)[5]. On August 20, Sánchez Arcas presented his credentials as extraordinary envoy and the plenipotentiary ministry of the Spanish Republic and the President of the Polish Republic, Mr. Bolelaw Bierut. Who was this Spanish diplomat elected to constitute and launch the first Embassy in exile? He was the member of the Spanish Communist Party (PCE) from 1936 and subordinated to the interests of his leadership, also responsible for the organisation of the first Polish embassy which was supposed to be the "coverage" in the struggle against Franco. Sánchez Arcas, born in Madrid in 1897, was recognised as a successful architect linked to the organization, so-called "Generation of '25" led by his partner and friend -Luis Lacasa and the architecture rationalist movement of the thirties. He was the member of the Iberian Artists Society, who participated in the construction of the City University, succeeded also in was one of his major professional project, the construction of the Clinical Hospital based in Madrid. When the Civil War started, he held some relevant to the Popular Front government positions, including the position of the Assistant Secretary to the State Ministry of Propaganda Del Vayo (April 1938). He crossed the French border in March 1939 and moved to Versailles, to the intellectual house of Wolkowich, where he remained until April, when he set off to Leningrad to meet his daughters, whom he had previously sent on trips organized by the Republicans, who took children to school camps based in the USSR. The family moved to Moscow and were welcomed into a "rest house " until the government got

---

5 AAPE was ruled by General Karol Świerczewski, the symbol of unity with Polish and Spanish communism – killed in 1947.

him a shared apartment and employed at the University of Architecture. In the fall of 1941, he arrived in Ufa, a city to which the university had to move because of the threat of Nazi invasion. He returned to Moscow in 1943, at the dawn of the Stalinist apogee. Two years later, he was appointed by the Government of the Republic in Exile as a Spanish diplomat based in Poland. The former Spanish Embassy building was destroyed during the war, so they finally moved it to an apartment in the Hotel Polonia, practically the only operating in a capital utterly desolated. He came accompanied by the Secretary of the Embassy, the Basque, Francisco Andrés Iturbide. The endowed Giral Government donated the legations with the monthly budget of 127,500 francs processed through the Basque Delegation based in New York, with whom he had to deal with in the scope of the salaries and any other expenses. This monthly allowance will not cover the maintenance of the Embassy, which turned to complicate its operation due the difficult post-war living conditions.

The Spanish Embassy in Poland remains open until the early 1950s and will be supported by Oskar Lange, the Polish Ambassador at the UN and a personal friend of Sánchez Arcas. During this time, their primary mission was to protect the Spanish residents in Poland, who, according to the study of Ciechanowski were mostly taken to work in Germany and the other territories controlled by the Third Reich during the war[6]. According to the official documentation, their aim was to encourage all the Spanish to get united, regardless of "their political label,". In 1946, the President Giral organised a meeting with the group of intellectuals, among whom, there were Pablo Neruda, Jose Bergamin and Elya Ehrenburg. In 1948, he was accompanied by Pablo Picasso and Paul Eluard while attending the Peace World Congress of Intellectuals. It was Sánchez Arcas, who showed much interest in constituting the relations with representatives accredited by the central-eastern capitals and who attend the public events, such as "The Passion" organised in Warsaw, April 1947. The invitations sent by the President of Parliament constituted the form of propaganda addressed against the Franco regime, as demonstrated in the article about the real reasons for the political mission of Manuel Sánchez Arcas in Warsaw (Ciechanowski 2007). The Spanish, with the Kominform help seemed to represent something more than PCE and the Parisian Government. With the departure of

---

6 Ciechanowski 2007: 69. However, Eiroa San Francisco (2001) offers more estimations, only two of them specify the number of the Spanish who did not take part in the legalisation. The documents, provided by Ciechanowski seems to contain more real data.

the Spanish Communist from the Republic government in exile, led since early 1947 by the Socialist, Rodolfo Llopis and six months later by Alvaro de Albornoz, the representative of the Republican Left, Mr. Sánchez Arcas the relations were eventually got much than strained. The Tito-Stalin conflict finally broke them definitely. When Sánchez Arcas was informed that the Government of the Republic in exile maintained some relations with the Yugoslav government known as the "fascist gang composed of U.S. imperialism agents, the enemies of our nation, (...) and the Spanish democracy" he submitted his resignation to the President, Diego Martínez Barrio. On the 22nd Februarz 1950 his resignation was approved. Although relinquished his duties, Manuel Sánchez Arcas remained in Warsaw together with his wife and daughters until 1958, working in the research department of the Ministry of Health and living in the city under reconstruction. The Government of Paris, applied for the accreditation for Elfidio Alonso Rodríguez, the politician and canary journalist who was sent to lead the republican *ABC* during the Civil War. Linked to Republican, he took as the vice Secretary of the Public Works in the government of Juan Negrin and visited Warsaw as the Spanish representative accredited, in 1950, by the Congress of the Peace Party. The Polish government, fully subject to the guidelines and Moscow directives, did not sent any answer. In this way, any diplomatic relations between the Polish Stalinist government and the Spanish government in exile finished, though they had never been officially broken up. I started, however, a stage in which Poland was to become the second European country who was receiving the Spanish emigrants, escaping from the communist persecution held in the western part of Europe.

3. Spanish exile in Poland: post operation Bolero-Paprika refugees

With the beginning of the fifties, the communism became to be the black beast of the western countries which launch so called "witch hunt", through the operation directed against them. So when in September 1950, the French government decided to outlaw the communism, many of those who exiled to France at the end of the Civil War, were forced to begin a process of "re-migration" that mainly affect the countries situated behind so called "Iron Curtain", mainly in Czechoslovakia and Poland. Therefore, this "second" exile got more political and corresponded mainly to the communist militants.

On September 7, 1950, the French government launched the "Operation Bolero - Paprika", a process of persecution directed against the foreign communist militants in the context of the Cold War threat to the national security. The operation affected between 256 and 285 Spanish Communists, among which there were the leaders known in France as PCE, as well as the Warsaw Hospital personnel, workers and the members of the communist ideology. The operation PCE was banned in France and many detainees were deported to Corsica and North Africa (Algeria). In ideologically broken Europe, upon request of the General Secretary of the Party, Dolores Ibárruri, many deportees will receive a political asylum in the so called "democracies". On the same day, the 20th, Ibárruri was writing, from Prague - in Russian and Spanish, to the Polish President, Mr Boleslaw Beirut asking him to grant the Spanish communists asylum. Also the families of the deportees, wrote a letter to the President of the Polish Ministry Council, "applying fervently" for granting their families "its entitlement to have the asylum in this great and generous country"[7]. After having approved their request and get the extradition of the Spanish, the Polish diplomatic representation in Paris was responsible for organizing this process and their reception. The "popular republics" had only eight months to deal with this particular case, as the victory of the right party was predicted to win the elections in France, scheduled in June 17th, 1951, what might cause a risk of exiles' comeback to the Franco regime.

Of the 108 deportees, 40 Spanish were welcomed in Poland. They were joined by 81 families: a total of 121. Most of them belonged to PCE, but also were affiliated to the PSUS and JSU[8]. Two boats came to Gdynia (Poland), the first group brought the group from Corsica and the second, the Polish ship called "General Walter" brought the group from North Africa (Algeria). The deported arrived, as well as those who had received the asylum in Czechoslovakia and Hungary, and reached the port of Gdynia w here they were taken by train to Warsaw. Those who left Poland went by train to Budapest and Prague. The exiles began a new life in the central-eastern country, joined within small Spanish colony that was already residing in the country. Since 1952, most of their relatives were coming to visit them. Almost all were based in Warsaw, except for a small group that was established in the city of Katowice- then so- called Stalinogrod-, located in the mining area of the Silesia region, in

---

7 Pethö (2008) reproduces the circulars from the Archive PCE.
8 Spanish exile in Poland, 57 belonged to PCE, 20 al PSUC, 13 JSU, 3 a "other related parties" and only 12 were not related to any political option.

the south of the country. The following data presents their distribution, according to the age and gender. It seems that there were the majority of the males, older than 15:

	Warsaw	Katowice
older than 15:	76	26
older than 15:	39	nd

	Warsaw	Katowice
Males :	46	16
Females:	30	13

The Polish Government, upon the request of PCE, helped in the search for home and work, but they themselves had to get adapted to a different lifestyle, try to integrate into society through the Polish natives customs, culture and language, which seemed to be so different and which turned to be the most important obstacle in the process of their socialization. They also had to get known the heavy industry production procedures, in which the women, for example, had to take jobs as regular employees. Thus, they with respect to their jobs, they worked mainly in car factories, as the FSO (e.g. Casás Consuelo and her husband - Carlos Marroyán) or vodka. Also, the Spanish have been located in the building industry, in chemical factories based in Kędzierzyn and the port warehouses located at the Odra river. They also took jobs in radio stations (Spanish-language public radio), which referred to the relative percentage of the students who belonged to the " school political party"[9]. It is worth mentioning that in 1954 two architects, among them, Manuel Sánchez Arcas who got the job in Warsaw and stayed there by the time he decided to his next destination - Berlin.

	Warsaw	Katowice
Factories:	36	18
Office:	8	4
Radio personal:	11	0
	Warsaw	**Katowice**
Architects:	2	0
Medical doctors:	0	1

---

9 Intervie with Consuelo Casás, published in *El Siglo* (12 enero 2009).

Students:	14	0
Not defined:	0	6
Unemployed:	5	0

But how the PCE was handled within the political life of its "exile"? In a totalitarian model of the control, as well as the communist, everything seemed to be run out by the central organizations. There were two core "groups" of the party, one based in Warsaw and one in Katowice, supervised by Enrique Lister who was also dedicated to run the rest of the republics. Each group was divided into smaller groups of the party, in Warsaw - there were 5 groups and in Katowice - 2. Each group was led by its director (Louis, in Warsaw). The direction of the collective was formed by the group leaders and the committee of three people (Luis, Sánchez Arcas and Clement), although, when Enrique Lister appeared in his first year, it got a bit less effective and operative as it just discussed the political problems. The direction of each group kept relations with the directive organs of PCE based in Prague, having the foreign section of the Central Committee of the PC or regional organization based in Poland. In line with prevailing Stalinism, it was ideological control training so members were convened regular meetings and study circles; had to study the history of the PC of the USSR, resolutions and reports provided to Kominform on the problems of Spain or the construction of socialism... In some occasions, the non-party Spanish members, usually the wives of the regular members got also the invitations. Then, the bosses performed a kind of evaluation referred as well as to the party members as the groups themselves. Also, the classes of Spanish were offered in the scope of reading and writing, grammar studies, as well as the classes of the basic math were available, and especially-in the early years, the classes of Polish language courses were addressed to such groups to facility them the integration with the Polish nation. The group from the Polish capital, whose data is available in the archives of PCE, nearly did not participate in the activity of the ideological background. It was not until the Lister's visit to Warsaw on June 4th, 1952, when the committee was reorganized to launch a new activity: although it remained Luis Sánchez Arcas as the leader of this committee appointed to lead the study circles, Clement (his surname is unknown but he is known to work in the radio) became responsible for materials and Puigcerber issues management becoming a new member and representative of the workers, whom he worked with in a factory. However, the committee has never highlighted any profuse political debate. In 1953, Louis joined the High College of the party and Clemente took over the responsibility of the committee. Culturally, the "clubs" got centralized in the scope of all exiles activities of the exiled, organising the trip to the museums, conferences, anniversaries, parties (for children, New Year's Eve festivals), concerts, gatherings, meeting, cinemas and a library that offered the possibility to read Spanish books and press, not only on policy issues but also literature. The club, also called "Spanish Home" was held by the Polish Communist Party - "sister party" - which was facing installation payments, renting and expenses, electricity, heating or cleaning. The Warsaw consisted of three rooms with no communication between them and had also the library.

We do not have any official data statistics on the geographical origin of the Spanish in Poland, although there exist some different press articles referred to a large number of Aragon and Catalan presence among the exiles. They remained, for more than one decade, in the neighbouring country, with the aforementioned difficulties of getting adapted to a different culture and language. However, the children of these exiles, many of whom were born in Poland and will be integrated smoothly into the host society, sharing games, school and training with Polish children. Some refugees ended up with questioning the basic principles of the authoritarian system built by Stalinism and joined the ranks of the democratic opposition. The Spanish had to cope with the demands of the communist totalitarian political model, until the mid-sixties some of them began to consider their return to Spain. The lack of material support of their family members who had left Spain, prevented occasionally them from a permanent return to homeland. The Polish Emigration in the economic terms, was not comparable to the American or Swiss one: it has just to manage to maintain a livelihood bringing enough savings to start a new life in the Spanish development realities, which was not possible. And while some of them returned to Spain, we know that more than 46 families were still living in exile, based in Warsaw of 1978 (*Los últimos de Varsovia...*). About 130 Spanish of the three generations found in Poland, their home land country.

4. Bibliography

Alted Vigil A. 2002, *El exilio español en la Unión Soviética*, "Ayer" 47: 129-154.

Bolloten B. 2004, *La Guerra Civil española: Revolución y contrarrevolución*, Madrid: Alianza.

Cabeza Sánzhez-Albornoz S. 1997, *Historia política de la Segunda república en el exilio*, Madrid: Fundación Universitaria Española.

Ciechanowski J.S. 2007, *Las relaciones entre la Polonia comunista y la República española en el exilio. Razones políticas de la misión de Manuel Sánchez Arcas en Varsovia (1946-1950)*, "Ayer" 67: 49-79.

Dreyfus-Armand G. 2000, *El exilio de los republicanos españoles en Francia. De la Guerra Civil a la muerte de Franco*, Barcelona: Crítica.

Egido Leon Á., Eiroa San Francisco M. 2004, *Los grandes olvidados. Los republicanos de izquierda en el exilio*, Madrid: CIERE.

Eiroa San Francisco M. 2001, *Las relaciones de Franco con Europa Centro-Oriental (1939-1955)*, Barcelona: Ariel.

Los últimos de Varsovia, "Cambio 16" (30 abril 1978).

Moradiellos E. 2001, *El reñidero de Europa. Las dimensiones internacionales de la Guerra Civil*. Barcelona: Península.

Payne S. 1995, *La primera democracia española*, Barcelona: Paidós.

Pethö S. 2008, *El exilio de comunistas españoles en los países socialistas de Europa centro-oriental (1946-1955)*, Universidad de Szeged. Facultad de Filosofía y Letras (PhD thesis no edited).

Rubio J. 1977, *La emigración de la Guerra Civil de 1936-1939. Historia del éxodo que se produce con el fin de la II República española*, Madrid: Editorial San Martín.

Samper M. 2005, *La oposición durante el franquismo. 3. El exilio republicano*, Madrid: Encuentro.

Soldevilla Oria C. 2001, *El exilio español (1808-1975)*, "Cuadernos de Historia" 88, Madrid: Ed. Arco Libros.

Southworth H.R. 1963, *El mito de la cruzada de Franco*. París: Ruedo Ibérico.

Questions of Polish Identity in the Context of European Integration

KONSTANTY ADAM WOJTASZCZYK
UNIVERSITY OF WARSAW

Poles are a nation that has developed its national identity while in possession of a state and while stateless, during both partitioning and occupation. This development is also contributed to by the Polish diaspora – those many groups of Poles living outside Poland's borders. The phenomenon of Polish national identity has been subjected to major challenges in the face of limited state sovereignty under socialism and in a relationship of dependence with the USSR. The regaining of independence in 1989 opened up new prospects for fostering national identity. Polish membership of the European Union has placed on the agenda issues of the relationship between Polish national identity and European identity.

1. National identity - conceptualization of the concept

National identity is a multifaceted concept and defined in different ways (Łastawski 2000). It can be most generally accepted that national identity is a feeling of separateness from other nations, shaped by nation-building factors such as national symbols and colours, languages, awareness of origin, national history, national consciousness, blood ties, relationship with the cultural heritage, culture, territory and national character (Huntington 1981: 60 ff.).

Thus national identity on the one hand connects a national community (Rainer Lepsius 1990: 233 ff.) as it integrates it and leads to common action: the building of common functioning. On the other hand, elements that building national identity separate one community from others. The state plays a special role in shaping national identity; through its strategies for development and specific policy objectives, it reinforces national values and integrates the power of their influence. An important benchmark for national identity is a nation›s cultural heritage and historical memory. These decide the ideas, values, myths and symbols created and perpetuated in the history of the nation that are stored in human consciousness and perpetuated in national culture.

2. The origins and development of Polish national identity

Polish national identity emerged in connection with the formation of the Polish nation in various conditions, from the golden years of its own state, through its partitioning, occupation and external dependency.

By the end of the eighteenth century, the term "nation" was used a primarily in relation to narrow social groups. The Polish aristocracy saw only itself as a nation. Burghers and peasants did not count. It was only with the adoption in the Constitution of 3rd May 3 of the principle of universal equality that it became possible to pull within the concept of nation all members of the community. The development of the Polish nation was accompanied by the formation of its identity, for which a particular reference point were common territory, ethnicity, culture, community, the common political organization and emotional ties.

A significant factor affecting the development of the Polish national identity was – and is – the state. In a historical sense, this means both the condition of its existence and the struggle for its recovery, and the bond with it for those beyond its borders.

Table 1. Historical stages of development of the Polish state

Historical period	Form of state
960 - 1795	Monarchy: The Piast Dynasty 960-1370 The Andegawen Dynasty 1370-1386 Jagiellonian Dynasty 1386-1572 Polish-Lithuanian Commonwealth 1569-1795 (The "Noble Republic" from 1572)
1795-1918	Stateless nation (the period of partitioning)

1918-1939	The Republic – The Second Republic
1939-1945	German-Soviet Occupation
1945-1989	The People's Republic – socialist state with limited sovereignty
1989 onwards	The Third Republic from 1997, with a parliamentary-cabinet system

Source: author's own study.

Poland's stormy history meant that for long periods the Polish nation was deprived of a state either by partitioning (1795-1918), or by the occupation by other countries (1939-1945), or had limited sovereignty due to external factors (1945-1989). A nation without a state persisted and perpetuated its national identity, mainly through nurturing its spiritual and material culture, and through action (uprisings, protests) in pursuit of independence (for example, the November Uprising of 1830, the January Uprising of 1863, the Silesian uprisings after World War I, the Warsaw Rising in 1944 and the activities of the Solidarity movement from 1980 to 1989).

The modern Polish nation, as a result of changes in the external borders and territorial transfers, is homogeneous. Polish nationality constitutes 97.09 % of the Polish population. This is a new situation in comparison to previous historical periods, particularly the period of the Polish-Lithuanian Commonwealth or Second Polish Republic (1918-1939). In the interwar period, Poles constituted an estimated 65 per cent of the general population, Ukrainians 16 per cent, Jews 10 per cent, Belarusians five per cent, Germans four per cent, with the remaining one per cent being composed of Russians, Czechs, Lithuanians and others. The Second Republic was thus a true cultural and ethnic mosaic. This diversity has been a source of serious conflicts; almost all ethnic minorities expressed dissatisfaction. The Germans dreamt of joining the German State, The Belarusians demanded the parcelling out of Polish estates. The Ukrainians never gave up plans to create their own state, and the Jews had to fight National-Democratic anti-Semitism.

Noticeable now is just a trace of the Jewish people in the current composition of the Polish society compared with the interwar period, when this minority numbered in the millions. This disappearance is mainly due to the extermination of Jews by the Nazis and the forced emigration of Polish Jews from the Polish People's Republic for political reasons. This is a serious loss in terms of civilization, because Polish and Jewish culture had for centuries been closely intertwined.

An important determinant of the state is its borders. The contemporary Polish borders are close to those of coverage Piast Poland. From the tenth to twelfth century Polish territory was an area of about 250 thousand square kilometres. The largest country in the history of the area covered 990 thousand square kilometres (in 1634). The territory of the Second Polish Republic ultimately stood between 1920 and 1922 and included 388.6 thousand square kilometres. Today's Polish borders were designated after World War II by the victorious powers (USSR, USA, and Great Britain). Near Warsaw lies the geometric centre of Europe, the point of intersection of lines connecting Cape Nordkinn (Norway) and Cape Matapan (Peloponnese, Greece), and Cabo da Roca (Portugal). The territory of the state covers an area of 312 683 thousand square kilometres. This puts Poland ninth in Europe by area. Modern Poland from the west borders Germany (467 000 km²), south of the Czech Republic (790 000 km²) and Slovakia (541 000 km²), east of the Ukraine (529 000 km²), Belarus (416 000 km²), Lithuania (103 000 km²) and Russia (210 000 km²). The total length of Polish borders (land and sea) is 3496 km. Both the size of the territory as well as the external borders of the Polish state underwent dynamic changes in the process of historical development.

Figure 1: Polish borders - historical and modern

Source: Google (date: 30.09.2013)

A key factor in the formation of the Polish national identity is culture. Its development has been determined on the one hand by openness to Western European culture and on the other, under the conditions of annexation and foreign occupation, by the nation, which took steps against Germanification, Russification and Sovietisation.

Cultural factors also include both language and religion, but also the other products of spiritual and material culture.

An important link in nation-building is language. From a historical perspective for the preservation and strengthening of Polish national identity use of the Polish language was decisive for the cultural education of the nation, and is today an effective link between the diaspora and the Polish homeland. The Polish language is a natural language belonging to the East Slavic group[1], as part of the Indo-European family. It is estimated that Polish is the language of around 44 million people in the world: Polish and Polish citizens living abroad (*World Almanac and Book of Facts* 1999; Dalewska-Greń 2002: 584). The Polish language is influenced by other languages: currently most significantly by English and formerly by Latin, Greek, German, Czech, Russian, Turkish, French, Italian Russian, Hungarian and Yiddish (Krajewski 1976: 81, 233-234, 474). On the other hand, the Polish language has influenced languages such as Ukrainian, Belarusian, Lithuanian, Russian, Yiddish, Hebrew, Czech, Romanian, Hungarian (Szul 2009: 245). 1696 years of Polish language became the official language of the Grand Duchy of Lithuania (Davies 1991: 40-41). From the mid-sixteenth century to the early eighteenth century Polish was the language of the court in Russia (Szul 2002: 213; Bardach 1991: 123-124). In the seventeenth century, Polish was also spoken by the courts of Moldavia and Wallachia (Łużny 1966: 13). In the same century the Polish language was common in Ukraine (Walicki, 2009: 14; Bruckner 1918: 162).

The Catholic religion plays a vital role in the Polish national identity. The largest religious community in Poland is the Catholic Church, to which approximately 33.5 million people belong[2]. According to the Polish Public Opinion Research Center (CBOS) in 2012, ninety three per cent of respondents said they considered themselves Catholics, though in terms of outlook only eight per cent of Poles are fully aligned with the doctrine of the Catholic Church (CBOS: Poles and ...). The beliefs of

---

[1] The group of the East Slavic languages are Czech, Slovak, Kashubian, Lower Sorbian, Upper Sorbian and extinct Elbe.
[2] Data for 2011. Source: Polish Central Statistical Office, 2012.

many Poles are characterised by far-reaching selectivity and syncretism, outlook and religious views of many also combining traditional Catholic concepts with those of non-Christian religions, such as belief in reincarnation (26 per cent) or destination (66 per cent). According to CBOS 2012 years 45 per cent of Poles follow Church recommendations in matters of faith, 47 per cent declared themselves to be non-believers, undecided or indifferent to religion (CBOS: *Polacy wobec...*) In Poland, about 40 per cent of all believers practise regularly, the highest rate in Europe after Malta. The Roman Catholic Religion is tightly bound up with the Polish national identity through all historical stages of development of the Polish nation.

The internal unification of the Polish nation was contributed to by the Christianization process initiated by the baptism of Mieszko I in 966 AD. At that point a community that had been differentiated in terms of religion and culture was united and brought together. Christianity became the national faith, standing together with society at difficult times of war, partition, and other complex historical events. The adoption of one religion also led to social integration. Primary intra- and inter-tribal relations transformed in social interdependence, which in turn led to the development of the nation.

The Church fulfilled a special role in times loss of national sovereignty, uniting Poles around national goals, protecting and nurturing Christian-humanistic values. In the countries of Eastern and Southern Europe, the Pole is identified as a Catholic and the Roman Catholic religion as "the Polish religion".

Alongside the Roman Catholic Church there are also other religious organizations. However, from the perspective of the above data on the domination of Roman Catholic faith, their position is insignificant. Among the other major religious groups are the Orthodox Church, (over one million followers), Protestantism (about 150 thousand followers), restorationism, a particular Association of Jehovah's Witnesses (over 129 thousand followers) (GUS: *Wyznania religijne...*).

The Polish national identity is also maintained outside the country, among the Polish diaspora (known as the "Polonia"). According to estimates, 21 million Poles and people of Polish origin live outside Poland. The Polonia was formed as a result of emigration, outflows of refugees after nineteenth century uprisings (fleeing to France, United Kingdom, Switzerland, Germany, North America), emigration in the second half of the nineteenth century until 1939 (to France, Belgium Germany, USA,

Canada, Brazil, Argentina), and political exile as a result of World War II, as well as due to regime change, the emigration of Polish Jews in the face of anti-Semitic persecution, among others known, the so-called "post-March" years, 1968-1971, the political and economic emigration of the 1980s, and emigration after the political transformation in 1989 (to United Kingdom, Ireland, Germany, France, Netherlands, Belgium, Italy).

The Polish diaspora has settled in countries across the world. The largest Polish populations are in particular in: the U.S. – 10.6 million; Germany - 2 million; Brazil – 1.5 million; the United Kingdom – 1.3 million; the Ukraine – 1.1 million; France - one million; Belarus - 1 million; Canada - 800 thousand; the Russian Federation - 400 thousand; Argentina - 350 thousand; Lithuania - 350 thousand; Australia - 200 thousand; Ireland - 200 thousand; Czech Republic - 100 thousand; Kazakhstan - 100 thousand; Sweden - 100 thousand;, Latvia - 80 thousand; Belgium - 70 thousand; Austria - 50 thousand; Italy - 50 thousand; Greece - 50 thousand; South Africa - 35 thousand; the Netherlands - 20 thousand; Spain - 20 thousand; Spain - 20 thousand; Hungary - 20 thousand; Switzerland - 20 thousand; Denmark - 16 thousand; Norway - 8 thousand; Uruguay - 8 thousand; Slovakia - 6 thousand; New Zealand - 6 thousand; Georgia - 6 thousand; Moldova - 6 thousand; Mexico - 6 thousand; Chile - 6 thousand; Paraguay 6 thousand; Estonia - five thousand; Turkmenistan - five thousand; Uzbekistan - five thousand; Venezuela - four thousand; Israel - four thousand; Arab - three thousand; Finland - three thousand; Luxembourg - three thousand; Peru 3 thousand; Turkey - one thousand; Azerbaijan - one thousand; Syria - one thousand; Croatia - one thousand (*Polonia w liczbach*).

In Poland, the Association "Polish Community" is a non-governmental organization that aims to strengthen Poland's ties with Poles and people of Polish descent living abroad. It is an organization that promotes Polish national identity by: inspiring, supporting and conducting wide-ranging cooperation with the Polish homeland from abroad in the fields of education, science, culture, religion, economy, tourism and sport, to promote, support and maintain teaching of the Polish language as well as maintain the knowledge Polish among those living abroad, promoting within the diaspora knowledge about Polish culture and contemporary social and political phenomena in the country, deepening knowledge of the Polish community in Poland and abroad, promoting Polish heritage outside the country, helping to ensure pastoral care in Polish and defending the rights of the Polish minority (Świat *Polonii*).

Another important project of the Polish state is the creation of the "Polish Card" (Act of September 7, 2007...), a document confirming a person's belonging to the Polish nation that can be given to a person with neither Polish citizenship or nor permission to settle in Poland who declares himself to belong to the Polish nation and meets certain statutory requirements. A cardholder, among other things, is exempt from the obligation to obtain a work permit (Act of 20 April 2004...), may undertake and carry on business on the same terms as a Polish citizen (Act of 2 July 2004...), may study in Poland, pursue doctoral studies and other forms of education, and participate in research and development work (Act of 27 July 2005...), take advantage of various forms of education (Act of 7 September 1991...), use the Polish state health service in medical emergencies (Act of 27 August 2004...) and benefit from a 37 per cent discount on the public railways (Act of 20 June 1992...) as well as free admission to state museums.

In addition to language and religion, characteristic features of the Polish national identity are Sarmatian characteristics, traditions as the bulwark of Europe, a tradition of multinational cooperation, a willingness to make sacrifices for their freedom and that of others, and combining the efforts of Polish at home and abroad.

The Sarmatian characteristics of the Polish nation find their roots in Polish history from the late sixteenth to the second half of the eighteenth century (Mankowski 1946). Sarmatism was a mix of Eastern and Western cultures, which emerged from the belief that the Polish nobility was descended from the Sarmatians - the ancient people residing between the lower Volga and the Don (Jelski 1898). From them, the nobility had inherited a love of liberty, hospitality, benevolence, courage and bravery. Sarmatism in the Polish context shaped values at family, social and national levels; it was a system of life dress, customs, architecture, painting and religion. Sarmatians believed in a special role for Poland - a place for freedom and a golden "bulwark of Christianity" under attack from the infidels. Sarmatians believed in the rule of law, autonomy and election of officials. The close relationship with Catholicism meant acceptance of God's providence and mercy, participation in religious ceremonies and the particular cult surrounding Mary, the saints and the Passion. With the wars of the seventeenth century, began to grow xenophobic attitudes and a particular image of foreigners in the eyes Sarmatians – the French, cunning Italians, greedy and thick-skinned Germans and touch Spaniards. Sarmatism through a combination of political ideology, baroque influences and oriental culture has created a particular kind of lifestyle, mentality and customs. Its characteristic features are still manifested in the modern Polish nation.

The Polish national identity is infused with a deeply-held belief that Poland is the bulwark of Christianity (Tazbir 2004), one of the Polish myths about the special mission of Poland. As such, it is believed that it falls to Poland to selflessly defend Europe from the "Eastern barbarians". This view emerged in the seventeenth century. Tatar raids and later the Turkish threat, defending against Orthodox Muscovites, communism and fascism all strengthened the belief that Poles are the guardians of Catholicism. Treatment of Polish as *antemurale christianitatis* goes alongside Poles view of themselves as fulfilling a special mission. Such thinking sometimes gives rise to religious intolerance.

Historically, Poland has a strong tradition of international cooperation, institutional and informal. In the past, this meant both dynastic systems, as well as the building of the Republic as a multi-ethnic state, in particular with the establishment of the Polish-Lithuanian Commonwealth in 1569. This was an example of real union. In wartime Poland was settled by different peoples. The idea was also mooted of Poland as a composite state, encompassing states from the Baltic Sea to the Black Sea. For the Polish state, as a consequence of geopolitics, international cooperation has been vital. This is no less true today and is manifested above all in Poland's membership of NATO and the European Union.

Of particular significance in the manifestation of the Polish national identity is the motto on the banners of the insurrectionists of 1831 - "For our freedom and for yours" (in full: "In the name of God for our freedom and for yours"). During the November Uprising, Polish and Russian adorned the banners, with the intention of showing that this was an action against the despotism of the tsar, and not against the Russians people. This was a motto calling for Poles to show solidarity in armed conflicts in Europe and the wider world. Its underlying ideological meaning remains important for the Polish nation in modern times[3].

3. The European identity

The European identity and its characteristics and determinants are much-discussed, but understanding these concepts is not entirely clear.

---

[3] Polish military awards given to combatants supporting the Republicans in the Spanish Civil War were engraved "for your freedom and for ours" (Journal of Laws 1956, No. 46, point 207).

It too has undergone transformation in various stages of European history (Juchniewicz 2000). The European identity, and in particular those characteristics as relate to the area comprising the countries of the European Union signify in particular:
- Greek intellectual traditions, especially in their political and cultural dimension;
- Roman legal traditions, especially in the field of civil and administrative law and the political system;
- Judeo-Christian values constituting a particular reference point for the European outlook, strategy and policy, particularly in the social dimension;
- observance of the democratic rule of law, including both national and supranational levels; this means for instance the principles of: subsidiarity and proportionality, solidarity, loyalty and legal hierarchy, as well as legal forms of functioning of institutions in the multi-level political system of the European Union, hierarchy and observance;
- political, economic and social pluralism;
- civil society, whose participation is an essential to the legitimacy of both the multi-level political system of the European Union and ongoing process of European integration;
- a guarantee of observance – and punishment of violations of – freedoms and human rights and citizens' rights;
- Market freedoms, including the freedom of movement of goods, services, capital, people and enterprise and other rules governing the operation of the single European market;
- International cooperation respecting human rights and the peaceful settlement of disputes
- The building of a European security zone.

In the interpretation of European identity there are two approaches: essentialist and constructivist.

An important prerequisite for the functioning and strengthening of the European identity is a shared understanding of the concept. So far, such a shared formula is missing. In the interpretation of European identity there are two approaches: essentialist and constructivist.

Table 2. Two dimensions of European identity

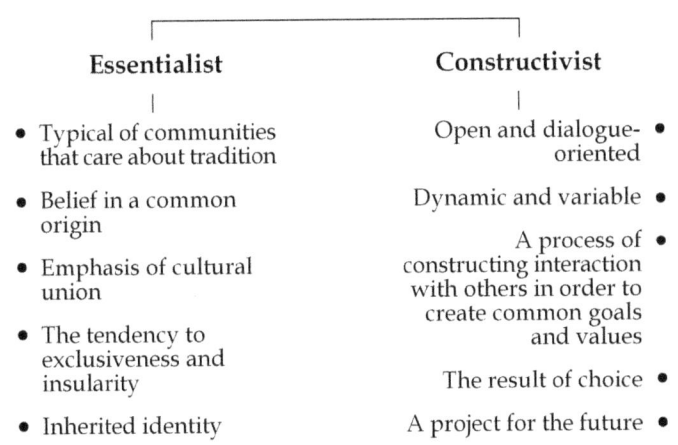

Source: Z. Mach, *The European Identity: a Work of Evolution or a Political Construct?* (http://ec.europa.eu/cgi-bin/etal.pl, 29 June 2009).

As a result of Poland's membership of the European Union, the Polish national identity has to a certain degree undergone a transformation:
• Polish society's historical "'Europeanness' deficit complex" has been largely overcome. The formerly prevailing view in Poland saw the country as either on the periphery of Europe, or as a Christian bulwark (or part thereof in a cultural sense), associated with the Mediterranean culture. EU membership has given the country a greater sense of empowerment and influence on the processes of development, and given Poles a feeling of being Europeans;
• the processes of Europeanization in various spheres of public life in Poland, including the political system, laws and sectoral policies, is affecting Polish national identity on various levels;
• the relationship between the Polish national identity and European identity are in a constant process of formation. This process is characterized by great dynamism both in public life and in the consciousness of the nation.

It is possible to conclude – having past experience in mind – that the strengthening and development of the European identity has a greater chance of success under the constructivist approach, where national and European identity are not placed in opposition, but a community is built around strategies and structures agreed at different levels.

Figure 2: Euro-enthusiasts, eurosceptics and euro-realists on the Polish political scene

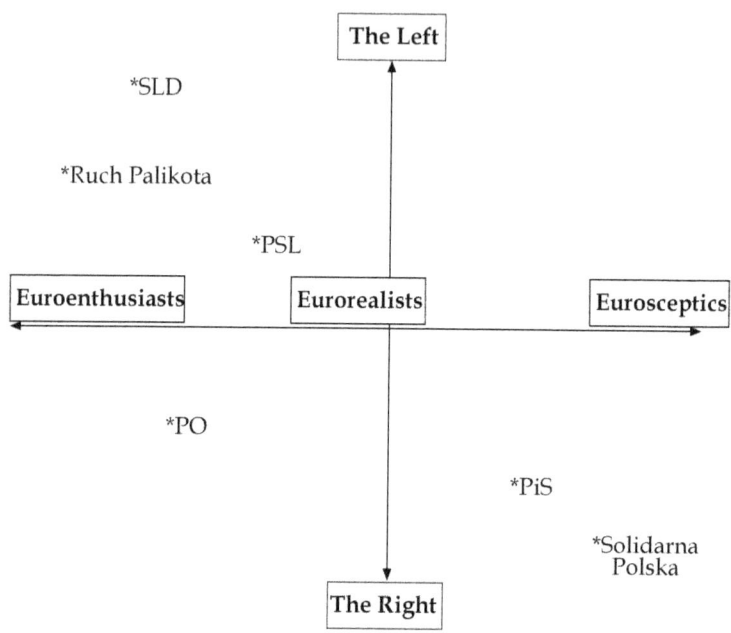

- SLD – Democratic Left Alliance
- Ruch Palikota – The "Palikot Movement" (centre-left)
- PSL – Polish Peasant Party (centre-left)
- PO – The Citizens' Platform Party (centre-right)
- PiS – The Law and Justice Party (right-wing)
- SP – The United Poland Party (right-wing)

Source: author's own work

4. Polish national identity and European identity

Polish national identity is a tied to the values and culture of the homeland (Skotnicka-Iliasiewicz 2002). Accession to the European Union and 10 years of membership have given rise to a variety of attitudes and assessments of Polish participation in the European integration undertaking (Szpociński 1998). The views expressed in society and the political elites are diverse and fit into three camps: Euro-enthusiast, Eurosceptic and Euro-realist (Łastawski 200: 1).

The euro-enthusiasts represent the so-called "European point of view" and are not concerned with questions of national identity; they are satisfied with Polish membership of the European Union, pointing to the chances of accelerated civilizational development of state and society, as well as the benefits of the Single Market. Among the Euro-enthusiasts are chiefly young people with secondary and higher education, residents of large cities, of liberal and left-wing views.

Eurosceptics relate either negatively or very reluctantly to European integration and at the same time see national and European identity as clearly opposed. They see European integration as a threat to sovereignty and national identity. Eurosceptics are predominantly the elderly, residents of small towns and rural areas, less-educated, of right-wing or extreme right-wing views.

The euro-realists are the most rational in their approach to the relationship between the Polish national identity and European identity. They stress the benefits and challenges of membership. Among euro-realists are people of diverse age and place of residence (town and country), though they are generally people with higher and secondary education.

5. Poland *vis-a-vis* the European Union's development dilemmas

The European Union faces real development dilemmas, associated primarily with the aftermath of the recent crises that have enveloped most Member States as well as the EU's structures (Wojtaszczyk 2012). These many crises have been overlapping: economic and financial, political, social, psychological as well as crises of leadership. Compounding these are the consequences of globalization and other world-level challenges. The phenomena associated with the crises, the cost of overcoming them, and the search for new forms of integration, have all increased the role of states in EU decision-making processes. Similarly, national interests have overshadowed values that have been shaped through the historical process of European integration.

From the perspective of Polish national interests, change in the European Union should lead to:
- modernization of the EU mainly through EU law, and not through non-EU laws;
- preservation of the decisive role of EU institutions – and the European Commission in particular – in decision-making processes;

- Poland joining the economic and monetary union once the country has resolved its internal problems and the fulfilled the convergence criteria;
- efforts to limit the formation of extra-treaty institutions created for use within limited formulas for cooperation;
- strengthening of supranational mechanisms in shaping the Common Foreign and Security Policy;
- shaping of budgetary perspective and EU budget in in which mechanisms for structural and regional policy are not marginalised;
- the incorporation of energy policy into EU mechanisms;
- action to increase the number of forms of democratic legitimacy in the processes of European integration and the accountability of EU officials;
- the development of policy towards the EU's eastern neighbours, by increasing funding for its implementation and accelerating the creation of institutional ties with those countries non-EU countries, and
- conclusion of a new economic agreement with the U.S...

6. Conclusions

Formed through the historical process, the Polish national identity possesses certain universal features typical of European countries, but due to Poland's difficult history (partitions, occupation and restricted sovereignty under socialism) also possesses unique characteristics.

The unusual historical experiences of the Polish state - lack of absolutism and the particular role of the nobility, and later magnates, were phenomena unprecedented in Western Europe. The long period of statelessness or its foreignness created a political culture typical of Polish - the opposition of society (US) and state (THEM) (Lewandowski 2008).

The cohesiveness of the Polish national identity, thanks to historical developments, has been helped by the dominant language and the Catholic religion. Polish membership of the European Union also affects directly the Polish national identity (Sułek 1998: 14). The openness of Polish society to the patterns and models of Western democracies has grown (Piskozub 1995). The rules of the market economy and first-hand experience of the common market have become widespread. From the perspective of a constructivist model of European integration, euro-enthusiasm, euro-scepticism and euro-realism all co-exist in the European Union project – today and in the future.

7. Bibliography

Bardach J. (ed.) 1991, *Przemiany w Polsce, Rosji, na Ukrainie, Białorusi i Litwie*, Wrocław: Zakład Narodowy Ossolińskich.

Bruckner A. 1918, *Wpływy polskie na Litwie i Słowiańszczyźnie wschodniej*, [in:] *Polska w kulturze powszechnej - część II*, ed. by F. Koneczny, Kraków: Krakowska Ekspozytura Biura Patronatu dla Spółek Oszczęd. i Pożyczek.

CBOS: *Polacy wobec Kościoła oraz nauczania Papieża Benedykta XVI* (http://cbos.pl/SPISKOM.POL./2012/K04912.PDF//pal; dostęp 18.02.2013)

Dalewska-Greń H. 2002, *Języki słowiańskie*, Warszawa: Wydawnictwo Naukowe PWN.

Davies N. 1991, *Boże igrzyska: historia Polski*, t. 2: od roku 1795, Kraków: Społeczny Instytut Wydawniczy „Znak".

GUS: *Wyznania religijne, stowarzyszenia narodowościowe i etniczne w Polsce 2006-2008* (http://www.stat.gov.pl/cps/rde/xbar/gus/oz.wyzn.rel.stow.nar.i.etn.w.pol.2006-2008.pdf; dostęp 29.06.2013)

GUS 2012, *Mały Rocznik Statystyczny* (http://www.stat.gov.pl/cps/rde/xber/gus/oz/malyrocznikstatystyczny2012pdf.//pol; dostęp18.02.2013)

Huntington S. 1981, *American Politics. The Promise of Disharmony*, New York: Harvard University Press.

Jelski A. 1898, *Zarys obyczajów szlachty*, Kraków: Drukarnia Związkowa.

Juchniewicz K. (ed.) 2000, *Od podziału do jedności. Inicjatywy integracyjne w Europie XX w.*, Kłodzko: Kłodzkie Towarzystwo Oświatowe.

Krajewski K. 1976, *Piśmiennictwo polskie od średniowiecza do oświecenia*, Warszawa: WSiP.

Rainer Lepsius M. 1990, *Interessen, Ideen, Institutionen*, Opladen: Westdeutscher Varlag.

Lewandowski E. 2008, *Charakter narodowy Polaków i innych*, Warszawa: Muza.

Łastawski K. 2000, *Polska tożsamość narodowa u progu XXI wieku*, (http://archiwum2000.tripod.com/475Lastaw.html; dostęp 29.06.2013); i *Polska tożsamość narodowa we współczesnym procesie integracji europejskiej*; (http://docs.google.com/gniew?url=http%3A%2F%2Fwww.wojskopolskie.pl%2FSK, dostęp: 29.06.2013)

Łużny R. 1966, *Pisane księgi Akademii Kijowsko-Mohylańskiej a literatura polska. Z dziejów związków kulturalnych polsko-wschodniosłowiańskich w XVII-XVIIIw.*, Kraków: Instytut Filologii Wschodniosłowiańskiej UJ.

Mach Z., *Tożsamość europejska – dzieło ewolucji czy konstrukt polityczny*, (http://ec.europa.eu/cgi-bin/etal.pl; dostęp: 29.06.2009).

Mańkowski T. 1946, *Genealogia sarmatyzmu*, Warszawa: Wydawnictwo Łuk.

Piskozub A. 1995, *Polska w cywilizacji zachodniej*, Gdańsk: Wydawnictwo Uniwersytetu Gdańskiego.

Polonia w liczbach (http://liveweb.erchive.org/http://archiwum.wspol notapolska.org.pl/?id=pwko00)(pol.); dostęp 27.03.2013)

Sułek A. 1998, *Niezmienne kryteria polskości*, „Gazeta Wyborcza" z 23 września 1998.

Szociński A. 1998, *O polskiej tożsamości narodowej w perspektywie wejścia do Unii Europejskiej*, „Rocznik polskiej polityki zagranicznej".

Świat Polonii – Stowarzyszenie Wspólnota Polska (http://wspolnotapolska.org.p; dostęp 27.03.2013)

Tazbir U. 2004, *Polska przedmurzem Europy*, Warszawa: Wydawnictwo Książkowe Twój Styl,

Ustawa z dnia 7 września 2007 o Karcie Polaka (Dz. U. z 2007 roku, Nr 180, poz. 1280).

Ustawa z dnia 27 lipca 2005 roku – Prawo o szkolnictwie wyższym (Dz. U. z 2005, Nr 164, poz. 1365).

Ustawa z dnia 27 sierpnia 2004 r., o świadczeniach opieki zdrowotnej finansowanych ze środków publicznych (Dz. U. z 2004 r., Nr 210, poz. 2135).

Ustawa z dnia 2 lipca 2004 roku, O swobodzie działalności gospodarczej (Dz. U. z 2007 r., Nr 155, poz. 1095).

Ustawa z dnia 20 kwietnia 2004 roku o promocji zatrudnienia i instytucjach rynku pracy (Dz. U. z 2004 r., Nr 99, poz. 1001).

Ustawa z dnia 20 czerwca 1992 r., o uprawnieniach do ulgowych przejazdów środkami publicznego transportu zbiorowego (Dz. U. z 2002 r., Nr 175, poz. 1440).

Ustawa z 7 września 1991 r., o systemie oświaty (Dz. U. z 2004 r., Nr 256, poz. 2572).

Walicki A. 2009, *Naród, nacjonalizm, patriotyzm. Kultura i myśl polska. Prace wybrane*. Tom1, Kraków: Universitas.

Wojtaszczyk K.A. 2012 (ed.), *Modernizacja Unii Europejskiej*, Warszawa: ASPRA-JR.

Skotnicka-Iliasiewicz E. 2002, *Czynniki formacji i deformacji tożsamości narodowej Polaków*, [in:] *Tożsamość narodowa Polaków w przyszłej Europie*, ed. by P. Gulczyński, B. Loba, Warszawa: Fundacja Instytut Lecha Wałęsy.

Szul R. 2009, *Język. Naród. Państwo, Język jako zjawisko polityczne*, Warszawa: PWN.
World Almanac and Book of Facts 1999, World Almanac Books, Mahwah.

Spain – Europe: a Strange Relationship

JOSÉ DÍAZ NIEVA
SANTO TOMÁS UNIVERSITY

1. Introduction

On June 12, 1985 the Treaty of Accession of Spain to the European Economic Community was signed, by which Spain formally entered it. The agreement would enter fully into force on January 1, 1986. Stronger Europe was talked about enthusiastically; with more open roads; with less distances. The fact was presented as a new chapter for a young and seductive Spain. A president of the National Confederation of Agricultural chambers wrote: "Today we celebrate with hope the signing of the Treaty of Accession of Spain to the EEC, not because it makes Spain more European nor because we dream that the EEC be our manna, but simply because this accession more unites our people, cultures, economies, concerns and safety" (ABC, 13/6/86: 67).

Now, 26 years later, we face a European Union plunged into an economic crisis that can break some of the pillars upon which this new Europe was built...

But without examining these institutional and political problems which will be discussed by other authors of this project, what we can moot is the identification of Spain with the old Europe and this new Europe that is still consolidating. We must ask ourselves and reflect on the Spanish and European identity, or encounters and clashes between the two.

It may be nearly impossible to try to explain, in a moment of apparent dissolution of the Spanish state, what is meant by Spain and what is its political and historical identity. And much more complicated would be to frame it in the context of Europe that is torn between its political and institutional projection and its historical configuration as a pillar of Western culture. Although apparently they seem different problems, at bottom they have one thing in common: a loss of identity following ideological principles emerged from modernity.

For a long time there was a saying that claimed that Spain ended in the Pyrenees; as if Spain was not part of Europe physically and culturally, as if Spain lived apart from the changes occurring in the old continent, remaining isolated and enraptured with itself. But again the question would arise: What Europe are we talking about?

At the bottom it's a matter of mentalities and values, as we would say now. During the debate on the preamble to the so-called Constitution of the European Union, a whole arduous polemic arose around one of its paragraphs; precisely the one that somehow tried to point out what united all its members, and which says that it originated *"Drawing inspiration from the cultural, religious and humanist inheritance of Europe, from which have developed the universal values of the inviolable and inalienable rights of the human person, democracy, equality, freedom and the rule of law."* Many were those who claimed why the text made no express mention of that religious past mentioned openly and unequivocally, the word "Christian". One could coincide with many when they said that European identity not necessarily depended on the inclusion of one simple word in a text with constitutional pretensions. It is clear that Europe contains a legacy shaped by Greek philosophy, Roman law and the Christian religion; and this despite that many others disregard adding other elements, such as the Enlightenment, natural science or liberal democracy. And it is here where one can personally disagree.

It's not an unimportant question to ask ourselves, in a matter of identities, what Spain and what Europe we are talking about. The Spain of Cádiz 1812 or the Spain of III Council of Toledo. The Europe of the cathedrals or the Europe of the Enlightenment. It is in this debate where divergences or convergences of the two are clearly shaped.

2. Today's Spain

In the discussion of today's Spain we can highlight the concern of the Spanish people, at least according to the indicated by the barometer of the Sociological Research Council, about three issues to stand out. 88.6% see the economic situation as bad or very bad. There is no doubt that deep economic crisis, the squandering of public administration, the closure of small and medium enterprises, unemployment or unpaid mortgage and their consequences, are issues that affect citizens living anguished by the fact of not knowing an uncertain future and on which depend their loved ones.

In the background would stand the opinion about so-called political class and political parties. Cases of corruption, illegal financing, bribery, lack of competence to hold public office, trying to convert what should be a vocation for service in a species of professional caste, that often turns its back to social reality and unknowns, or is deaf to concerns of their voters..... have caused that one in four Spanish, 26.9%, see the political class and the parties as one more problem for Spain.

The same studies claim that the number of Spanish supporters of a state with central government only, with no autonomous communities, significantly increases month by month, reaching a rate of 24.5%. These studies indicate that only 29.4% would favor the existing regional decentralization model. The theme of the unity of Spain as a state until recently was not an excessively worrying issue for Spaniards, who were comfortably immersed in a welfare state that guaranteed them an adequate standard of living. Evidently the problem of a possible secession or independence of a part of the territorial integrity of Spain implies, or rather is the result of, a loss of consciousness - not necessarily homogeneous - of a collective past (*El Mundo*, 05/07/2012).

The theme of disintegration of national unity is not a recently appeared topic, although it is noteworthy that it focuses primarily on very specific areas of Spanish territory: Catalonia and Basque Provinces, and to a lesser extent Galicia. This item has a legal dimension and other clearly political dimension. Let's approach briefly both, although concentrating on the Catalan case.

To address this point, at least in its legal dimension, we should build an approximation to the constitutional text of 1978, whose title VIII ("Territorial Organization of the State") went on to redefining throughout its 16 articles (143 to 158) the territorial structure of the Spanish state. It, too, acknowledged the existence of some communities called historical (precisely Catalonia, Basque and Galicia) that, on the other hand, were not granted any special status, except as provided in Additional Provision 1 referring to Basque Country and Navarre, to protect and respect the so-called "historical rights of chartered territories".

A subject to note is the one concerning the allocation of powers to autonomous entities, scattered in fifteen articles and three additional provisions; the rules applicable to the exercise control of the autonomies, which appear in five different articles; or references to Statutes (norms that autoregulate the functioning of them), which can be traced in ten articles and one additional provision. In short, a real chaos.

But what reaches the climax of paranoia is concerning the allocation of powers. A well-known political scientist of the moment indicated how the article 149 enumerated up to 32 different competencies that the constitutional text defines as "exclusive of the state" and how the article 148 enumerates others which could be assumed by the Autonomous Communities. So far everything would seem coherent and in pure constitutionalist logic. The absurd and insane would be found in Article 150.2: "The State may transfer or delegate to the Autonomous Communities, by organic law, the powers relating to state ownership that by its very nature can be transferred or delegated". That prominent political scientist came to the logical conclusion that one article would have been enough to address this complex issue: "The State will transfer to the Autonomous Communities the powers it deems appropriate" (Fernández de la Mora 1986: 123 -124).

There is no doubt that the Constitution, precisely because of the problem discussed above, establishes a State *sui generis*, and in constant change, in which it's established a very wide (unfinished and with the possibility of permanent expansion) administrative decentralization and, especially, the policy for different regional bodies that integrate its national territory. But it should be made clear that in no way one could say that it is a federal state. The Constitution is unequivocal in this point, as it raises no doubt, that it recognizes the sovereignty of the Spanish people as a whole, and only as a whole.

The new territorial map quickly was outlining until reaching 17 autonomous communities: On December 18, 1979, the Congress of Deputies approved the autonomous statutes of Basque and Catalonia; in 1981, those of Galicia, Andalusia, Asturias and Cantabria; in 1982, those of La Rioja, Murcia, Valencia, Aragón, Castile-La Mancha, Canary Islands and Law of Improvement of Navarre's Jurisdiction; finally, in 1983, those of Extremadura, the Balearic Islands, Madrid and Castile and León. Later the statutes of the autonomous cities of Ceuta and Melilla would have to be added, which were approved in 1995.

From that date until today jurisdictional conflicts have been on a daily basis, but the problem has worsened in recent years. If we refer to the particular case of Catalonia, we should refer to the reform of its own statute of 2006. At this point, and leaving aside the problems derived from financing or investment in infrastructure (and even those derived from equalizing idiomatically the Castilian and Catalan in rights and duties; passing the latter from being optional to mandatory, consolidating the position of Catalan as the "language of normal and preferential use" of public administrations in Catalonia and "normally used for teaching and learning in education"), we should refer to the wording of its preamble. In it Catalonia was declared a *nation*. The controversy was served, especially if we look at its article 8: "Catalonia, defined as a nationality, in the first article, has the flag, the feast and anthem as national symbols".

The topic gains new impetus in 2012, with regional elections to renew the Catalan parliament. The then candidate for reelection, Artur Mas, presented an electoral program based on three pillars: economic recovery combined with job creation; maintenance of the welfare state; and transition to national independence. For the first time, own State is marked as the main objective, although it was stated that "within the framework of the European Union", but redefining its ties with Spain.

Until this moment Catalan regionalists, or at least the most moderate sectors to which Mas was supposed to belong, had not gone beyond a generic and vague defense of a supposed right to self-determination. By contrast since then the sovereignist project was openly raised, pledging to boost a consultation so that Catalans decide their collective future.

The first chapter of the program is dedicated precisely to justify this shift in its political line: "It's time for Catalonia to start the course towards its own State", in which it's stressed that "Catalonia is a nation with more than a thousand years of history", which lacks "instruments of state" in order to "live better".

It seems as if Catalonia was a territory that was once occupied by a foreign power, Spain that had oppressed its inhabitants, denying them rights, squeezing its natural resources and imposing the invader's habits and customs. This is not the time to reconstruct the history of Catalonia to see the falsity of the claim of "a nation with more than a thousand years of history", though it also can't be overlooked.

A recent book on this subject demonstrates how Catalonia has never been a free and independent state, "was never an isolated political reality". Being part of the Gothic Kingdom, it was integrated into the Carolingian Empire, and then belonged to the Crown of Aragon in the XII century, and since the Catholic Kings, already in the early XVI century, links its fate to Castile.

Although, perhaps, one of the biggest falsities of this myth of Catalan nationalism refers to the events of September 11, 1714, when Bourbon troops enter the city of Barcelona, which had positioned itself in favor of the Archduke Charles of Habsburg in the race for succession to the throne of Spain. This fact is unknown, and has become the icon of Catalan resistance to the Spanish presence in those lands. A historical fact was rewritten, the struggle between Spaniards in their support for one of pretenders to the crown became the Catalan resistance in their struggle against Spanish oppression.

Of course, the problem is not new, and have emerged in the heat of Romanticism that devised a false sense of nationalism that only tried to develop, unsuccessfully, in both Republican experiments of contemporary Spain: In 1873, when Baldomero Lostau tried to proclaim a Catalan Republic within the intent of constructing a Spanish Federal Republic. And in 1931, when Francisco Macià proclaimed the Catalan Republic, linked to a union of Iberian people, or in October 1934, when, in view of the right wing's victory in previous year's elections, they tried to proclaim another ephemeral Republic, immersed in an inexistent Spanish Federal Republic.

It is clear that nationalism needs a sentiment on which to settle, at least if we build on the theories of Johann Gottlieb Fichte and his *Speeches to the German Nation*. And it is precisely what has been building in recent years in Catalonia, especially following the educational transfers to Catalan autonomous authorities.

There is no doubt that current Spain has a problem in this regard; not so much in the territorial integrity, but in its peaceful coexistence. The boom of nationalism of these dimensions raises the question of where we are heading and where this process of disintegration might lead.

But another identity problem has to do with the way we, Spaniards, have to assume our own historical past, or in other words: When the Spanish nation emerged?

There would be many who could claim that the Spanish nation emerged in 1812, with the drafting of the Constitution of Cádiz. Before this constitutional text, what the law today calls "Spain" would simply be a mosaic of quite diverse territories which only would have in common the monarchic institution, a Personal Union of kingdoms. A Royal Union in the best of cases. Félix Rodríguez Mora, who defines himself as a self-taught historian, writes: "The preceding diversity and plurality, heterogeneity of languages and cultures, the abundance of institutions that limited and moderated, effectively in some cases, the power of the monarch, were negative on the military, economic, fiscal, administrative and cultural field for the Spanish elites. If Spain was to be a great power, uniformity was necessary".

More temperately, and with better foundation, the historian Fernando García de Cortazar says that the national earthquake of the Cádiz Cortes and the Constitution of 1812, already boiled in the XVIII century, brewing in the discourse of enlightened reformers, spellbound by the example of the French Revolution: "In 1812 the Spanish nation emerges from a legal brotherhood of peninsular kingdoms rebelled against Napoleonic imperialism, liberal union of historical reality which remounted intellectually to medieval times and formally to modern state" (Garcia de Cortázar 2001: 9).

But some may forget, or don't want to accent, or simply omit, that other Spain which was born in those distant medieval centuries. For some the Spanish nation arises, or is formed, in Cádiz of 1812. For others the Spanish nation emerges many centuries earlier, in 589, at the Third Council of Toledo. In that year the Visigothic king Leovigild converted to Catholicism and adopted this religion as the official faith of the kingdom. From that date until 711, the kingdom was unified under one crown, one cultural legacy and unified law of Greco-Roman heritage, and one common religion: Catholicism. It is precisely the Faith, Catholicism, which from that time will draw our historical development. Without understanding or trying to forget this reality, our past can't be written in a comprehensible way.

How could one explain the history of Spain during these eight centuries that stop in 711, after the Saracen invasion, until 1492, with the conquest of Granada, the last of the territories occupied by Islam. How this reconquest and the crusading spirit could be explained, without reference to the Faith which united all the Spanish: Catholicism.

How can you explain one of the greatest feats of mankind, the conquest and evangelization of the whole continent, America, without making reference to a belief that united all the Spanish: Catholicism.

How can one refer to resistance to anti-Machiavellianism, Erasmism and Protestantism of an entire pleiad of intellectuals, now forgotten or strongly fought, without reference to the beliefs of the latter: Catholicism.

How to explain the Council of Trent and the Catholic Reform without any reference to Catholic Spain, support of its King Philip II, and participation of the Jesuits, Diego Laínez, Alfonso Salmerón and Francisco Torres, the Dominicans Melchor Cano and Domingo de Soto, the theologian Gaspar Cardillo de Villalpando, or bishop of Granada,

Pedro Guerrero. Undoubtedly Spanish theologians and prelates were the most important in its development, both because of their number and their influence on decision making.

How can one explain European history, at least in regard to the Thirty Years' War, without any reference to Catholicism of the kings of Spain and its people, and its support for the Holy Roman Emperor against Protestant rebellion.

How to explain the Independence War, the Spanish people's uprising against Napoleon's troops without making reference to the devotion and religiousness of people who saw how unholy French troops plundered and burned their churches.

It's Faith, not the constitutional pact, that built the Spanish nation, and it was precisely the constitutional pact that has contributed to dissolve, or at least dilute, this nation which they claim to have constructed and strengthened.

After all, as Marcelino Menéndez Pelayo writes: "Spain, evangelizer of half of the world; Spain hammer of heretics, light of Trent, sword of Rome, birthplace of St. Ignatius ...; that is our greatness and our unity; we have no other. On the day it will finally lose its way, Spain will return to cantonalism of the Arevaci and vectors or kings of the taifas" (Menéndez Pelayo 1992: 1424).

3. Spain and Europe yesterday

It is often a cliché to say that "Europe ends at the Pyrenees", as if Spain had lived with its back to Europe. Undoubtedly such a statement would seem a contradiction; even more if we go in the early ninth century, when a new Europe began to awaken from a long slumber of three hundred years, from that distant 476, when Rome, or what remained of it, fell by the incursions of Odoacer and his hordes. For this we must go back to an event of great significance for the Christian order and for the future of medieval Europe: the discovery of the tomb of St. James, "son of thunder".

According to Concordia de Antealtares, - the first written testimony of the facts, dated in 1077, and whose authorship is not accurately known – there was a hermit named Pelagius (Pelayo), who lived in Solovio, in the forest of Libredón, who discovered the exact place where the remains of the apostle were. Near the place where he was, there were a Roman necropolis and a Visigothic one, both hidden under a layer of mud and lush vegetation.

One night of 813 he began to observe some intense and insistent glows above the place. He immediately informed of the finding Theodomir, the bishop of Iria Flavia, on whom depended those places. He, knowing the facts, decided to move to the site, finding that the light revealed a place where a Marble Ark was buried, under which rested three corpses, that were attributed to St. James the Greater and his disciples Theodore and Athanasius. Tradition has it that after the death and resurrection of Christ, the apostles began to proclaim his doctrine around the world; James would have brought the word of Jesus Christ to a distant place of the Roman Empire, Hispania, a real Finis Terrae of the moment.

After the revelation, Theodomir visited the court of King Alfonso II the Chaste, wanting to inform him of what happened. The king decided at the time to organize a trip to the place, and is accompanied by his chief nobles. Having arrived at the cited "Field of Stars" (Compostela), he ordered the construction of a small church, first antecedent of the present cathedral. Theodomir would move there, later, his episcopal see.

Other sources refer us to the Archbishop Turpin *(legendary version of Archbishop Tilpin of Reims, contemporary of Charlemagne)* who describes how the Emperor Charlemagne had a revelation about the location of the Holy Sepulchre: Apparently "a gentleman of splendid appearance and much more beautiful than one can say, appeared to him ... at night", talking to him while he dreamed: "What are you doing, my son?". To which the surprised Emperor would have replied: "Who are you, sir?".

The answer of the strange and mysterious figure was prompt: "I'm St. James, disciple of Christ, the son of Zebedee, brother of John the Evangelist, whom the Lord deigned to choose with his ineffable grace, by the Sea of Galilee, to preach to the people; the one killed with a sword by the king Herod, and whose body lies ignored in Galicia; still shamefully oppressed by the Saracens".

Charlemagne fell asleep thinking about the star path that he saw at nights, and which extended from the Wadden Sea to Galicia; where was hidden the body of the apostle James; and that strange dream revealed the exact location where he was, ordering "free my way and my land", just like the son of Zebedee and Salome indicated.

But this is not the time nor the place to argue about who took part in the discovery of the tomb, neither much less to question if the remains found are really those of James the Greater. Instead, what we want to highlight is the importance of the event in that distant age, and how it served as a link of unity for that first Europe.

Undoubtedly the enormous prestige provided by the presence of the apostle's relics was cleverly used by Astur-Leonese monarchs to consolidate their kingdom and become known to the rest of Christendom. Santiago would also become the third pilgrimage place for Christianity, after the Holy Land and Rome; and in this the Cluniac Reforms would play an important role.

The Way of St. James became big pilgrimage route in the XII and XIII centuries thanks to the concession from Rome of Compostelan Holy Years, with the possibility that pilgrims obtain the plenary indulgence. The Bull Regis Aeterni granted by the Pope Alexander III in 1179, only confirms Compostelan privilege granted by the Pope Callistus II in 1120.

The term *peregrinus* (one who walks in strange lands, without rootage) would become distinctive appellation of someone "going to St. James' house or returning from it" (Dante, *Vita Nuova*), differing from the "romers" and "palmers", who were going to Rome or to Jerusalem. Men of all classes and conditions peregrinated there, from simple vassals to lords, kings and men of the Church. Cid the Champion; the Dukes of Lancaster; William X, Duke of Aquitaine; Allard or Adelard, Viscount of Flanders, Louis VII of France, the philosopher Ramon Llull, or Guy de Burgundy, future Callistus II. Some of them would later be raised to the altars: St. Francis of Assisi, Saint Dominic de Guzmán, St. Francis of Seine, Saint Elizabeth, Queen of Portugal, Saint Vincent Ferrer, St. Olaf II of Norway.

Clearly this was another Europe. It was a Europe immersed in spiritualism and religion, and St. James' Way was one of its most significant manifestations. Its weight was such that the European Parliament had to consider it as one of the essential elements of the Christian dimension that permeates the member countries of the European Economic Community (29-1-1993). Perhaps for this reason, years ago, the then Economic Community showed great institutional sensitivity to St. James' Way, aware "of the role these itineraries ... have played in the development of certain cities, in creating religious and secular institutions ..., noting that religious and cultural contacts resulting from this significant movement of pilgrims throughout Europe have been a first step towards interculturalism and European unity" (*Assembly of the Council of Europe, 28/06/1984*).

It is evident that Christianity would become unitive cement of a society resulting from the slow decline of the Roman Empire and thus the hallmark of Europe that began to come out of one of the most critical and dark periods of its history. And in that Europe went through Spain, and Spain felt identified with Europe, religiously, politically, culturally.

How not to refer to the School of Translators created under the impetus and determination of Alfonso X, the Wise, and which brought together a group of Christian, Jewish and Muslim erudites who developed important scientific work by rescuing ancient texts and translating them into Latin, laying thus the cornerstones of scientific renaissance in medieval Europe. Until then the men of science of the moment from all over Europe shifted, such as the Englishmen Robert Retines, Adelard of Bath, Alfred and Daniel of Morley and Michael Scot; the Italian Gerard of Cremona, or Germanics Herman Dalmatin and Herman the German.

Interesting, in this regard, is the testimony of a young English clergyman, Daniel of Morley, who narrates in a private letter the reasons why he traveled in mid-twelfth century to Toledo in search of instruction: *"the passion for study made me leave England. I remained some time in France. There I only saw the savage installed with grave authority in their school seats having in front of them two or three stools loaded with huge works that reproduced Ulpian lessons in golden letters and with lead pens in hands wrote seriously in their books. Having understood the situation, I started thinking about ways to embrace the Arts of Quadrivium that clarify the Scriptures. And as nowadays in Toledo the teaching of the Arabs, which consists almost entirely of the Quadrivium Arts, is passed to the crowds, I hurried to get there to hear the lessons of the greatest philosophers of the World. Since some friends invited me to return to England, I left Spain with a lot of precious books. Nobody should be shocked if now to discuss the creation of the world I invoke the testimony not only of the Fathers of the Church but also of the pagan philosophers, because although the latter are not among the faithful, some of their words should be incorporated into our teaching"* (cf. Rodríguez de la Peña).

Universities were certainly another of the medieval contributions to the Christian West that over time would spread as a form of higher education throughout Europe. In their formation, the creation of Bologna and Paris served as a model for the ones established later. The first Spanish university of Palencia would appear in 1208, by Alfonso VIII of Castile, from the cathedral school of this city; but its existence was short-lived, the *studium* where liberal arts and theology were taught ceased to exist in 1250. But meanwhile, Alfonso IX of León had founded a university in Salamanca. Spain joined thus this Europe which was showing interest in promoting culture.

Salamanca students were recruited usually in neighboring dioceses, and those who wanted to broaden their education travelled to Bologna to study law, to Paris, to study theology, or to Montpellier - medicine. It is in this university transfer in which we should seek origins of one of the most prestigious university institutions of Bologna, the College or «Casa Hispánica» (Spanish House), founded on September 29, 1364, by Cardinal Gil de Albornoz.

One could speak of the Spain of Renaissance or the Spain of Charles I (V of Germany) and Philip II and their European links. And while it's true that Spain represented anti-Europe of Erasmism, or Protestantism, so it is that men of science and art moved to it. It couldn't be sustained that Spain turned its back on Europe. Sometimes Spain looked at it with almost mimetic desire. The kings, the nobles, higher clergy, businessmen and lawmen have set their eyes beyond the Pyrenees and have continued to enjoy the arts, literature, fashions, tapestries, silks, cloths, harnesses and all kinds of foreign products. During those years Italian, Flemish or German architects, sculptors, painters continued to work in Spain.

4. The complex of Spain

In the late XIX century emerges in Spain the so-called Regenerationism, an intellectual movement that tried to reflect on the causes of what was considered the decadence of Spain as a nation. In reality it was the crisis of a political system founded by Antonio Cánovas del Castillo during the Restoration, based on the stable alternation of parties that had provided the country with a false stability and behind which lay big political corruption that prevented to see people's misery, poor geographical distribution of belated industrial revolution, caciquism, electoral fraud, the triumph of economic and political oligarchy, which had relegated the dynamic role of bourgeoisie to Catalan and Basque entrepreneurs, tricky ecclesiastical confiscations which generated unproductive latifundia, a large class of day laborers.

Having made the diagnosis, the regenerationists rushed to find solutions. So, Joaquín Costa, leader and driving force of the movement, would be the first to advocate that problems of Spain and its secular delay should be corrected from a European perspective. Thus, Spain should break chains that bound it to tradition and perpetuated it in the yearning for its past glories in order to move towards modernity and future that represented, for them, Europe: "Our fundamental problem and since many years – centuries perhaps–, can be enclosed in this formula: To equal Europe, physically as well as spiritually; that the Spanish rise up from their subjugated status to the dignity of man, that they reach the fullness of freedom, political and moral, or in other words: to stop hunger, hunger for bread, hunger for education, hunger for justice, these three coefficients required for freedom" (Costa 1914: 63).

But Costa would not be the only one, beside him one could mention Lucas Mallada, with his work *The ills of the country and the future Spanish revolution* (1890), or Ricardo Macías Picavea and his book *The national problem* (1899), whose theses were similar to the ones presented here.

But if regenerationists defended the overcoming of our national decline through Europe, after the disaster of 1898, and the loss of the last vestiges of the Spanish overseas empire, the new generation of intellectuals, who has been called Generation of 98 came to advocate the opposite. There was no need to Europeanize Spain; we should Hispanize Europe. The major supporter of this theory would be Miguel de Unamuno, for whom it was not necessary to look for solutions outside the Spanish soil. In a rather ironic form, given his agnosticism, he speaks in the first person, in his work *Mist*, when he says: *"Yes, I am Spanish, Spanish by birth, education, body, soul, language and even profession and work; Spanish first of all and above all, and Spanishness is my religion, and heaven I want to believe in is a celestial and eternal Spain, and my God, that of Our Lord Don Quixote, a god who thinks in Spanish and in Spanish he said: Let there be light!, and his word was Spanish word...!"* (Unamuno 2002: 241).

But it was not always like this, in one of his early works, *En torno al casticismo* (The Return to Love of Purity), just the opposite appeared, the desire to bring Spain closer to Europe, hence this "Die Don Quixote!". Nevertheless that initial attitude will change when one discovers the tradition of a millenary nation revealed in its art, language, habits. Then he feels that the new national mission is to Hispanize this so distant and unknown Europe: "I have a deep conviction that true and profound Europeanization of Spain, that is, our digestion of that part of European spirit that could be made our spirit, doesn't begin until we try to impose us in the spiritual order on Europe, to make it swallow ours, in exchange for its, until we try to Hispanize Europe" (Unamuno 1986: 906).

Conversion similar to that suffered by Ramiro de Maeztu, who wrote about it: "I also wanted then – referring to his youth – Spain to be and be stronger, but I wanted it to be different. Only later I realized that being and strength of being are the same thing, and that wanting to be another is the same as wanting to stop being" (Maeztu 1998: 237).

The history of Spain, especially in recent times, and being a passionate nation, is characterized by going from one extreme to another, from white to black without crossing any shades of gray. Thus we come to the Generation of 14. This new generation of Spanish intellectuals would return to, how could it be otherwise, the problem of Spain and Europe. Among these thinkers stood out the figure of the philosopher José Ortega y Gasset.

Ortega differs from the writers of the Generation 98 to connect with the regenerationist postulates. For him, Spain was a problem that can only be solved through Europe. Europe is, for Ortega, the Spirit, the Culture by antonomasia, that rises in the face of barbaric nature, represented by Africa. Europe is a fruit of «divine inspiration» of the towns created by the Roman Empire. From here have resulted four or five major European nations (France, Germany, England, Italy, Spain) that have followed the course of their destiny spreading across the earth, but never losing their unity. A unity not only spiritual («cultural») but also political.

Ideas that are repeated in September 1949, when the Spanish philosopher delivered a lecture entitled *Meditation of Europe* before a group of students who listen to him: "Europe, gentlemen, is science above all: friends of my time, study! Europe is also moral sensibility, but not of the old Christian morality of intentions, but this other morality of action, less mystical, more precise, clear which prefers political virtues to personal ones, because it has learned that it is more fruitful to improve a city than an individual. (...) Since we can't learn these virtues in Spanish, we are forced to seek them wherever they may be. Taking a stick to make way, let's set off on a journey across the world and let's peregrinate in search of the saints of the earth. And then, on our return, let's kindle the pure soul of the people with words of idealism that those men of Europe have taught us".

5. Spain and Europe today

Needless to say that now we're not interested in medieval Europe nor that other Europe that Spain confronted in the field of ideas throughout the XVI to XVIII centuries. It's contemporary Europe that we finally should refer to. The Europe of the European Union, despite the redundancy. To this end we must go back briefly to the origins of it, to the European Economic Community.

Let us recall that the original EEC was born on March 25, 1957, following the signing of the Treaty of Rome. Originally it was formed by six countries that until not so long ago had been old rivals: Federal Republic of Germany, Italy, France, the Netherlands, Belgium and Luxembourg.

It would be difficult to determine exactly what vision of European integration had the officials responsible for Spanish foreign policy in those first years, existing significant divergences between different sectors that supported Franco. Faced with European enthusiasm of some of his collaborators, Franco seemed to feel certain aversion to the integrationist project and above all the European one. Nevertheless an application was made, on February 9, 1962, in a letter signed by the Minister of Foreign Affairs, Fernando María Castiella, for the opening of negotiations in view of an *"association susceptible to reach in due time full integration after saving indispensable stages so that Spanish economy could be aligned with the Common Market conditions"*. But because of a regime considered authoritarian this application was not accepted, since one of the requirements for joining the European Economic Community was that all countries should have democratic regimes. Yet, years later, in 1970, the preferential agreement would be signed, allowing a large reduction in tariffs.

The second attempt to enter the EEC, was in 1977, after Franco's death, and in Spain that lived immersed in a process of political transition. Everything indicated that Spain already met political requirements for accession, but was again rejected; although on that occasion the reasons had more to do with the Spanish economic context and institutional context of the EEC.

With the first government of Felipe González, and Fernando Morán being Minister of Foreign Affairs, the Treaty of Accession to the European Communities, as already noted, was signed. Spain would become a full member of the Europe of the Twelve, though perhaps not on most desirable terms, for the speed with which they wanted to conduct negotiations.

For a good part of the Spanish population, joining the EEC meant breaking with an external image that associated it with a recent dictatorial past; passing to become part of the club of modern European democracies. Meanwhile, the country's access to the European common market would force to renew regulation of the Spanish economic system, which would pass from isolation to free trade with its new community partners. The truth is that critical voices were few and with little or no media coverage.

In the years immediately following this 1986, Spain will combine a strong acceleration of economic growth with a strong restructuring of certain production sectors. Indeed, thanks to European aid policy, designed to reduce imbalances in Europe, Spain became recipient of large sums of money via structural and social cohesion funds (European Regional Development Fund -ERDF-, European Social Fund -ESF-, European Agricultural Guidance and Guarantee Fund -EAGGF). But on the other hand, liberalization of our economy ended the traditional Spanish protectionism, forcing a hard reconversion. This would lead to address the negative aspects of our incorporation: the initial loss of many jobs and sharp decline in some productive sectors, such as fishery, agriculture, mining or steel industry.

When in 1992 the Treaty of Maastricht was signed, which changed the name of EEC for European Union, the European integration process will intensify, setting itself as the final objective a political union, to be achieved gradually. In addition, the Treaty proposed for 1999 the Monetary Union with the introduction of a common currency: the euro. The government of José María Aznar was one of the main driving forces of this new Europe, making his country as one of the first to adopt the new currency, which in 2002 replaced the Spanish peseta as a currency.

At that time Spain had become, nobody knows by what strange magic, not just one of the promoters of the European Union, but the most pro-European country of the old continent. It must be because of that infatuation of Spanish people that makes them go from one extreme to another without knowing middle ground. One proof of this is the approval by referendum of the unsuccessful project of the European Constitution.

Indeed, the referendum on the Treaty which intended to establish a Constitution for Europe was held in Spain on February 20, 2005, being approved with high majority vote. 76.73% of the Spanish voted YES to the question *"Do you approve the Treaty establishing a Constitution for Europe?"*. Only a little over two million four hundred thousand people (17.24%) chose No; option which failed to prevail in any of the 17 autonomous communities; achieving meaningful voting in some of them: in the Basque Country, 33.66%; Navarre, 29.22%; Catalonia, 28.07%.

These results clash with those obtained by the proposal in other countries where was held: In France (29 May) the result gave the victory to NO with 55% of voters against and participation of 69%. In the Netherlands (1 June) official results showed that 61.5% of voters rejected the Constitution, with electoral participation of 63.3%. The same happened later on in Ireland (June 12, 2008), where the proposal was defeated by 53.4% of votes, with attendance of 53.1%. Of the countries in which the popular consultation was held, only the minuscule principality of Luxembourg accompanied Spain, where Yes prevailed by a margin of 13 points (YES: 56.52%; NO: 43,48%); in any case the difference between both options was much lower than that obtained in Spain, or if you prefer the Eurosceptics obtained a better result than that obtained by the Spanish.

Since then Spain has continued to support the formation process of the European Union and its citizens have been one of the most pro-European nations. In the last Eurobarometer Spanish citizens, with 33%, would be among those who feel more European inside the entire EU, only behind Luxembourg, Malta and Germany. This was evidenced by the Eurobarometer survey in autumn 2012 on the Spanish perception of the European Union. They are among those who feel more European inside the entire EU, only behind Luxembourg, Malta and Germany, since 33% said "yes, sure", I feel European, a percentage that has been increasing in recent years. Data that would conflict with the paragraph of European citizenship, which would be below the average in terms of existence of bonds with the rest of EU countries, being the social bond most frequently mentioned (37%), followed by tourism (28%) and television (27%). The main source of information on issues related to the EU is television (50%), followed by Internet (30%) and daily press (24%).

About the European Citizens' Initiative, which allows EU citizens to propose an initiative of their interest to the European Commission, 71% of the Spanish see little or no probability of making use of it, as recorded by the survey. As for living conditions, Eurobarometer points out that one in every five Spanish families (18%) almost always have trouble making ends meet, and another 28% also occasionally have financial problems to cover satisfactorily their monthly payments. Among the main achievements of the EU, the Spanish cite "free circulation of people, goods and services" (45%) and "peace among member states of the Union" (35%) (*El País*, 01/03/2013).

6. Spain – Latin America

We can't conclude these brief remarks without making reference to the Latin American world. From October 12, 1492 until December 9,

1924 those territories and Spain were the same reality; but since that date and the early twentieth century the relations between the so-called "Motherland" and its former overseas territories were reduced to the simple exchange of diplomatic credentials. On some occasions relations were interrupted, as in the case of Chile and Peru, after an absurd war waged by Spain (1865-1866) against its ancient provinces. In both cases, diplomatic relations were, as expected, interrupted for some years.

But one must wait for the beginning of the XX century to see these relations somehow expanded thanks to initiatives like the creation in 1885 of the Latin American Union or the Spanish Cultural Institute of Buenos Aires, which begins its first steps in 1910, precisely with the acts of celebration of the first centenary of Argentine independence. Likewise, one could make reference to the organization of congresses and exhibitions, the Latin American Exhibition of Seville, in 1929, being the most significant.

Yet, these relations were somehow institutionalized in an official entity not before the first Francoist years. In 1946 the so-called Institute of Hispanic Culture was born. Nevertheless this organization only limited its activity to cultural cooperation and granting of scholarships. Many prominent intellectuals and politicians of the decades of 50's, 60's and 70's were favored by them.

This situation changed in 1981 when the World Bank stated that Spain was no longer receiving international aid to be considered as a developed politically and economically country. This phase is related to the economic and political crisis of various Latin American countries (the lost decade). In this situation, Spain lends itself to invest economically and to serve as a model of political transition. As the first concrete step one could refer to the Secretary of State for International Cooperation and for Latin America, which began operating in 1986, just one year after our entry into the EEC.

But one would have to wait for the celebrations of the V Centenary of the Discovery of America to see these relations increased, and this thanks to the Ibero-American summits, the first of which was held in the city of Guadalajara (Mexico) between 18 and 19 July of 1991. Conferences have become, despite its difficulties, in a privileged forum for political consultation and arrangements, whose purpose is to reflect on the challenges of international environment as well as to promote cooperation, coordination and regional solidarity. Spain tries to become, thus, a key player in relations between Europe and Latin American countries.

Spain has now become one of the main investors in Latin America, with significant presence in key sectors of the process of economic development and modernization such as banking, energy, communications, construction and management of infrastructure, tourism and provision of public services. Although this effort has not always been welcomed by certain political groups that have seen behind these actions some kind of Spanish neocolonialism.

7. Conclusion

As a conclusion, one could only state that undoubtedly today's Spain and its people, and this fact can't be explained rationally, have become one of the staunchest supporters of the European Union, of its defense, strengthening and even expansion.

But despite that, and returning to the starting point, this illusion of disproportionate Europeanism is preceded by an important identity loss of our past, our culture, our way of being, feeling and throbbing. It is logical, therefore, to think that this Europeanism comes only to fill the void left by the slow and permanent identity loss. Nevertheless, the effects of the economic crisis and the interference of the European institutions in our policies on such matters could have an opposite effect in the short term.

8. Bibliography

Alonso A. 1985, *España en el Mercado Común, Del Acuerdo del 70 a la Comunidad de los Doce*, Madrid: Espasa-Calpe.

Barraycoa J. 2011, *Historias ocultadas del nacionalismo catalán*, Madrid: Libros Libres.

Blanco Vila L. (ed.) 1995, *El Camino de Santiago* [Cursos de Verano de El Escorial, 93-94], Madrid: Universidad Complutense.

Costa J. 1914, *Crisis política de España*, Madrid: Biblioteca "Costa".

Díaz Nieva J., Núñez Martínez J. 2006, *El fortalecimiento de la democracia a través de la cooperación española en Iberoamérica*, "Historia Abierta", 37: 18-22.

Fernández E. 1998, *El Pensamiento y la obra de Joaquín costa*, Working Paper n° 145, Barcelona: ICPS.

Fernandez de la Mora G. 1986, *Los errores del cambio*, Barcelona: Plaza y Janés.

Garcia de Cortazar F. (ed.) 2001, *La nación española: historia y presente*, Madrid: FAES, Madrid, 2001.

García V., José G. 2009, *Un apunte histórico sobre el Real Colegio de España en Bolonia*, "Nueva Revista" 123: 58-65.

González Martín M. 1989, *El III Concilio de Toledo: Identidad católica de los pueblos de España y raíces cristianas de Europa*, Anales de la Real Academia de Ciencias Morales y Políticas 68, 1989: 67 -84.

Maeztu, R. De 1998, *La defensa de la hispanidad*, Madrid: RIALP.

Martínez L., Pedro A. 1985, *La política europea del Ministro Fernando María Castiella*, en "Movimiento Europeo" 11-12: 141-158.

Menéndez Pelayo M. 1992, *Historia de los heterodoxos españoles*, Madrid: CSIC: 1424.

Mora F.R. 2002, *Cádiz 1812. La creación a viva fuerza de "la nación española"*. http://felixrodrigomora.net/cadiz_1812_la_creacion.pdf

Ochoa de M., Francisco J. 2007, *La europeización de España desde la cultura y las categorías del juicio. Reflexiones en torno a Ganivet, Unamuno y Ortega*, "Revista Castellano-Manchega de Ciencias Sociales" 8: 193-213.

Ortega y Gasset J. 1949, *Meditación de Europa*, Madrid: Revista de Occidente.

Pereira Castañares J.C. 1992, *España e Iberoamérica: un siglo de relaciones (1836-1936)*, "Mélanges de la Casa de Velázquez", 28(3): 97-127.

Rodríguez de la Peña A. 2006, *Los orígenes de la Universidad: las piedras y las almas de las universidades medievales*, "Arbil" 85. http://www.arbil.org/(85)univ.htm

Sebastian Lorente J. J. 1994, *La idea de Europa en el pensamiento político de Ortega y*

Gasset, "Revista de Estudios Políticos" 83: 221-246.

Unamuno M. 2002, *Niebla*, Madrid: Espasa Calpe.

Unamuno M. 1986, *Ensayos*, Madrid: Aguilar.

The Euro Area Crisis: Selected Problems of Institutional Solutions. Implications for Poland

JAN MISIUNA
WARSAW SCHOOL OF ECONOMICS (SGH)

KAMIL ZAJĄCZKOWSKI
CENTRE FOR EUROPE, UNIVERSITY OF WARSAW

The consequences of the financial and economic crisis in the EU have proven to be much broader, more intense and deeper than predicted, as they are not limited to the functioning and the mechanisms of the euro area. Other phenomena that affect the entire process of European integration in the form of the EU have become more pronounced as well (Kuźniar 2013: 158). The European Union has been experiencing several different crises – the crisis of the euro area, economic stagnation, signs of a social crisis, a crisis of political leadership, as well as a slowdown of the entire project of integration. The crisis of the euro area affects Poland as well, although we should clearly stress that it is not a direct influence. It is, however, primarily a political challenge (the attempt to remain in the so called European vanguard or the hard core of the EU) and an economic challenge (Poland's position towards the projects and initiatives of the euro area concerning the EU's economic governance and their possible implications for Poland). This article is divided into two parts. The first one concerns the nature of the euro area crisis and the actions undertaken by the EU in order to strengthen the Economic and Monetary Union (in particular, the discussion therein concerns the significance of the European Stability Mechanism and the two pillars of the banking union). The second part of the article concerns Poland and presents the country's macroeconomic situation in the last years, identifies the positive and negative aspects of the Polish economy, points out which sectors of the Polish economy have been affected by the crisis of the euro area the most, and it also presents Poland's position towards the systemic and institutional changes related to economic governance in the EU.

1. EU's position towards the crisis of the euro area

The 2008 economic crisis has revealed important systemic phenomena that affect the euro area and show its structural weakness (manifested by the greatest government debt since World War II). During the crisis, market mechanisms allowed only a limited response to asymmetric disturbances. The scope of influence of the so called automatic stabilisers, that is social expenditure and progressive taxation systems in the Member States, is rather limited as well. The coordination mechanisms in the euro area have not proven themselves either during the crisis. We should also bear in mind the specificity of the euro area. It's essential characteristic is the centralisation of the monetary policy on the EU level combined with decentralisation of fiscal policies in the Member States. Hence, at the EU level, there are no suitable financial instruments which would, on the one hand, introduce structural changes in the economy of the euro area and, on the other hand, allow for reactions to crisis situations in the individual countries of the euro area (in response to asymmetric shocks).

The EU took two types of measures in response to the economic crisis – temporary *ad hoc* measures and long-term measures aimed at the establishment of stronger institutional and systemic foundations of the EMU. As regards the former, they were focused on launching bailout mechanisms for the most crisis-ridden countries – the so called PIIGS (from the first letters of the names of these countries: Portugal, Italy, Ireland, Greece, Spain), and Cyprus. It seems that the actions of the EU and the international community in the form of the Troika (European Commission, IMF, ECB) have halted the financial collapse of these countries and calmed down the financial markets for a time (situation as of August 2013). Expressing any definite statements or judgements in this regard seems, however, rather premature and unjustified. Furthermore, these states face an even more serious problem – a comprehensive and structural reconstruction of their economies.

The long-term actions of the EU are based on the action plan of the European Council agreed upon by the heads of state and government on

14 December 2012 and directly referring to the report *Towards a Genuine Economic and Monetary Union*, presented by Herman Van Rompuy just before the summit, on 5 December 2012[1], as well as to the action plan titled *A Blueprint for a deep and genuine Economic and Monetary Union: Launching a European debate*, presented by the European Commission in November 2012 (Press release: 28 November 2012).

The European Council's action plan is in fact a plan of comprehensive deepening of the euro area in four main dimensions: financial, budgetary, economic, and political. In the financial dimension, the goal is to ensure security of the euro area's banking system through the establishment of the Banking Union; in the budgetary dimension, it is about ensuring budget stability through centralisation of the fiscal policy, which could include the element of Communitisation of government debts of the euro-area members and the element of financial assistance in return for reforms promoting macroeconomic balance between the economies of the euro area; in the economic dimension, it is about actions aimed at ensuring growth, employment and social cohesion due to better coordination of economic policies; in the political dimension, it is about strengthening the mechanisms of democratic legitimacy of decisions made in the sphere of finance. Referring only briefly to each of these tasks, we should emphasise the enormousness of the challenges that are facing the EU.

The establishment of the integrated financial framework, the so called banking union, still leaves many questions unanswered. We know that the banking union should have three primary constituents: common supervision, a common deposit guarantee system, as well as a common system of recovery and orderly resolution of banks. Tomasz G. Grosse wonders, rhetorically, if the banking union and the accompanying regulations concerning the banking sector can actually meet the expectations concerning the reform of the financial system in Europe. He believes this to be rather difficult, as the reform is neither the sole, nor the most important goal in the political game accompanying the establishment of the banking union (Grosse 2013: 4).

One of the main elements of the new system of the euro area is the Treaty on Stability, Coordination and Governance in the Economic and Monetary Union (also called the Fiscal Compact), accepted by 25 heads

---

[1] The report was drawn up by the President of the European Council, Herman Van Rompuy, in close collaboration with the President of the European Commission, the President of the European Central Bank and the President of the Eurogroup.

of state and government of the EU Member States on 30 January 2012 and signed by them on 2 March 2012 (the UK and the Czech Republic have opted out). The Fiscal Compact entered into force on 1 January 2013, after ratification by 12 out of the 17 states of the euro area. The treaty itself is to improve the budget discipline more effectively than, for example, the Stability and Growth Pact. It establishes new, more automatic sanctions for breaking discipline, including the new expenditure rule[2]. Apart from economic consequences, the adoption of the Compact entails several political challenges as well. Roman Kuźniar points this out by writing that with the Fiscal Compact, 'the spectre of a two-speed Europe has become a fact [...]. Federalisation of the euro area heralds a division of the EU into a 1st league and a 2nd league' (Kuźniar 2013: 160).

The EU is still struggling with the problem of low or even scanty economic growth and the systematically increasing number of unemployed people in the EU (higher than ever in the history of the EU, especially among the young generation). The IMF predicts that in 2014 the economic growth in the euro area will be 0.9 percent and in the entire EU – 1.2 percent (*World Economic Outlook Update: Growing Pains*: 2013). As a result of this bad economic situation and the lack of any noteworthy results in combating the crisis, the people of many European capitals are becoming distrustful of Brussels and some even exhibit confrontational attitudes. We can observe an ever greater lack of faith in the sense of the idea of the EU and an increase of nationalist sentiments (a return to the idea of nation states in the search for solutions to problems). These attitudes are further exacerbated by the fact that hastened integration in the euro area was taking place without democratic legitimisation. The conservative reaction of the societies comes therefore as no surprise. The action plan of the European Council of December 2012 mentions the need to provide it with a democratic mandate. However, the idea that cooperation at the level of national parliaments should be closer in order to achieve this seems unlikely to contribute to overcoming the crisis of the foundation of European integration – the society's conviction of the rightness of further European integration. What is more, the crisis in the EU happened at a time when the EU's leaders are weak, without any vision, and in the case of several important states of the euro

---

[2] For Poland, the Compact will be binding only once we adopt the euro. In the draft of the ratifying act, the government proposed the procedure specified in Article 89 of the Constitution, which provides for ratification of the agreement by the President upon consent of the Sejm and Senate given by ordinary majority of votes. The Sejm gave its consent on 20 February 2013 and the President ratified the Fiscal Compact on 23 July 2013.

area, euphemistically speaking, irresponsible ("Rocznik Strategiczny" 2011/2012: 57), This weakness of European leaders is very well shown by one of the caricatures published in *The Economist* of 2 April 2011, which shows four European leaders (Sarkozy, Berlusconi, Merkel, and Zapatero), each having some disability crippling their governance.

The measures taken by the EU and its Member States are the most serious attempt to conduct a reform of governance of the euro area since its establishment, using the mechanisms introduced by the Treaty of Lisbon (Article 136 TFEU concerning the surveillance and coordination of the economic policy in the euro area)[3]. While the crisis forced the countries to implement reforms, the Member States' and their societies' lasting dislike and scepticism of deeper financial and fiscal integration (cf. the establishment of the fiscal and banking union) gives rise to doubts about whether the reformatory trend will be maintained (Grosse 2010; Borkowski 2013: chapter VI).

The crisis of the euro area has revealed a structural weakness of the European Union. At the same time, it has long-term consequences for the international position of the EU in international relations. The question is, to what extent. To a certain degree, this will depend on the political will of the individual Member States to implement reforms of the EU's economic governance.

One of the key elements of these reforms is the establishment of the European Stability Mechanism and the aforementioned banking union. As it has been proposed in the document *Towards a Genuine Economic and Monetary Union*, they are to constitute the basis of an integrated financial framework. It would comprise uniform European banking supervision, a common framework of bank deposit guarantees, as well as recovery and orderly resolution of banks, with the European Stability Mechanism as the fiscal safeguard mechanism for the states of the euro area.

2. The European Stability Mechanism

The European Stability Mechanism (ESM) is one of the elements of a more comprehensive reform of the model of economic governance in the European Union implemented to counteract the crisis. The establishment of the crisis mechanism – initially a temporary one[4] and

---

3 For more on the geostrategic implications of the crisis in the euro area see the subsequent editions of "Rocznik Strategiczny" (2009/2010; 2010/2011; 2011/2012; 2012/2013), especially Chapters I, II and III.
4 With the signing of the agreement with Greece in May 2010, concerning the granting of bilateral loans, the decision was announced on the establishment of a temporary stabilisation mechanism consisting of

eventually a permanent one – is a safeguard mechanism protecting against imbalances in the different countries (Trzcińska 2013: 7). On 11 July 2011, the countries of the euro area signed the Treaty establishing the European Stability Mechanism[5] (a modified version of the Treaty taking into account further changes aimed at improving the effectiveness of the Mechanism was signed in February 2012). In September 2012, the Treaty establishing the ESM entered into force[6] and on 8 October 2012, the ESM was finally launched[7]. The European Stability Mechanism has the status of an international financial institution established under an intergovernmental agreement between the countries of the euro area, therefore all the countries that have the common currency are its members. At the same time, countries joining the euro area are required to join the Mechanism as well. The ESM's goal is to obtain financing and offer support – although subject to many rigorous restrictions depending on the form of assistance provided – to the countries of the euro area which either suffer or are at risk of suffering serious financial problems and when this is necessary in order to preserve the financial stability of the euro area as a whole and of its members. The most important decisions will be made by the ESM Board of Governors, composed of the ministers of finance of the euro area countries[8]. The total subscribed

---

two components: the European Financial Stabilisation Mechanism (EFSM) which gathers funds in the financial markets through issuing debt securities guaranteed by the EU budget, as well as the European Financial Stability Facility (EFSF), providing assistance only to euro area countries, financed through the issuing of debt instruments guaranteed by the countries of the euro area. Cf.: http://www.nbp.pl/publikacje/integracja_europejska/programy_pomocowe.pdf (22.02.2014).
5 Eventually, in December 2010, the European Council decided to establish a permanent mechanism of financial assistance for the countries of the euro area which replaced the provisional EFSF and EFSM. The establishment of the ESM involved the need for a limited revision of the Treaty on the functioning of the European Union (TFEU), which was executed under the simplified revision procedure. It enables a revision of the primary law of the EU without convening a convention, and, hence, without the conference of representatives of the governments of member states. The decision to amend the treaty is adopted unanimously by the European Council after consulting with the European Commission (EC), European Parliament (EP) and the European Central Bank (ECB). On 24 March 2011, the decision was made to amend Article 136 TFEU by adding Point 3, which will allow the countries of the euro area to establish a stability mechanism serving the protection of the stability of the euro area as a whole (Gostyńska, Tokarski 2011; Trzcińska 2013).
6 The prerequisite for launching the ESM was ratification of the ESM agreement by the countries that would provide at least 90 percent of the fund's capital. This condition was fulfilled on 27 September 2012, when the Bundestag ratified the agreement. The Bundestag's decision was possible because 'on 12 September the Federal Constitutional Court (FCC) in Karlsruhe ruled on motions aimed at blocking the ratification of the following three laws: the law establishing the European Stability Mechanism (ESM), the law relating to the fiscal compact and the law which makes it possible to adopt the European Council Decision amending Article 136 of the Treaty on the Functioning of the European Union (TFEU) with regard to a stability mechanism for eurozone member states' (Frymark 2012).
7 Despite full functionality of the ESM, the EFSF was not immediately liquidated – it kept operating until July 2013. The EFSF continued to finance the assistance programmes which had been agreed upon before the signing of the Treaty establishing the ESM, that is the programmes for Greece, Ireland and Portugal. The European Stability Mechanism (ESM) inaugurated, 8.12.2012, http://ue.eu.int/homepage/showfocus?focusName=the-european-stability-mechanism-(esm)-inaugurated&lang=en (20.02.2014).
8 Apart from the Board of Governors, the other organs of the EMS are the Board of Directors and the Managing Director responsible for its current operations. The Board of Governors can elect a President

capital of the ESM is EUR 700 billion, of which EUR 80 billion is paid-up capital (contributed in five equal instalments between 2012 and 2014), and EUR 620 billion is paid-in capital. In other words, this means that the countries of the euro area will provide the fund in Luxembourg with a total capital of EUR 80 billion. The remaining EUR 620 billion will have to be obtained by the ESM on its own, by selling bonds in international financial markets guaranteed by the governments of the 18 countries of the monetary union[9]. Revenue from financial sanctions against the countries of the euro area that fail to observe the rules of budget discipline and the principles of economic policy will be handed over to the ESM, thus increasing its paid-up capital. The ESM's liabilities are not counted among the liabilities of the shareholder states and, as a result, do not affect the size of the deficit and debt of the countries of the euro area (differently than in the case of the EFSF). All countries participating in the ESM are obliged to pay up capital, even if they do not qualify for receiving assistance or are receiving assistance from the ESM.

The share of the individual states of the euro area in the ESM's capital is calculated on the basis of the ESM's contributions key, based on the ECB's capital key, with the poorest countries, that is those with a GDP per capita of less than 75 percent of the EU average, benefiting from a temporary correction for a period of 12 years after their entry in the euro area.

The assistance offered under the ESM mainly takes the form of loans, granted to countries on the condition of implementing a rigorous plan of fiscal and general economic reforms. Other forms of assistance are: opening a credit line, purchasing bonds issued by the given country on the primary or secondary financial market, as well as the possibility of participation in the process of recapitalisation of the struggling financial institutions. Consequently, the economies suffering from financial difficulties are to receive, first of all, a shot of liquidity which is necessary in order for them to conduct the relevant reforms (Gans 2013).

---

and Vice-President or give this function to the President of the Eurogroup. The board has done that and the office is now held by Jeroen Dijsselbloem. The meetings of the Board of Governors can also be attended by the EU Commissioner for Economic and Monetary Affairs and the Euro, the President of the ECB and the President of the Eurogroup (if he or she is not a member of the President of the ESM Board of Governors at the same time), however, with no voting right. The non-eurozone EU Member States can participate in assistance ad hoc, parallel to the ESM (by offering bilateral loans), thus obtaining the right to become observers at the meetings of the Board of Governors concerning the assistance provided and its monitoring. In such a case, the euro area countries support the granting of the creditor status to them, equal to the ESM status. *ESM Board of Governors elects Jeroen Dijsselbloem as its Chairman*, 11 February 2013,http://www.consilium.europa.eu/uedocs/cms_data/docs/pressdata/en/ecofin/135408.pdf (20.02.2014).
9 The ESM finances its actions by obtaining funds in the capital markets – by issuing medium- and long-term debt securities with maturity dates of up to 30 years.

Starting with 1 March 2013, assistance from the ESM is conditional upon the ratification of the Treaty on Stability, Coordination and Governance in the Economic and Monetary Union (TSCG) by the country applying for assistance, and, subsequently, implementation of its provisions in its national law. Linking the ESM to the TSCG was the consequence of their complementary role within the framework of budget policy, enforcing a more reasonable fiscal policy and greater solidarity in the monetary union (Trzcińska 2013: 15).

As Agnieszka Trzcińska notes, the changing challenges faced by the EU economies make the role of the Mechanism evolve as well, with its mandate and extent of competences undergoing a gradual reformulation; initially the European Stability Mechanism was intended only for rescuing individual countries when the stability of the entire euro area was at risk, but nowadays it is also becoming a safeguard for the banking sectors and constitutes an important element of the integrated financial framework (Trzcińska 2013: 3-4).

After the establishment of the Single Supervisory Mechanism (SSM) in November 2014, the European Stability Mechanism – according to the conclusions of the European Council of October 2012 – will be able to perform capital infusions to banks (direct recapitalisation), so the costs of such operations would not burden the national budgets as it used to (presently, the ESM can provide loans for recapitalisation of credit institutions only to governments, so this aid increases the debt of the state and local government sector)[10]. After the establishment of the uniform resolution system, the ESM would perform the function of its fiscal safeguard.

3. Single Supervisory Mechanism

The first element of the Banking Union is the Single Supervisory Mechanism (SSM), which was finally approved by the Council of the European Union in October 2013 and which will start operating in November 2014. The countries of the euro area will automatically become members of the SSM. Under the SSM, the ECB will be responsible supervising 6,000 banks in the euro area, but it will directly control only large banks, with

---

[10] *Strengthening economic and monetary union: progress on legislative files*, 15.03.2013, http://www.european-council.europa.eu/home-page/highlights/strengthening-economic-and-monetary-union-progress-on-legislative-files?lang=en (20.02.2014); *Council adopts regulations on single supervisory mechanism (SSM)*, 15.10.2013; http://www.consilium.europa.eu/homepage/showfocus?focusName=council-adopts-regulations-on-single-supervisory-mechanism-(ssm)&lang=en (20.02.2014).

asset value of more than 30 billion euro and accounting for at least 20 percent of the GDP of the country in which they have their seat, but also the banks that had asked for public assistance from the emergency funds of the EFSF or EMS and ones that received such assistance. It is expected that the ECB will be directly supervising approximately 130 credit institutions, which account for almost 85 percent of the total banking assets in the euro area. This number has been calculated by applying the consolidated approach, under which a banking group comprising various credit institutions is counted as a single institution. Supervision of smaller banks will largely fall to national institutions. They will also supervise on a day-to-day basis, for example, the protection of customers, protection against money laundering and payment services[11].

As the supervisor in the euro area, the ECB will be granted new competences, e.g. to impose fines on banks that do not respect its decisions. Furthermore, with the approval of national regulators, the ECB will grant and revoke banking licences. The ECB will be evaluating the takeovers in the sector and in certain circumstances will be able to order banks to increase their capital. The ECB will also have the competence to conduct inspections in the financial institutions that it supervises[12].

A Supervisory Board will be established in the ECB and will be responsible for preparing the supervisory tasks[13]. Its decisions will be subject to approval by the ECB Governing Council.

Non-eurozone countries can establish close cooperation between their banking supervision institutions and the ECB. This allows them to fully participate in the Supervisory Board. They will not, however, be admitted to the ECB Governing Council.

The SSM strengthens the role of the European Central Bank, which is to play the control role thus weaken the national supervisions. Cezary Kowanda stresses, however, that the EBC's power will not be absolute at all, even if only for the fact that it will be controlling only the largest banks; this is one of the many indications of the German influence on

---

[11] *Council adopts regulations on single supervisory mechanism (SSM)*, 15.10.2013, http://www.consilium.europa.eu/homepage/showfocus?focusName=council-adopts-regulations-on-single-supervisory-mechanism-(ssm)&lang=en (20.02.2014); *Banking supervision*, http://www.ecb.europa.eu/ssm/html/index.en.html (20.02.2014); *ECB: Banking Union starts with top lenders' health checks*, 23.10.2013, http://www.euractiv.com/euro-finance/ecb-banking-union-starts-top-len-news-531245 (20.02.2014).

[12] http://www.stefczyk.info/wiadomosci/gospodarka/pe-przeglosowal-wspolny-nadzor-bankowy,85 15910102#ixzz2t0iHdR7X (22.02.2014).

[13] It will be composed of: a Chair (appointed for a non-renewable term of five years); a Vice-Chair (chosen from among the members of the ECB's Executive Board); four ECB representatives; one representative of the national competent authority of each participating country. The right to approve the Chair and Vice-Chair of the Supervisory Board as well as the right to initiate the procedure of dismissing the Chair will be the competences of the Council and the European Parliament.

the banking union, as under these conditions the highly popular savings banks (*Sparkasse*) and state banks (*Landesbank*), with a balance total of less than EUR 30 billion, will be excluded from the ECB's supervision (Kowanda 2013) As a matter of fact, for Poland, the ECB's supervision is important regardless of whether we join the banking union or not. Many of the banks operating in Poland belong to large European institutions which will be subjected to ECB control anyway, as their seats are in euro area countries. Among the banks dominated by Polish capital, the only one large enough to be controlled by the ECB is PKO BP (Kowanda 2013).

4. Single Resolution Mechanism

The second element of the banking union is the Single Resolution Mechanism (SRM). The relevant draft regulation was agreed upon on 18 December 2013 at the meeting of the EU's ministers of finance (ECOFIN). Two days later, on 20 December 2013, these agreements were adopted at the EU summit. The SRM is to guarantee financial stability should a bank declare bankruptcy and minimise the costs incurred by the tax-payers and the real economy. The mechanism will comprise the Single Resolution Board (Council of the European Union, Press Release: 18 December 2013)[14] and the Single Bank Resolution Fund. The latter body will be established gradually and will reach full financial capacity in 2026. The fund will be financed from bank levies raised at national level (i.e. the banks themselves would pay contributions to the fund). Initially, until the fund reaches financial capacity of 1 percent of all guaranteed deposits, i.e. until the end of 2025, there would exist a network of national divisions of target funds – the so called national compartments[15]. In these 10 years, the national compartments would be gradually communitised and merged into a single fund. After 10 years, the size of the fund would

---

[14] The Board will be composed of representatives of national resolution authorities of all the participating countries, an executive director and four full-time appointed members. Its task will be to devise a plan to improve the situation of banks at risk of bankruptcy or specifying actions related to liquidation of collapsing financial institutions. The plan will become the basis for the bank's restructuring or liquidation, unless within 24 hours, upon a motion of the European Commission, the Council of the European Union decides by a ordinary majority of votes to veto the plan or propose changes to it. If the Council of the EU does not react within 24 hours after the Board makes its decision, the decision enters into force. *Council agrees its position on the single resolution mechanism*, 19.12.2013, http://ue.eu.int/homepage/showfocus?focusName=council-agrees-its-position-on-the-single-resolution-mechanism&lang=en (18.02.2014); (Council of the European Union, Press Release: 18 December 2013).

[15] Initially, the contributions paid by the financial sectors of the individual states are to be collected in national envelopes and will be used to assist the national banks, and only later will be gradually moved to the European pool. See: Popławski 2014 and *Banking Union – Single Resolution Mechanism (SRM)*, European Commission, September 2013, available at: http://ec.europa.eu/internal_market/finances/docs/banking-union/dg-markt-factsheets-srm_en.pdf (18.02.2014).

be EUR 55 billion for the euro area. Until sufficient funds are collected in the Single Bank Resolution Fund, governments would be able to impose additional fees on banks (as suggested by Germany)[16] and if this is not enough, they would be able to use national funds. Should the government have insufficient funds at its disposal, it can ask the EMS for a loan. Later, that is after 2025, when the Resolution Fund collects all payments, it will be able to loan additional funds. These loans would ultimately be reimbursed, however, by the same banks through levies, also ex-post. It has been agreed that the method of operation of the Fund will be specified in a separate intergovernmental agreement, not forming a part of the regulation, which would have to be concluded by the euro-area members and other willing non-eurozone states by 1 March 2014. The intergovernmental agreement would enter into force once ratified by the member states participating in the SSM/SRM that represent 80 percent of contributions to the Single Resolution Fund. The regulation itself, based on Article 114 TFEU, is subject to the ordinary legislative procedure; consequently, in January 2014 the Presidency commenced negotiations on this issue with the European Parliament, so that they can be concluded before the end of the Parliament's term of office, that is by May 2014. It should be noted that, even once approved by the Council and the Parliament, the regulation on the Single Resolution Mechanism will become binding only when the intergovernmental agreement on the Single Bank Resolution Fund enters into force. It is assumed that if all the deadlines are met, the Single Bank Resolution Fund and the entire Resolution Mechanism could start functioning from January 2015 (Council of the European Union, Press Release: 18 December 2013; J.P. Durante: 2013).

The SRM, and particularly the Single Resolution Board, is to be responsible for the resolution plans of all the trans-border banks and those directly subject to ECB supervision (in total, approximately 330 banks). National regulators responsible for resolution (representatives of financial supervision authorities from the individual countries) are to be responsible for the remaining, typical national banks. However, the Single Resolution Board would always be responsible for the resolution of banks requiring the use of the single fund[17].

---

[16] One of the controversial issues was the financial safeguarding of bank resolution in the period when the Resolution Fund will accumulate funds. Germany is arguing against using the EMS for this purpose, so that German taxpayers would not pay for the difficulties of Spanish banks, for example.

[17] Council of the European Union, *Council agrees general approach on Single Resolution Mechanism*, Brussels, 18 December 2013, 17602/13, http://www.consilium.europa.eu/uedocs/cms_data/docs/pressdata/en/ecofin/140190.pdf (22.02.2014).

The SRM is supplemented and complemented by the Banking Recovery and Resolution Directive (BRRD), the so called bail-in rule, on which the Parliament and Council finally agreed on 11 December 2013. Under this directive, from 2016 the private sector will have to cover a minimum of 8 percent of the liabilities of a bank requiring financial aid, before assistance will be provided from state or euro area funds[18]. Furthermore, certain rules, which will be binding from 2016, will regulate the order in which losses related to bank restructuring will be covered. The debts of the bailed-out banks are to be covered first by creditors and shareholders, then by holders of deposits of more than EUR 100,000, and only then – should the fund still be insufficient – from the bank recovery fund (European Commission, MEMO December 2013).

Those non-EU countries that join the SSM will have the opportunity to join the SRM. However, these countries will not be able to apply for a loan from the EMS. So far no specific solution to this problem has been presented for countries non-eurozone countries. Some assistance can be provided to them from balance of payments assistance instruments (BoP), under which the EU grants EUR 50 billion aid for improving the balance of payments. There are, however, limited possibilities of applying for assistance from this instrument only for the banking sector. In December 2013, due to strong opposition from Germany, among others, the ministers of finance did not approve the changes in the BoP programme that would make it easier to provide such targeted assistance[19].

The governments of the EU Member States have reached a compromise regarding the establishment of new institutions responsible for orderly resolution of banks and the financing of these processes. This compromise, as noted by Jacek Ramotowski, is so distant from the initial plans that it raises questions about the effectiveness of the banking union; the new institutions could prove to be just empty shells and the mechanisms and procedures to be so lengthy that they would make it impossible to be effective; what is more, the distant perspective of when the funds for liquidation proceedings or payment of guaranteed deposits

---

[18] Council of the European Union, *Bank recovery and resolution: Council confirms agreement with EP*, Brussels, 20 December 2013, 18093/13, available at: http://www.consilium.europa.eu/uedocs/cms_data/docs/pressdata/en/ecofin/140277.pdf (last accessed on: 22 February 2014); P. Tokarski, *An EU Banking Union: How Damaging Will the Comprehensive Assessment of Banks Prove to Be?*, Bulletin PISM, no. 141 (594), 20 December 2013, http://www.pism.pl/publications/bulletin/no-141-594 (22.02.2014).

[19] *Unia bankowa – szanse na równe zabezpieczenia dla krajów spoza euro (Banking Union – A Chance for Equal Safeguards for Non-Eurozone Countries)*, http://www.obserwatorfinansowy.pl/dispatches/unia-bankowa-szanse-na-rowne-zabezpieczenia-dla-krajow-spoza-euro/ (20.02.2014); *Ustalono finansowanie likwidacji banków w euro landzie (Financing Bank Resolution in the Euroland Has Been Decided)*, PAP, 18 December 2013, http://www.ekonomia.rp.pl/artykul/706164,1073489-Ustalono-finansowanie-likwidacji-bankow-w-eurolandzie.html (22.02.2014).

are to be collected means that at least for the next couple of years, governments will nonetheless have to bail out banks using their taxpayers' money (Ramotowski 2014).

In the opinion of Cezary Kowanda, Germany has done everything in its power to delay the situation when the contributions paid by its banks will be the ones used to rescue institutions in other Member States (Kowanda 2013)

The Polish Minister of Finance Mateusz Szczurek noted that the common system of financial safeguarding of bank resolution in the banking union will be developing gradually and until it is fully operational, the stability of the banking system will still be, to a certain extent, connected with the solvency of the state (PAP 2014).

The problem of the small pool of available funds so far remains unsolved. It is estimated that the present crisis has cost the EU EUR 1.6 trillion provided to banks as aid and according to some assessments, EU banks could still have bad debts of approximately EUR 1 trillion. Hence, the funds from the EMS and the EUR 55 billion from the resolution fund are obviously not enough to lend the banking union sufficient credibility as the EUR 55 billion will be just enough to rescue two medium-sized banks (Popławski 2014). Therefore, the compromise proposal of the banking union is not a breakthrough and if the banking crisis gets worse, finding sources of funds for the indebted institutions will require very time-consuming negotiations. The crisis in Cyprus, in turn, shows that the entire process of providing assistance to banks may not take longer than a couple of days (Popławski 2014).

In this context, the construction of the Single Resolution Board gives rise to some concerns. It would not be the Single Resolution Board and not the European Commission, but the Council of the EU that would have the last say in matters regarding bankruptcy and restructuring. The *Financial Times* calculated that as much as 126 people could participate in the decision-making process; consequently, when there is no common consent, it would be necessary to hold nine meetings of different groups and 143 votes.

Moreover, there is a danger that the final decision on a bank's bankruptcy could be purely political, because governments could protect their zombie-banks for the same reasons they have done that so far (PAP, 6 February 2014) Meanwhile, the essence of the concept of liquidation of a bank in the form of resolution is that this operation must be conducted very quickly with the decision-making groups as small as possible. It is all about maintaining rigorous secrecy and preventing valuable assets from being withdrawn from the banks. Furthermore, this is to prevent a domino effect in the entire system and a sudden withdrawal of deposits, which could take place when a bank declares bankruptcy (PAP, 6 February 2014)

Furthermore, it should be noted that the development of the banking union is founded on different legal bases. The first and second pillar are founded in Article 114 of the Treaty on the functioning of the European Union. The basis for the functioning of the Single Resolution Fund is an intergovernmental agreement. This solution was advocated by Germany, which argued that an agreement ensures more legal reliability. The European Parliament, however, is strongly against this solution and it believes that the fund should be based on an EU treaty.

The third stage of the banking union was supposed to be common deposit guarantee scheme, but due to Germany's opposition, the EU will most probably make do with a directive harmonising the deposit guarantee schemes in the EU, namely the Deposit Guarantee Scheme Directive (DGSD). Uniform rules concerning the protection of deposits of up to EUR 100,000 have been agreed upon, but this threshold had already been applied in most countries, including Poland. Now it is only to be confirmed.

5. Implications of the Euro Area Crisis for Poland

The Euro Area Crisis, as an element of the global financial crisis, has had significant influence on Poland, which is not surprising when the economic interconnectedness of Poland with its European partners is taken into account. There is nothing particularly novel in the above sentence, however, it still might be interesting to look at the macroeconomic data behind it.

5.1. *The economic situation of Poland in the European context in the period preceding the global economic crisis*

Between 2002 and 2007, the last six years before the beginning of the global economic crisis, Poland's GDP grew at a rate not lower than 3.6 % annually. The value of Poland's GDP grew fastest in 2007 (6.8 %). The only exceptions from the high growth rate came in 2001 and 2002 when Polish GDP grew only by 1.2 % (2001) and 1.4 % (2002) (Eurostat,

Real GDP). In the same period, the GDP growth rate of the euro area countries was much lower: in 2003 the euro area's GDP grew by just 0.7 % (the lowest rate) and in 2006 the euro area's GDP grew by 3.3 % (the highest rate). The economy on the territory of the present day EU (EU-28) during that period grew faster than the economy of the euro area, however, its growth rate was much slower when compared to Poland's. In that period, the EU-28's GDP growth rate went from 1.3 % in 2002 to a maximum of 3.4 % in 2006 (Eurostat, *Real GDP*). Between 2002 and 2007 the rate of growth of Poland and the EU-28 were at the same level only in the periods when Polish economy grew at a particularly low rate.

In the period 2002–2007, the lowest value of inflation (HICAP) in Poland was 0.7 % (2003) and the highest was 3.6 % (2004). In the same period, inflation in the euro area oscillated between 2.1 and 2.2 %. Inflation in the EU as a whole was similar to the inflation in the euro area (the lowest was 2 % in 2003 and highest was 2.3 % in 2007) (Eurostat, *HICP*). What made Poland stand out when compared to the EU and the euro area was the fact that inflation in Poland was less stable. Inflation in the euro area did not change much each year and in the EU the changes were barely noticeable, while in Poland inflation levels changed significantly.

Between 2002 and 2004 the unemployment rate in Poland slowly fell (starting from 20 % in 2002 to 19.1 % in 2004). With each passing year unemployment in Poland fell lower and faster and in 2007, for the first time in many years, the unemployment rate in Poland was lower than 10 % (9.6 %). This huge drop in the unemployment rate still could not change Poland's position as a country with one of the highest unemployment levels in the EU. In the same period, unemployment in the euro area was at its highest (9.2 %) in 2004 and at its lowest (7.6 %) in 2007. Similar values were noted for the EU – 9.3 % in 2004 and a drop to 7.2% in 2007 (Eurostat, *Unemployment*). Even at a time when unemployment in Poland was the lowest in many years, it was still much higher than unemployment in the euro area and the EU.

5.2. The economy of Poland during the global financial crisis

Although the first symptoms of the incoming financial crisis were noticed already in 2007, they did not have much of influence on Poland's and the EU's economic situation. In the following years, however, it all changed and the consequences of the crisis were severely felt by the economies and societies of the EU Member States.

Between 2008 and 2013, the economy of Poland grew at a lower rate than in the last six years before the crisis. Even though in 2008 Polish GDP rose by 5.1 %, the very next year the GDP growth rate was only 1.6 %. In the next two years, the economy of Poland grew at almost pre-crisis rates (3.9 % in 2010 and 4.5 % in 2011). However, that dynamic growth ended quite soon and by 2012–2013 Poland's GDP grew only by 1.9 % (Eurostat, *Real GDP*), just above the values of growth during the last economic crisis of 2001–2002. What do those values tell about the shape of the Polish economy when compared to the euro area and the EU-28? Analysing the GDP changes for the euro area between 2008–2013, one can see the impact of the crisis much clearer. In 2008, the GDP of the euro area grew by just 0.4 % and the next year there was no growth at all: the GDP of the euro area in 2009 fell by 4.4 %. Growth returned in 2010 and 2011, but the rate was not significant (less than 2 %). What is more, the crisis returned in 2012 when the euro area's GDP fell again by 0.7 %. The growth rate for the EU as a whole during that period was similar to that of the euro area. There were two small differences, however. In 2008 the EU's GDP fell by 4.5 % (a bit more than in the euro area) and in 2012 the EU's GDP fell by just 0.4 % (Eurostat, Real GDP). Poland's economy, unlike that of the euro area and the EU, grew constantly during the crisis and in some years almost as if the crisis never came.

Poland's GDP growth during the economic crisis was accompanied by slightly higher inflation: 4.5 % in 2008 (highest inflation since 2001), 3.5 % in 2009, 4.3 % in 2011, and 3.7 % in 2012. In the years since the beginning of the crisis, inflation in Poland was lower than 3 % only in 2010 (2.6 %) and 2013 (0.9 %) (Central Statistical Office of Poland, *Roczne wskaźniki*). Inflation in the euro area during the crisis lost its stability: the highest level of inflation was 3.3 % in 2008 and the lowest level came just the very next year (0.3 %) along with a risk of deflation. In the years 2010–2013, inflation in the euro area was slightly higher, reaching 1.6 % in 2010, 2.7 % in 2011 and 2.5 % in 2012. However, in 2013 inflation in the euro area dropped to 1.4 % (Eurostat, *HICP*), which fuelled speculations whether the risk of deflation had returned (Distressed Volatility). Inflation in the EU as a whole was higher than in the euro area. Inflation in 2008 reached 3.7 % but by next year it fell to 1.0 % and never returned to a level higher than 3.1 % (2011) or lower than 1.5 % (2013) (Eurostat, HICP). When comparing the inflation levels in Poland and in the euro area and the EU-28, it seems clear that in contrast to the euro area, Poland has never faced a real risk of deflation. Moreover, there never was a serious risk of inflation getting out of control, which leads to the conclusion that the Polish economy performed well also in terms of monetary policy.

In the first year of the crisis, the job market in Poland performed well: the unemployment rate in 2008 fell yet again to 7.1 %. However, starting with the next year unemployment slowly grew, reaching 8.1 % in 2009. Between 2010 and 2013 the unemployment rate was higher than in the preceding period but relatively stable (9.7 % in 2010 and 2011 and then it went up to 10.3 % in 2013). Unemployment was therefore higher than just before the beginning of the crisis (and in the first year of the crisis), but still much lower than at the turn of the century. In 2008, unemployment in the Euro Area (7.6 %) was at the same level as in 2007 and similar to the level in Poland, however, it grew at a much faster rate: in 2009 it reached 9.6 %, and – as in Poland – remained stable in 2010–2011 at 10.1 %. The unemployment rate grew again in 2012 (11.4 %) and 2013 (12.1 %). Unemployment in the euro area was higher than in the EU: in 2008 unemployment in the EU reached 7.1 % and in the following years it grew to 9.0 % in 2009, 9.7 % in 2010 and 2011, and 10.5 % in 2012, and 10.9 % in 2013 (Eurostat, *Unemployment*). Unemployment in the analysed period slowly grew with a period of stability at the beginning of the decade. The unemployment rate in Poland during crisis is lower than in the Euro Area and in the EU, however, what needs to be stressed is the fact that there are important differences between EU Member States and between countries in the euro area, e.g. in 2013 unemployment in Spain reached 26.4 % and in Germany it fell to 5.3 %: the lowest level since 1991 (Eurostat, *Unemployment*).

5.3. Poland's and the EU's future economic growth

Let us stress that even advanced modern economy, although some economist may disagree, cannot foresee with absolute certainty what the economic future is going to be. This fact, however, should not stop us from trying to predict the economic outlooks for the next 2 years for Poland, the euro area and the EU.

The European Commission forecasts that Poland's GDP in 2014 will grow by 2.9 % and by 3.1 % in 2015. Poland's growth in the coming years will be rooted in the same factors as in the last years, i.e. low labour costs and exports to new dynamic markets (European Commission 2014: 88). In the same period the euro area's economy will grow by 1.2 % in 2014 and 1.8 % in 2015 and the EU's GDP will grow by 1.5 % in 2014 and 2.0

% in 2015 (European Commission 2014: 1). If the forecasts are true, than Poland's economy will again grow faster than that of the euro area and the EU as it has done for many years now.

The Polish Monetary Policy Council (*Rada Polityki Pieniężnej*) set an inflation target of 2.5 % (plus/minus 1 percentage point) for 2014, exactly the same as it did for each year since 2004 (National Bank of Poland 2013: 10). The European Commission forecasts that inflation in Poland in 2014 will reach 1.4 % and 2.0 % in 2015 (European Commission 2014: 89). According to the European Commission, inflation in Poland will be higher than inflation in the euro area (1.0 % in 2014 and 1.3 % in 2015) and in the EU-28 (1.2 % in 2014 and 1.5 % in 2015) (European Commission 2014: 1). The forecasts show that inflation in the euro area and in the EU-28 will reach levels below the optimal inflation level of 2.0% set by the European Central Bank. The economic data suggest also that, as in previous years, in Poland as well as in the EU there will be no risk of inflation, still some risk of deflation remains.

What will be the influence of decent economic growth and low inflation on the Polish labour market? The European Commission forecasts that the unemployment rate will improve in 2014 and 2015, but the change will not be significant. In 2014 the unemployment rate in Poland will reach 10.3 % and 10.1 % in 2015: almost exactly the same level as in 2013. The Euro Area's labour market will remain stagnant as well: unemployment will reach 12 % in 2014 and 11.7 % in 2015. The situation will not be any different in the EU-28 with the unemployment rate at 10.7 % in 2014 and 10.4 % in 2015 (European Commission 2014: 1). The overall forecast for the European and Polish job markets is simple: stagnation (with important regional differences, as already noted).

5.4. The economic crisis and the industry: a case study of car manufacturing in Poland

We used macroeconomic data to present the general economic situation of Poland and the European Union during the crisis, but what was the impact of the crisis on the most important branches of industry? Car manufacturing is one of the largest branches of industry in Poland, bringing in technical and organizational know-how and producing goods mostly for export, particularly to the European Union (Ministry of Economy 2012: 148), therefore, whatever happens in the EU's economy has direct influence on car making in Poland. Due to the export dependence of Polish car makers, the best indicator of this sector's condition seems to be the value of exported goods. In the years before the onset of the crisis, exports of cars and car spare parts from Poland grew rapidly: from 4.5 bn euro in 2000 (the value of export to the EU-15: 3.8 bn Euro) to 15.7 bn euro in 2007 (the value of export to the EU-15: 9 bn Euro) (Polski Związek Przemysłu Motoryzacyjnego 2008: 56). In 2008, when the economic crisis in the euro area just started, exports of cars and car spare parts from Poland grew to 20.7 bn euro and constituted 17.8 % of total Polish exports (Polski Związek Przemysłu Motoryzacyjnego 2013: 166). The crisis hit the car manufacturing industry in 2009: the value of exports dropped and with it production and employment. Although in 2009 the value of cars and spare parts exported from Poland fell to 17.7 bn euro, the car makers' share in Polish exports grew to 18.1 %. In the next few years the value of car and spare parts exports slowly grew and by 2011 reached 21.9 bn euro, thus reaching a higher level than before the crisis. However, at the same time the share of cars and car spare parts in Polish exports fell and by 2011 dropped to 16.2 %. In 2012, the value of cars and parts exported fell to 20.5 bn euro and the share in total exports dropped even further to 14.4 % (Polski Związek Przemysłu Motoryzacyjnego 2013: 166).

The largest drop in exports of cars and car spare parts from Poland happened during the worst period of economic downturn in the EU and the euro area (2009). Therefore, one can safely assume that the economic crisis in the EU directly influenced the car manufacturing industry in Poland and due to its importance for local exports and economy, it had a significant impact on the economic situation of Poland. The crisis and economic downturn were also responsible for a drop in Polish car and car spare parts exports in 2012. However, the situation was further worsened by the decision of Fiat to move production from Poland to Italy (Polski Związek Przemysłu Motoryzacyjnego 2013: 157): a move that was caused by the poor financial condition of the company due to the crisis and the pressure of the Italian government to save jobs in Italy at the expense of Fiat subsidiaries in other countries.

5.5. The factors influencing the economic situation of Poland during the crisis

At the height of the crisis in 2009, the economies of almost all EU Member States constricted. Latvia was hit particularly hard with the GDP falling by

17.7 % (Eurostat, *Real GDP*). The only exception from the pan-European trend of economic decline was Poland, which grew throughout the crisis. What was the reason behind the growth of the Polish GDP at a time when the EU's did not? Many factors have influenced the Polish economic growth during the crisis, but it seems that the most important of them all was the transfer of money from the EU in the form of structural funds, cohesion founds and single farm payments.

During the crisis, many countries decided to prepare and implement stimulus packages, including large public investments. In Poland the money transferred from the EU played the same role as stimulus packages in other countries. During the first year of the crisis (2007), net transfer (money transferred from the EU minus Polish contribution to the EU budget and money returned to the EU) from the EU to Poland amounted to 4.852 bn euro (Ministry of Finance 2007). In 2008 that amount fell to just 3.986 bn euro (Ministry of Finance 2008): the lowest level during the crisis. However, in 2009, when the EU's GDP fell by 4.5 %, the net transfer of money from the EU budget to Poland amounted to 6.011 bn euro (Ministry of Finance 2009). With each year the amount transferred annually from the EU to Poland grew and by 2012 reached 11.87 bn euro (Ministry of Finance 2012). Altogether, net transfers from the EU to Poland between 2007 and 2012 totalled at 44.679 bn euro.[20] It may be said – although at a risk of certain oversimplification – that the net transfers from the EU together with the money provided by the Polish government and local governments to co-finance certain projects prepared with the support of the EU acted as a stimulus package for Poland's economy during the crisis. Thanks to this package Poland could grow when other countries in the EU suffered due to the crisis.

5.6. Public policy actions in the face of the crisis

In November 2008, reacting to the global economic crisis, the Polish government prepared the *Plan for stability and development* (*Plan stabilności i rozwoju*), containing not only actions to be undertaken, but also measures that were already in place. The *Plan for stability and development* included actions to stimulate investments (particularly trough increased absorption of money from the EU budget) and consumption (through tax cuts enacted in 2006). Measures to protect the job market were also

---

[20] Own calculations, using data provided by the Polish Ministry of Finance.

undertaken to further stimulate demand (National Bank of Poland 2009: 38), including the *Act on softening the impact of the economic crisis on employees and entrepreneurs* (*Ustawa o łagodzeniu skutków kryzysu ekonomicznego dla pracowników i przedsiębiębiorców*) (Dz. U. of 2009, No. 125, Item 1035, as amended), which additionally regulated working time, contracts, benefits and public subsidies for increasing the competences of employees[21]. The *Plan for stability and development* also included other measures aimed at increasing demand, such as special funds to help those who lost jobs, pay house mortgage premiums and provide public support for medium and large companies working on important developmental projects for the Polish economy. The government *Plan for stability and development* was supplemented by measures introduced in October 2008 by the National Bank of Poland (*Narodowy Bank Polski*) in *The Confidence Plan* (*Plan zaufania NBP*), in particular actions aimed at reducing the risks in interbank financial markets (including bank liquidity risks) (National Bank of Poland 2009: 38).

5.7. Poland's positions vis a vis EU reforms in reaction to the euro area crisis

The European Union decided to implement certain reforms, described earlier in the paper, in reaction to the impact of the economic crisis: most importantly the Treaty on Stability, the Coordination and Governance in the Economic and Monetary Union (Fiscal Compact), the Single Resolution Mechanism (Banking Union) and the European Stability Mechanism. What was Poland's position regarding some of those measures?

During the negotiations of the Fiscal Compact, Poland insisted that every EU Member State should be allowed to take part in Euro Area Summits. Poland proposed that the leaders of all EU Member States should participate in Euro Area Summits and that the ministers of finance of all Member States should participate in eurogroup meetings. The Prime Minister of Poland argued that exclusion from those meetings would mean inability of certain Member States to influence decisions impacting the economy of the entire EU, which in turn would cause deep divisions within the EU ("Wprost"). France opposed the Polish position arguing that only the euro area countries should have the right to debate and

---

21 The *Act on softening the impact of economic crisis on employees and businessman* was replaced in 2013 by the *Act of 11 October 2013 on particular actions aimed at protecting jobs* (*Ustawa z dnia 11 października 2013 r. o szczególnych rozwiązaniach związanych z ochroną miejsc pracy*) (Dz. U. of 2013, Item 1291).

decide on euro area policies ("Gazeta Wyborcza"). In the end, however, the Fiscal Compact contains provisions fulfilling the Polish propositions: the EU Member States that have not adopted the euro but have ratified the treaty will participate in some Euro Area Summits, particularly those on competition policy and further reforms ("Rzeczpospolita"). Still, the Fiscal Compact met with stiff local opposition and the ratification process was even debated by the Constitutional Tribunal of Poland (Polish Constitutional Tribunal, *Procedural Decision*)[22], which could mean that future governments of Poland will decide to terminate the treaty.

The Polish government's position towards the Banking Union underlines the importance of two questions. The first one revolves around the effectiveness of the Banking Union that is still under construction, yet the government of Poland expressed hope that the Banking Union will be effective once all the parts of the Union are in place. The second question deals with the macroprudential policy of the European Central Bank. From the Polish perspective, the European macroprudential policy needs to take into account 'the situation of each state so that it could help counter the effects of asymmetrical shocks and different reactions of all the economies to common shocks' (Governement Plenipotentiary).

From the Polish perspective, the Banking Union should not interfere with the 'retention and increasing of the strength of local financial markets oversight institutions as well as with the protection of the local financial sector against further effects of the euro area crisis' (Szpringer 2013: 3). Additionally, it is important for Poland to retain a high level of safety of local banks, thus local oversight institutions should not be limited by decisions taken at the EU level. The European oversight institutions should also not limit the possibilities of taking preventive measures by local oversight authorities, therefore some decisions made by the European oversight institutions that could affect subsidiary companies in different Member States should be first consulted with local oversight authorities (Szpringer 2013: 4).

The position of the Polish government towards bank resolution was different than the position of the European Commission: 'due to the fact that most banks in Poland are subsidiaries of foreign banks, Poland wants an equal position in the process of banking resolution, while the European Commission wanted to give one vote to the country where the

---

[22] Joining the ESM resulted in similar actions, see: Polish Constitutional Tribunal, *Judgement of 26.06.2013*, File No. K 33/12, http://otk.trybunal.gov.pl/orzeczenia/teksty/otkpdf/2013/K_33_12.pdf 11.02.2014

seat of the holding is registered and one vote to all the other countries where the subsidiaries of a bank are active' (Euractiv.pl). The Polish proposition was designed to strengthen the protection of interests of Poland as a country that receives large financial investments (Kowanda).

Whatever the problem debated in the EU, it seems that the Polish government has decided to take an active part in the negotiations and reforms of the European Union caused by the economic crisis. The rationale behind this policy choice is securing adoption of solutions that take into account Polish interests, economic situation and reality.

6. Conclusions

The economic development of Poland in the 21st century was much faster than the economic development of the euro area and the whole EU. By the 2010s, Poland even managed to limit its very high unemployment, although that was possible primarily due to large emigration. The global economic crisis slowed down the Polish growth, but did not stop it. The factors that were responsible for Poland's good economic situation during the crisis are, among others: cheap workforce, export oriented economy and, last but not least, the large net transfer of funds from the EU budget that acted as a very large stimulus package for the economy. The prospects of the Polish economy for the next 2 years are good with further growth of GDP and low inflation, however, the unemployment rate seems to remain stagnant at around 10 %. During the time of the global economic crisis and the necessary reforms of the European institutions, the government of Poland remained active and concentrated on protecting at the European level the local financial, economic and political interests. The actions of the Polish government often stood against the positions of larger EU Member States and managed to organise strong support for the solutions it favoured. All in all, Poland fared fairly well during the turbulent times of the global economic crisis.

7. Bibliography

Borkowski P.J. 2013, *Międzyrządowość w procesie integracji europejskiej (Intergovernmental Method in the Process of European Integration)*, Warszawa: Aspra-JR.

Central Statistical Office of Poland, *Produkt krajowy brutto w 2013 r. szacunek wstępny (Gross Domestic Product in 2013, a preliminary estimate*), http://www.stat.gov.pl/gus/5840_12449_PLK_HTML. htm (11.03.2014).

Central Statistical Office of Poland, *Roczne wskaźniki cen towarów i usług konsumpcyjnych w latach 1950-2013* (*Annual indicators of the prices of commodities and consumer services in 1950–2013*), http://www.stat.gov.pl/gus/5840_1634_PLK_HTML.htm (11.03.2014).

Council of the European Union, Press Release, Brussels, 18 December 2013, 17983/13, http://www.consilium.europa.eu/ueDocs/cms_Data/docs/pressData/en/ecofin/140193.pdf (20.02.2014).

Distressed Volatility, *These Charts Show Why Deflation Risks Remain In The Euro Zone #ECB*, http://www.distressedvolatility.com/2014/01/these-charts-show-why-deflation risks.html (11.03.2014).

Durante J-P, 2013, *Euro area: the Single Resolution Mechanism for the Banking Union is born*, http://perspectives.pictet.com/2013/12/20/euro-area-the-single-resolution-mechanism-for-the-banking-union-is-born/ (18.02.2014).

European Commission, December 2013, *Commissioner Barnier welcomes agreement between the European Parliament and Member States on Deposit Guarantee Schemes*, European Commission, MEMO, Brussels, 17 December 2013, http://europa.eu/rapid/press-release_MEMO-13-1176_en.htm (last accessed on: 20 February 2014).

European Commission, *European Economic Forecast, Winter 2014*, Brussels 2014.

Eurostat, *Real GDP growth rate – volume*, http://epp.eurostat.ec.europa.eu/tgm/table.do?tab=table&plugin=1&language=en&pcode=tec00115 (11.03.2014).

Eurostat, *HICP - inflation rate - Annual average rate of change (%)*, http://epp.eurostat.ec.europa.eu/tgm/table.do?tab=table&language=en&pcode=tec00118&tableSelection=1&footnotes=yes&labeling=labels&plugin=1 (11.03.2014).

Eurostat, *Unemployment rate by sex and age groups – annual average, %*, http://appsso.eurostat.ec.europa.eu/nui/submitViewTableAction.do;jsessionid =9ea7d07e30d696d9cb3e0bb34e8f84649c82cfde8588.e34MbxeSahmMa40LbNiM bxaMc3iPe0 (11.03.2014).

Francuskie media o stanowisku Tuska w sprawie paktu fiskalnego: To polski szantaż (*The French media about the Donald Tusk's position on the Fiscal Compact*), "Gazeta Wyborcza", 27.01.2012, http://wiadomosci.gazeta.pl/wiadomosci/1,114873,11042929,Francuskie_media_o_stanowisku_Tuska_w_sprawie_paktu.html (11.03.2014).

Frymark K. 2012, *Germany can ratify the European Stability Mechanism and the fiscal compact*, "OSW Analyses", 12 September, http://www.osw.waw.pl/en/publikacje/analyses/2012-09-12/germany-can-ratify-european-stability-mechanism-and-fiscal-compact (20.02.2014).

Gans M. 2013, *Europejski Mechanizm Stabilności* (*European Stability Mechanism*), 7 August, http://www.uniaeuropejska.org/europejski-mechanizm-stabilnosci (19.02.2014).

Gostyńska A., Tokarski P. 2011, *European Stability Mechanism in the Making*, "Bulletin PISM" 40 (257), 22 April 2011, http://www.pism.pl/index/?id=f7fa6aca028e7ff4ef62d75ed025fe76 (20.02.2014).

Government Plenipotentiary for Euro Adoption in Poland, *Implikacje reformy instytucjonalnej strefy euro dla procesu wprowadzenia euro w Polsce* (*Implications of the institutional reform of the euro area for the introduction of the euro in Poland*), http://www.mf.gov.pl/ko/ministerstwo-finansow/dzialalnosc/integracja-ze-strefa-euro/aktualnosci/-/asset_publisher/Rq0a/content/id/7384312;jsessionid=A1467A2608D54AA5E8669BD5B302A997# (11.03.2014).

Grosse T.G. 2010, *Euro w kryzysie: wnioski dla Polski* (*The Euro in Crisis: Conclusions for Poland*), "Polski Przegląd Dyplomatyczny" 2.

Grosse T.G. 2013, *Dylematy unii bankowej* (*Dilemmas of the Banking Union*), "Analiza natolińska" 2, http://www.natolin.edu.pl/pdf/analizy/Natolin_Analiza_2_2013.pdf (14.03.2014).

Kowanda C. 2013, *Kompromis dobry dla Niemców* (*A Compromise Would Be Good for the Germans*), 19 December, http://www.polityka.pl/tygodnikpolityka/rynek/1565427,1,unia-bankowa---czym-jest-i-co-nam-da.read (21.02.2014).

Kuźniar R. 2013, *My, Europa* (*We, Europe*), Warszawa: Scholar.

Milczarek D., Adamczyk A., Zajączkowski K. (eds.), *Introduction to European Studies. A New Aproach to Uniting Europe*, Publishing Programme of Centre for Europe University of Warsaw, Warsaw 2013.

Ministry of Economy, *Polska 2012: Raport o stanie gospodarki* (*Poland 2012: Report on the state of the economy*), Warszawa 2012.

Ministry of Finance, *Przepływy finansowe Polska – UE w 2007 r. (w Euro)* (*2007 Poland–EU financial flows, in euro*), http://www.mf.gov.pl/documents/764034/1007802/2007.pdf (11.03.2014).

Ministry of Finance, *Przepływy finansowe Polska - UE w 2008 r. (w Euro)* (*2008 Poland–EU financial flows, in euro*), http://www.mf.gov.pl/documents/764034/1007802/2008.pdf (11.03.2014).

Ministry of Finance, *Przepływy finansowe Polska - UE w 2009 r. (w Euro) (2009 Poland-EU financial flows, in euro)*, http://www.mf.gov.pl/documents/764034/1007802/2009.pdf (11.03.2014).

Ministry of Finance, *Przepływy finansowe Polska - UE w 2010 r. (w Euro) (2010 Poland-EU financial flows, in euro)*, http://www.mf.gov.pl/documents/764034/1007802/2010.pdf (11.03.2014).

Ministry of Finance, *Przepływy finansowe Polska - UE w 2011 r. (w Euro) (2011 Poland-EU financial flows, in euro)*, http://www.mf.gov.pl/documents/764034/1007802/2011.pdf (11.03.2014).

Ministry of Finance, *Przepływy finansowe Polska - UE w 2012 r. (w Euro) (2012 Poland-EU financial flows, in euro)*, http://www.mf.gov.pl/documents/764034/1007802/2012.pdf (11.03.2014).

National Bank of Poland, *Polska wobec światowego kryzysu gospodarczego (Poland towards the global economic crisis)*, Warszawa 2009.

National Bank of Poland, Monetary Policy Council, *Założenia polityki pieniężnej na 2014 r. (Monetary policy objectives for 2014)*, Warszawa 2013.

PAP 2014, *Szczurek: dla Polski nie ma sensu wchodzenie do unii bankowej 'na ślepo' (Szczurek: There Is No Point for Poland to Enter the Banking Union)*, PAP, 27 January, http://m.onet.pl/biznes/branze/finanse,q5bd8 (20.02.2014).

PAP 6 February 2014, *PE odgraża się ws. unii bankowej, ale zostawia otwartą furtkę do negocjacji (The EP Makes Strong Statements about the Banking Union but Leaves the Matter Open for Negotiations)*, http://wyborcza.biz/biznes/1,100969,15410825,PE_odgraza_sie_ws__unii_bankowej__ale_zostawia_otwarta.html#ixzz2tL2ria8n (22.02.2014).

Polish Constitutional Tribunal, *Procedural Decision of 21.05.2013*, File no. K 11/13, http://otk.trybunal.gov.pl/orzeczenia/teksty/otkpdf/2013/K_11p13.pdf (11.03.2014).

Polish Constitutional Tribunal, *Judgement of 26.06.2013*, File no. K 33/12, *http://otk.trybunal.gov.pl/orzeczenia/teksty/otkpdf/2013/K_33_12.pdf* (11.03.2014).

Polska nie podpisze paktu fiskalnego, jeśli podzieli on UE (Poland will not sign the Fiscal Compact, if it divides the EU), "Wprost", 27.01.2012, http://www.wprost.pl/ar/290219/Polska-nie-podpisze-paktu-fiskalnego-jesli-podzieli-on-UE/ (11.03.2014).

Polski Związek Przemysłu Motoryzacyjnego (Polish Automotive Industry Association), *Raport 2008*, Warszawa 2008.

Polski Związek Przemysłu Motoryzacyjnego (Polish Automotive Industry Association), *Raport 2013*, Warszawa 2013.

Polsko-hiszpańskie konsultacje ws. energetyki i unii bankowej (Poland-Spain consultations on energy policy and the banking union), "Euractiv.pl", 16.07.2013, http://www.euractiv.pl/gospodarka/artykul/premierzy-polski-i-hiszpanii-o-energetyce-i-unii-bankowej-004864 11.03.2014.

Popławski K. 2014, *The shape of the banking union confirms Berlin's privileged position in the eurozone*, "OSW Commentary", 10 January, http://www.osw.waw.pl/en/publikacje/osw-commentary/2014-01-10/shape-banking-union-confirms-berlins-privileged-position (20.02.2014).

Press release 2012, European Commission, IP/12/1272, Brussels, 28 November.

Szpringer Z. 2013. *Unia Bankowa (Banking Union)*, "Infos. Zagadnienia społeczno-gospodarcze", no. 8 (145), 18.04.2013.

Ramotowski J. 2014, *Unia bankowa coraz mniej ambitna (The Banking Union – Less and Less Ambitious)*, "Obserwator finansowy" 2 January 2014, http://www.obserwatorfinansowy.pl/forma/analizy/unia-bankowa-coraz-mniej-ambitna/ (21.02.2014).

"Rocznik Strategiczny", 2011/2012, Warszawa 2012.

Trzcińska A 2013, *Europejski Mechanizm Stabilności jako stabilizator w planowanej unii finansowej (European Stability Mechanism as a Stabiliser in the Future Financial Union)*, 25 March, http://www.nbp.pl/badania/seminaria_files/10iv2013.pdf (23.02. 2014).

Ustawa o łagodzeniu skutków kryzysu ekonomicznego dla pracowników i przedsiębiorców (Act on softening the impact of the economic crisis on employees and entrepreneurs) (Dz. U. Z of 2009, No.125, Item 1035, as amended).

Ustawa o szczególnych rozwiązaniach związanych z ochroną miejsc pracy (Act on softening the impact of economic crisis on employees and businessman was replaced in 2013 by the *Act of 11 October 2013 on particular actions aimed at protecting jobs*) (Dz. U. of 2013, Item 1291).

World Economic Outlook Update: Growing Pains, International Monetary Fund, 9 July 2013, http://www.imf.org/external/pubs/ft/weo/2013/update/02/index.htm (28.02.2014).

Zajączkowski K. 2014, *Międzynarodowy potencjał gospodarczy Unii Europejskiej w dobie wyzwań globalnych (International Economic Potential of the European Union in an Age of Global Challenges)*, [in:] *Unia Europejska jako aktor na scenie globalnej. Razem czy osobno? (The European Union as an Actor in the Global Arena. Together or Apart?)*, ed. by B. Góralczyk, Warszawa: Centrum Europejskie UW: 111-155.

Spanish and Polish Economies: Two Faces of Great Recession in Europe

JOSÉ MANUEL CANSINO
UNIVERSITY OF SEVILLE

MANUEL ORDÓÑEZ
UNIVERSITY OF SEVILLE

1. Introduction

Despite not very significant differences in terms of area, population and demographic density (Table 1), Spain and Poland showed a remarkably different pattern of economic development during the last decade.

Table 1. Main geographical, population and demographic aspects of Spain and Poland

	Spain	Poland
Area (km²)	504,645	312,679
Total population	47,265,321	38,538,447
Density (people per km²)	93.66	123

Source: Eurostat

These two countries have a similar religious background –the Catholic religion is the most widespread denomination within both their populations - and just a little similarity in the deregulation process of their economies. The Spanish economy has been a market economy since the 1960s, but with strong regulation in most of its productive sector. Poland was a centrally planned socialist economy until the end of 1980s, following which its economy became a transition economy, and now it is also a market one. Finally, both Poland and Spain are Members States of the European Union –EU – (Spain since 1986 and Poland since 2004) although Spain is also a member of the Eurozone whereas Poland is not.

Despite these considerable similarities in geographical, demographic and cultural aspects, experts point out a very different behavior of their economies in the last decade, mainly when the great recession (Eichengreen and O'Rourke 2009) began in the majority of developed economies of the world.

This chapter focuses on structural differences between the Spanish and Polish economies to allow discovering some reasons which can explain their very different behavior and, perhaps, let us present some recommendations to policy makers. To achieve that, a key sector approach is developed following Rasmussen's (1956) method. The database used is provided for WIOD, as described below.

The structure of the chapter is as follows. After the introduction, Section 2 offers macroeconomic overview for the three economic areas considered; Spain, Poland and UE-27. Section 3 describes the database used and Section 4 provides a description of the methodology. Results are shown in Section 5. Section 6 concludes.

2. A comparative macroeconomic overview

Poland is the only EU economy with a positive real Gross Domestic Product growth rate during the past decade, also when the great recession started (Table 2).

Table 2. Real GDP growth rate (%)

	2000	01	02	03	04	05	06	07	08	09	10	11	12	13	14
EU (27)	3.9	2.1	1.3	1.5	2.5	2.1	3.3	3.2	0.3	-4.3	2.1	1.6	-0.3	-0.1	1.4
Euro area (17)	3.8	2.0	0.9	0.7	2.2	1.7	3.2	3.0	0.4	-4.4	2.0	1.5	-0.6	-0.4	1.2

Spain	5.0	3.7	2.7	3.1	3.3	3.6	4.1	3.5	0.9	-3.7	-0.3	0.4	-1.4	-1.5	0.9
Poland	4.3	1.2	1.4	3.9	5.3	3.6	6.2	6.8	5.1	1.6	3.9	4.5	1.9	1.1	2.2

Source: Eurostat

Poland's GDP per capita in Purchasing power parities (PPP) has increased by over 37 per cent while Spain's registered a low variation only. However, as Table 3 shows, the original values were very different.

Table 3. GDP pc in PPS (EU27=100)

	2001	02	03	04	05	06	07	08	09	10	11	12
EU (27)	100	100	100	100	100	100	100	100	100	100	100	100
Euro area (17)	112	111	110	109	109	109	109	109	109	108	108	108
Spain	98	100	101	101	102	104	105	104	103	99	98	97
Poland	48	48	49	51	51	52	54	56	61	63	64	66

Source: Eurostat

The inflation pattern shows a significant difference between these two economies. A low inflation rate was one of the conditions stipulated by the Maastricht Treaty[1] to allow becoming a member of the Eurozone; the Spanish inflation rate has been lower than Poland's since the beginning of the 21st century. Although the difference still persists, its range has been reduced and can be observed in Table 4 which contains the Harmonised indices of consumer prices (HICP) values.

Table 4. HICP - inflation rate (2005=100)

	2000	01	02	03	04	05	06	07	08	09	10	11	12
EU (27)	88.5	91.3	93.6	95.6	97.8	100	102.3	104.7	108.6	109.6	111.9	115.4	118.4
Euro area (17)	89.5	91.7	93.8	95.8	97.9	100	102.2	104.4	107.8	108.2	109.9	112.9	115.7
Spain	85.5	87.9	91.0	93.9	96.7	100	103.6	106.5	110.9	110.6	112.9	116.4	119.2
Poland	87.4	92.0	93.8	94.5	97.9	100	101.3	103.9	108.3	112.6	115.6	120.1	124.5

Source: Eurostat

---

[1] Formally, the Treaty on European Union or TEU, signed on 7 February 1992.

From the Government size perspective, the two economies considered are very similar, and this similarity has been visible for a long time already, as evidenced by the data offered by the OECD, presented in Table 5.

Table 5. General government total outlays % of GDP

	1995	2000	2001	2002	2003	2004	2005	2006
Poland	47.7	41.1	43.7	44.3	44.7	42.6	43.5	43.9
Spain	44.5	39.2	38.7	38.9	38.4	38.9	38.4	38.4
Euro area	53.0	46.2	47.2	47.5	48.0	47.5	47.4	46.7
Total OECD	42.6	38.7	39.7	40.3	39.9	39.3	39.3	39.0

	2007	2008	2009	2010	2011	2012	2013	2014
Poland	42.2	43.2	44.7	45.5	43.7	43.2	42.9	42.8
Spain	39.2	41.5	46.3	46.3	45.2	44.0	42.2	41.7
Euro area	46.0	47.2	51.3	51.0	49.5	49.5	49.4	49.1
Total OECD	39.1	41.0	44.5	44.0	43.2	42.6	41.9	41.1

Note: The data refer to the general government sector, which is a consolidation of accounts for the central, state and local governments plus social security. These data include outlays net of operating surpluses of public enterprises.
Source: OECD. Economic Outlook (2012)

Different consequences of the great recession in these two economies impact the Government accountability. Tables 6 and 7 show the pattern of general government deficit/surplus and how the general government gross debt has increased in Spain mainly.

Table 6. General government deficit/surplus in % of GDP

	1995	2000	01	02	03	04	05	06	07	08	09	10	11	12
EU (27)	:	0.6	-1.5	-2.6	-3.2	-2.9	-2.5	-1.5	-0.9	-2.4	-6.9	-6.5	-4.4	-4.0

Euro area (17)	-7.5	-0.1	-1.9	-2.6	-3.1	-2.9	-2.5	-1.3	-0.7	-2.1	-6.4	-6.2	-4.2	-3.7
Spain	-7.2	-0.9	-0.5	-0.2	-0.3	-0.1	1.3	2.4	1.9	-4.5	-11.2	-9.7	-9.4	-10.6
Poland	-4.4	-3.0	-5.3	-5.0	-6.2	-5.4	-4.1	-3.6	-1.9	-3.7	-7.4	-7.9	-5.0	-3.9

Source: Eurostat

Table 7. General government gross debt in % of GDP

	1995	2000	01	02	03	04	05	06	07	08	09	10	11	12
EU (27)	:	61.9	61.1	60.5	62	62.4	62.8	61.6	59	62.3	74.6	80	82.5	85.3
Spain	63.3	59.4	55.6	52.6	48.8	46.3	43.2	39.7	36.3	40.2	53.9	61.5	69.3	84.2
Poland	49	36.8	37.6	42.2	47.1	45.7	47.1	47.7	45	47.1	50.9	54.8	56.2	55.6

Source: Eurostat

Once Poland became a member of the EU, its international trade followed a similar pattern as the Spanish one since the second half of the 1980s. In both cases, the current account balance showed red figures, but the actual Spanish value close to zero from values close to 10 per cent of GDP and Poland's red figure shown in Table 8 require a deep analysis.

Table 8. Current account balance (Millions of current €)

	2005	2006	2007	2008	2009	2010	2011
Poland	-5,434.40	-9,872.26	-19,884.85	-26,231.73	-12,873.11	-18,032.11	-18,777.26
Spain	-62,574.47	-83,199.98	-108,462.80	-115,958.66	-52,358.98	-47,372.32	-38,959.69

Source: Word Bank. World Development Indicators.

Yet, the main difference between the Spanish and Polish economies in the past decade have been different patterns of unemployment rates. During the housing bubble, Spain was the EU country that generated the most employment. Most of that was motivated by the housing activity, but also by requirements from other productive sectors. After the bubble exploded, nearly four million people lost employment in Spain. The Spanish economy was the one that destroyed the highest number of jobs in the EU. Obviously, this is one of the reasons that explain the Spanish general government deficit and the gross debt level. Another reason is the Spanish banking sector crisis. The rate of unemployment in Spain rose to reach a level three times higher than that in Poland. Table 9 shows this dramatic difference.

Table 9. Unemployment rate

	1995 M12	2000 M12	2001 M12	2002 M12	2003 M12	2004 M12	2005 M12	2006 M12
EU (27)	:	8.5	8.7	9.0	9.2	9.2	8.8	7.8
Euro area (17)	10.7	8.3	8.3	8.9	9.1	9.4	9.0	8.1
Spain	19.6	11.0	10.7	11.5	11.3	10.3	8.8	8.3
Poland	:	16.7	19.2	20.1	19.9	18.4	16.8	12.1

	2007 M12	2008 M12	2009 M12	2010 M12	2011 M12	2012 M12	2013 M04
EU (27)	7.0	7.7	9.5	9.6	10.0	10.7	11.1
Euro area (17)	7.5	8.4	10.0	10.1	10.7	11.8	12.3
Spain	8.8	14.9	19.1	20.4	23.0	26.1	27.1
Poland	8.4	7.0	9.0	9.6	10.0	10.4	11.0

Source: Eurostat

3. Database

The data used in this chapter are taken from the World Input-Output Database (WIOD), a database developed to analyze the effects of globalization on trade patterns, environmental pressures and socio-economic development across a wide set of countries. The WIOD was opened to the public on April 16, 2012. The database covers data on 27 EU countries and 13 other major countries in the world for the period from 1995 to 2009. Also covers 35 productive sectors. These sectors are listed below.

Table 10. Productive sectors included in WIOD

Agriculture, Hunting, Forestry and Fishing
Mining and Quarrying
Food, Beverages and Tobacco

Textiles and Textile Products
Leather, Leather and Footwear
Wood and Products of Wood and Cork
Pulp, Paper, Paper, Printing and Publishing
Coke, Refined Petroleum and Nuclear Fuel
Chemicals and Chemical Products
Rubber and Plastics
Other Non-Metallic Mineral
Basic Metals and Fabricated Metal
Machinery, Nec
Electrical and Optical Equipment
Transport Equipment
Manufacturing, Nec; Recycling
Electricity, Gas and Water Supply
Construction
Sale, Maintenance and Repair of Motor Vehicles and Motorcycles; Retail Sale of Fuel
Wholesale Trade and Commission Trade, Except of Motor Vehicles and Motorcycles
Retail Trade, Except of Motor Vehicles and Motorcycles; Repair of Household Goods
Hotels and Restaurants
Inland Transport
Water Transport
Air Transport
Other Supporting and Auxiliary Transport Activities; Activities of Travel Agencies
Post and Telecommunications
Financial Intermediation
Real Estate Activities
Renting of M&Eq and Other Business Activities
Public Admin and Defence; Compulsory Social Security
Education

Health and Social Work
Other Community, Social and Personal Services
Private Households with Employed Persons

Source: wiod.org

For our research, Polish and Spanish National Input-Output Tables updated to 2009 were used together with an IO Table for the EU-27 area, constructed based on the multiregional IO Table for the same year, contained in the WIOD database. To do that, all areas other than EU-27 are grouped within a single area named "rest of the world". Other data from the WIOD were also used.

Figure 1 shows the basic structure of the IO tables constructed at basic prices

	35 sectors	Final demand	Exports	Imports	Output
35 sectors					
Taxes less subsidies on products					
Cif/ fob adjustments on exports					
Direct purchases abroad by residents					
Purchases in the domestic territory by non-residents					
Value added at basic prices					
International Transport Margins					
Output at basic prices					

Source: Own elaboration

4. Methodology

Following Rasmussen (1956), it is possible to identify the key sectors of an economy based on two indicators named backward linkage (BL) and forward linkage (FL).

BL measures the effect that a shock on the final demand of every sector causes over the total economy output. FL measures the effect that a shock on final demand of every sector causes over the specific output of one productive sector.

This methodology approach is based on the well-known Leontief's model (1966).

To calculate BL and FL values, we consider Leontief's inverse matrix, $M = (I-A)^{-1}$, where each of the elements named m_{ij} is a simple Leontief's multiplier and represents the quantities of i-sector input that are required to obtain one unit of goods produced by sector j.

Once multipliers are obtained, the multipliers aggregated by columns and rows are calculated. Each of the columns and rows multiplier will be calculated as follows:

$$M._j = \sum_{i=1}^{n} m_{ij} \qquad \forall j = 1, 2, \ldots, n \qquad (1)$$

$$M_{i\cdot} = \sum_{j=1}^{n} m_{ij} \qquad \forall i = 1, 2, \ldots, n \qquad (2)$$

Eq (1) shows the quantity of inputs that every sector needs to achieve output of sector j increased by one unit. Eq (2) shows the total output that sector i should provide if the rest of the sectors increase their outputs by one unit.

Multipliers obtained from (1) and (2) offer information on the backward and the forward effect of a specific productive sector. These multipliers allow calculation of the BL and FL indicators from:

$$BL._j = \frac{M._j}{\frac{1}{n}\sum_{j=1}^{n} m_{ij}} \qquad (3) \qquad FL_{i\cdot} = \frac{M_{i\cdot}}{\frac{1}{n}\sum_{i=1}^{n} m_{ij}} \qquad (4)$$

Once BL and FL are normalized, it is possible to conduct a comparison between different sectors. A value higher (lower) than one indicates that the sector has a backward effect or a forward effect that is above (below) the average value of all productive sectors.

If $BL_{.j}>1$, this implies that a shock in the final demand of sector j has an impact over the output of other sectors above the average value. If $FL_{i.}>1$, this implies that the effect of an increase in the final demand of the other sectors over sector's i output is higher than the average value.

Following to Cheneery and Watanabe (1958), it is possible to classify all the productive sectors of an economy into four subsets based on their BL and FL values (Figure 2). Sectors that appear in panel I are the key sectors of the economy.

Figure 2. Sector classification based on BL and BL values

	FL < 1	FL > 1
BL > 1	II. Relevant sectors with a strong backward effect	I. Key sectors
BL < 1	III. No relevant sectors	IV. Relevant sectors with a strong forward effect

Source: Own elaboration

However, BL and FL are average indicators. That implies that existence of two productive sectors with the same values of BL and FL, yet a different impact over the economy would be possible. Indeed, one of them could only impact a few sectors, along with a low impact over others. In this sense, impact of a sector with the same value of BL or FL could be dispersed over all sectors, but demonstrating a low level impact on each of them.

To capture how dispersed the sectors' impact is, Rasmussen (1956) defined two new estimators which measure the standard deviation of BL and FL. Eqs (5) and (6) define these new estimators named $D_{.j}$ and $D_{i.}$:

$$D_{.j} = \frac{\sqrt{\frac{1}{n-1}\sum_{i=1}^{n}\left(m_{ij} - \frac{1}{n}\sum_{i=1}^{n} m_{ij}\right)^2}}{\frac{1}{n}\sum_{i=1}^{n} m_{ij}} \qquad \forall\, j = 1, 2, \ldots, n \tag{5}$$

and

$$D_{i.} = \frac{\sqrt{\frac{1}{n-1}\sum_{j=1}^{n}\left(m_{ij} - \frac{1}{n}\sum_{j=1}^{n} m_{ij}\right)^2}}{\frac{1}{n}\sum_{j=1}^{n} m_{ij}} \qquad \forall\, i = 1, 2, \ldots, n \tag{6}$$

A reduced value of $D_{.j}$ reflects that the backward effect of sector j is delivered in a uniform way over the other sectors. A high value of $D_{.j}$ implies that the backward effect of sector j is focused on a reduced number of productive sectors.

$D_{i.}$ provides information on the major or minor degree of impact dispersion that a shock in the final demand of all the sectors has over sector i output. A reduced value of $D_{i.}$ indicates that sectors impact in an uniform way the output of sector i. On the other hand, a high value of this estimator shows that the final demand of a reduced subset of sectors explains the change in sector i output to the largest extent.

5. Results

Backward linkage and Forward linkage results are showed in Tables 11-13. Cells of sectors with critical values (closest to 1) are shaded. Sectors appear ranked fom the highest to lowest FL.

Table 11. BL and FL values of the Spanish economy by 2009

Sector	Forward linkage	Sector	Backward Linkage
30	2.44	3	1.25
17	1.90	15	1.23
12	1.70	12	1.20
18	1.67	16	1.20
26	1.62	18	1.19
28	1.53	6	1.18
23	1.47	14	1.18
20	1.42	11	1.15
21	1.37	5	1.15

29	1.09	8	1.15
8	1.05	10	1.15
27	1.01	13	1.12
3	0.98	9	1.11
9	0.94	26	1.11
7	0.93	4	1.10
34	0.92	25	1.08
19	0.90	24	1.07
10	0.86	17	1.07
1	0.83	7	1.06
6	0.77	2	1.05
13	0.77	23	0.99
16	0.76	19	0.96
11	0.75	27	0.92
14	0.71	1	0.90
22	0.70	22	0.89
15	0.68	20	0.88
31	0.67	34	0.88
4	0.64	30	0.86

33	0.61	21	0.80
2	0.58	33	0.77
25	0.57	28	0.77
32	0.56	31	0.75
5	0.55	29	0.73
24	0.52	32	0.61
35	0.49	35	0.49

Source: Own elaboration

Table 12. BL and FL values of the Polish economy by 2009

Sector	Forward Linkage	Sector	Backward linkage
30	2.12	3	1.27
21	1.93	25	1.23
20	1.79	6	1.19
23	1.56	15	1.18
17	1.54	8	1.18
18	1.45	26	1.17
3	1.21	16	1.16
1	1.20	24	1.15
12	1.18	12	1.15
19	1.17	18	1.12

2	1.15	10	1.11
28	1.13	9	1.11
29	1.09	14	1.09
26	1.05	7	1.08
8	1.05	13	1.07
27	1.04	1	1.06
34	1.00	11	1.06
7	0.98	5	1.02
9	0.91	17	1.01
11	0.87	23	0.97
6	0.84	22	0.97
10	0.83	4	0.95
13	0.69	28	0.94
16	0.69	34	0.93
22	0.69	29	0.91
14	0.66	21	0.89
31	0.66	20	0.88
33	0.62	30	0.87
15	0.61	27	0.86

Spanish and Polish Economies: Two Faces of Great Recession in Europe

4	0.57	2	0.85
32	0.57	19	0.85
25	0.55	33	0.81
5	0.54	32	0.69
24	0.54	31	0.68
35	0.53	35	0.53

Source: Own elaboration

Table 13. BL and FL values of the EU economy by 2009

Sector	Forward Linkage	Sector	Backward Linkage
30	3.38	15	1.31
20	1.62	8	1.23
12	1.56	3	1.21
28	1.54	12	1.20
26	1.43	6	1.18
17	1.40	5	1.15
21	1.28	13	1.14
23	1.22	16	1.14
29	1.15	14	1.14
18	1.11	24	1.13
9	1.08	10	1.13

27	0.95	9	1.13
8	0.95	4	1.11
7	0.94	25	1.11
34	0.92	7	1.09
1	0.92	11	1.09
14	0.90	18	1.08
15	0.90	26	1.04
3	0.90	1	1.02
2	0.89	17	1.00
13	0.83	23	0.95
10	0.82	22	0.94
19	0.80	19	0.92
6	0.75	20	0.92
11	0.73	28	0.92
4	0.67	27	0.91
22	0.67	34	0.88
16	0.64	21	0.86
31	0.62	30	0.84
32	0.60	2	0.82

Spanish and Polish Economies: Two Faces of Great Recession in Europe

5	0.59	33	0.80
25	0.59	31	0.78
33	0.57	29	0.70
24	0.57	32	0.65
35	0.50	35	0.50

Source: Own elaboration

The Spanish economy has five key sectors and so does the Polish economy, which is one key sector more as compared with the EU's economy; therefore, an initial key sector analysis does not allow drawing any relevant conclusions explaining the difference between the first and the second economy. The results need to be analyzed thoroughly.

The results obtained for $D_{.j}$ and $D_{i.}$ indicators do not offer any interesting information, useful in a comparative explanation of differences between the economies. The only exception is the major dispersion of BL in the Polish economy (2.8) compared to the Spanish one (3.3) in the first sector – a sector with a higher weight in the first economy as is shown in Table 15-. These results are presented in Table 14. Figures are similar in the three cases.

Table 14. Dispersion measures of BL and FL

Key sectors	Spain		Poland		UE-27	
	$D_{.j}$	Di.	$D_{.j}$	Di.	$D_{.j}$	Di.
Coke, Refined Petroleum and Nuclear Fuel	3.3	3.6	2.8	3.1	2.7	3.4
Basic Metals and Fabricated Metal	3.3	2.4	3.3	3.2	3.4	2.6
Electricity, Gas and Water Supply	3.9	2.1	3.3	2.1	3.8	2.6
Other Supporting and Auxiliary Transport Activities; Activities of Travel Agencies	3.3	2.3	3.1	3.5	3.4	2.6

Source: Own elaboration

Table 15 shows the common key sectors derived from results for the three areas being compared, and their importance measured as the ratio between the Sector Output and the total Output (discounted figures of imports and International Transport Margins).

Table 15. Common key sectors as a percentage of national total output

Key sectors	Spain	Poland	UE-27
Coke, Refined Petroleum and Nuclear Fuel	0.57	1.34	0.92
Basic Metals and Fabricated Metal	3.11	3.15	3.20
Electricity, Gas and Water Supply	3.13	3.97	2.84
Other Supporting and Auxiliary Transport Activities; Activities of Travel Agencies	2.32	1.23	2.01

Source: Own elaboration

Sectors 12 (Basic Metals and Fabricated Metal) and 17 (Electricity, Gas and Water Supply) show quite similar values both in the case of Spain and Poland, while sector 8 (Coke, Refined Petroleum and Nuclear Fuel) has a higher weight in the Polish economy compared with the Spanish one, whereas 26 (Other Supporting and Auxiliary Transport Activities; Activities of Travel Agencies) represents just an opposite case; consequently, figures in Table 13 do not allow drawing virtually any conclusions. Perhaps these four key sectors require a deeper analysis. This will be provided in Table 16.

Table 16 contains information on the destination of four key sectors specified above. It shows the role of the foreign sector in each of them.

Table 16. Exports of common key sectors as a percentage of sectorial output

Key sectors	Spain	Poland	UE-27
Coke, Refined Petroleum and Nuclear Fuel	34.73	20.94	14.46

Basic Metals and Fabricated Metal	22.88	42.71	14.14
Electricity, Gas and Water Supply	0.91	3.38	1.33
Other Supporting and Auxiliary Transport Activities; Activities of Travel Agencies	8.74	24.75	4.34

Source: Own elaboration

One ought to emphasize that figures in Table 16 contain very rich information. Sectors 12, 17 and 26 show a strong difference between the Spanish and Polish economies. Exports are much more important to the Polish key sectors than to Spanish sectors 12, 17 and 26. That means that domestic demand is not as relevant in the Polish economy as in the Spanish one, so when it falls as a consequence of a crisis period as the great recession one, the level of output suffers less damage in the former economy than in the latter. This is especially true when one of the main destination of Polish output is a strong economy as the German one. Data in the multinational Table of 2009 in the WIOD database support this conclusion.

In fact, when these economies are looked at as a whole, the role of the foreign sector therein is very different. Table 17 evidences the above thesis.

Table 17. Exports, output and export/output values by 2009

	Spain	Poland	UE-27
Exports (1)	293,683	166,039	2,389,643
Output (1)	2,682,451	757,742	29,143,489
Export/Output (2)	10.95	21.91	8.20

(1) Figures expressed in millions $. (2) Percentage of output

Source: Own elaboration

6. Conclusions

Poland and Spain show considerable similarities in terms of cultural background, political system, demographic and geographical as well as geo-economic aspects. However, from the economic perspective, these economies show very different patterns. In fact, Poland is the only EU economy with a positive real Gross Domestic Product growth rate during the past decade, also when the great recession started.

It is relevant for the economic analysis to compare these two economies and attempt to determine the factors which can explain the different way these two economies faced the period of crisis.

To achieve this objective, sector analysis following to one of the state of the art methodologies was conducted. The database used in the analysis was the WIOD, an extensive database containing information on 41 countries and 35 productive sectors for the period of 1995-2009. The year chosen for the analysis is 2009, as it is one of the most recent years the data are available for. Data of the EU-27 economy are used as a background for specific data concerning Spain and Poland.

Results of the key sectors analysis show that both the Spanish and Polish economies have just a few key sectors, similarly to the UE-27 economy treated as a whole. Therefore, differences regarding key sectors cannot explain dissimilar patterns in the case of Spain and Poland.

However, a more thorough analysis allows drawing interesting conclusions.

The main finding is that the role of the foreign sector in the Spanish and Polish key sectors can explain the different way in which these two economies faced the great recession.

The role played by the foreign sector is much more important in the case of Poland than in the case of Spain. This is true for three out of the four sectors considered. This fact makes domestic demand a determinant factor for the Spanish output; when it falls as a consequence of the crisis, the damage suffered is higher compared with Poland.

Likewise, the available data allow concluding that the main destination of Polish output (also for its key sectors' output) are strong economies such as the German economy.

From the point of view of policy makers, the lesson learned is that the role of the foreign sector in the total demand of national output ought to be reinforced.

Further development of the approach must consider more than one year of comparison, dispersion of FL and VL values through all the sectors and other available state of the art methodologies.

7. Acknowledgements

The authors are grateful for the funding received from the SEJ-132 project, from the Cátedra de Economía de la Energía y Medio Ambiente supported by the Fundació Roger Torne. The usual disclaimer applies.

8. Bibliography

Chenery H.B., and Watanabe T. 1958, International Comparisons of the Structure of Production. Econometrica, 26 (4), October: 487-521.

Eichengreen, B. and O'Rourke, K. H. 2009, A Tale of Two Depressions. September, 1 st. Available at http://www.voxeu.org/ Last access June, 2013.

Eurostat. http://epp.eurostat.ec.europa.eu. Last access June, 2013.

Leontief, W. 1966, "Input-Output Economics", 2ª ed., New York, Oxford University Press.

OECD Economic Outlook, Volume 2012 Issue 2 - No. 92 - OECD 2012. Last access June, 2013.

Rasmussen, P. 1956, *"Studies in Intersectorial Relations"*, Copenhagen: Einar Harks. Versión en español: *"Relaciones intersectoriales"*, Madrid: editorial Aguilar (1963).

Word Bank. World Development Indicators. http://data.worldbank.org (last access, july 2013)

World Input-Output Database (WIOD) (2012). http://www.wiod.org/database/index.htm (last access, june 2013).

Information about the Authors

Information about the Authors

Małgorzata Mizerska-Wrotkowska

Political scientist, doctor of humanities, assistant professor at the Institute of European Studies at the Faculty of Journalism and Political Science, University of Warsaw.

José Luis Orella

Doctor of history and political law; assistant professor of Contemporary History, chairman of the Arbil Forum (CEU San Pablo University, Madrid).

Józef Tymanowski

Doctor habilitatus of humanities in the field of political science, specializing in national security, head of the Department of European Sub-regional Studies in the Institute of European Studies at the Faculty of Journalism and Political Science, University of Warsaw.

Jacek Czaputowicz

Doctor habilitatus of humanities in the field of political science, professor of the University of Warsaw, the head of the Department of European Studies Research Methodology in the Institute of European Studies at the Faculty of Journalism and Political Science, University of Warsaw.

Juan Carlos Jiménez Redondo

Full professor of social movements, doctor of contemporary history, BA in history and political science (CEU San Pablo University, Madrid).

Konstanty Adam Wojtaszczyk

Professor, political scientist, lawyer, Director of the Institute of European Studies at the Faculty of Journalism and Political Science, University of Warsaw.

José Díaz Nieva

Political scientist, professor of history, doctor of history and law, member of the Society of History and Geography of Chile (Santo Tomás University, Santiago de Chile)

Cristina Barreiro

Professor of contemporary history, BA in journalism and doctor of history of the press (CEU San Pablo University, Madrid)

Jan Misiuna

Ph.D. in economics, M.A. in political science (European Studies) and cultural studies (American Studies), assistant professor at Department of Public Administration, Warsaw School of Economics (Poland).

Kamil Zajączkowski

Political scientist, doctor of humanities, assistant professor and coordinator for research and international cooperation at the Centre for Europe, University of Warsaw; recipient of the prestigious fellowship of the Polish Ministry of Science and Higher Education for the Best Young Scholars (2013).

José Manuel Cansino

Full professor of economics, Department of Economic Analysis and Political Economy, director of the Chair of Economy of Energy and Environment (University of Seville).

Manuel Ordóñez

Associate professor of applied economics (University of Seville).

www.ingramcontent.com/pod-product-compliance
Lightning Source LLC
Chambersburg PA
CBHW051044160426
43193CB00010B/1064